W9-ATZ-694

—————— To Make an ——————

Old Story New

What others have said...

If you don't know the plot-line of the Bible -- and even if you do -- I thoroughly recommend this epic retelling of the one story that everybody needs to know. It is respectful yet readable, insightful and invigorating. Best of all, it makes you want to read the original!

Revd. Canon J. John - international speaker and author.

Justyn Rees has reduced the story line of the Bible to a gripping tale, told with wit and warmth. This is the spinal cord of the world's oldest and most influential book, the story line from which the many branches of its doctrines, promises and privileges extend. It will be revealing to those who do not know the story, refreshing to those who do, and renewing to those who once knew, but have neglected it.

Charles Price - pastor of The Peoples Church, Toronto, and TV and radio host of Living Truth

I was gripped! From the beginning of creation to the end of Revelation I just couldn't wait to read more! Justyn has conveyed the Best Story Ever in up to date, everyday language. He has captured the drama, the wonder and the life changing impact of the Bible in a way that will make it a treasured book to receive, and to give away.

Julie Sheldon - international speaker, author and ballet dancer.

At last a book that simply tells the story – and just the story! It's brilliant! Now ordinary people, like me, can understand the Old Testament and how it links with the New; and realize how utterly fascinating, funny and relevant the bare-bones of the Bible's story actually is!

Jennifer Larcombe - author, conference speaker and Bible teacher.

Justyn Rees is a brilliant storyteller. The first line of each story engages the reader, and gently takes us into a world of wonder and exploration. Justyn exposes the emotion of each moment with subtle details that form a new picture in one's mind, capturing the moment with fresh understanding. One could imagine sitting near a quiet brook listening intently to every word, while Justyn unravels the next episode of this eternal story.

Richard Dodding - founder of Missions Fest Vancouver and director of the International Teachers Institute in Ukraine and Kazakhstan

There are not many books that are a 'Must Read' for everyone - but this book is. I don't know any other book that will make the Bible come to life like this does.

Max Sinclair - author, speaker and founder of Christian Vision for Men, UK (CVM)

Justyn Rees as a consummate story-teller has captured the essence of the Bible—true to the text, true to the Spirit, eminently readable. It captures our hearts and draws us into God's story so that it becomes our story, the very thing God had intended when God inspired people of old to write the sacred text. Take and read and you won't be able to put it down. Best of all, your faith will grow.

R. Paul Stevens - Professor Emeritus, Marketplace Theology, Regent College, Vancouver, BC.

Other books written by Justyn Rees:

TO MAKE A LONG STORY SHORT
A compelling retelling that makes the Bible's New Testament dance with life

HONEST DOUBT, REAL FAITH
A story of faith lost and recovered

LOVE YOUR NEIGHBOUR, FOR GOD'S SAKE
How to introduce Jesus to your friends and neighbours

CONTACT JUSTYN REES:
www.justynrees.com
jrees@upstream.ca

To Make an

Old Story New

THE EPIC SAGA OF THE BIBLE'S
OLD TESTAMENT RETOLD
WITH COLOUR AND WARMTH

Justyn Rees

WESTBOW·
PRESS
A DIVISION OF THOMAS NELSON
& ZONDERVAN

Copyright © 2014 Justyn Rees.

All rights reserved. No part of this book may be used or reproduced by any means, graphic, electronic, or mechanical, including photocopying, recording, taping or by any information storage retrieval system without the written permission of the publisher except in the case of brief quotations embodied in critical articles and reviews.

WestBow Press books may be ordered through booksellers or by contacting:

WestBow Press
A Division of Thomas Nelson & Zondervan
1663 Liberty Drive
Bloomington, IN 47403
www.westbowpress.com
1 (866) 928-1240

Because of the dynamic nature of the Internet, any web addresses or links contained in this book may have changed since publication and may no longer be valid. The views expressed in this work are solely those of the author and do not necessarily reflect the views of the publisher, and the publisher hereby disclaims any responsibility for them.

Any people depicted in stock imagery provided by Thinkstock are models, and such images are being used for illustrative purposes only.
Certain stock imagery © Thinkstock.

ISBN: 978-1-4908-3789-5 (sc)
ISBN: 978-1-4908-3788-8 (hc)
ISBN: 978-1-4908-3787-1 (e)

Library of Congress Control Number: 2014911518

Printed in the United States of America.

WestBow Press rev. date: 7/11/14

Table of Contents

1

The Origin

Once upon a time … But that's how a fairy tale would start. This story is history, established in time and space.

Before time and space, there was only God. Then God made time for once to be upon, with days and nights and seasons and years to mark its passage. And he made space big enough to accommodate all he was planning to create – sun, moon, stars, and, of course, the earth. There were lakes, rivers, and oceans teeming with multicoloured life. And there were continents and islands covered with green grass, flowers, and trees. Birds and insects flitted and buzzed through the air, and beasts of every shape and description lumbered or scurried along the ground.

Just exactly how God did this is a mystery that keeps scientists guessing, but the bottom line is, he spoke it. He ordered it into existence. It was as though his words were the source of reality. When it was all done, God took a day off to appreciate his creation. Yes, it was good. Very good!

But God wanted something in his creation to be a clear reflection of himself, perhaps not so much a physical likeness but rather an expression of his nature. The infinite size of space might have given a hint of his greatness, but that would have suggested God was remote, unreachable. Perhaps a mighty mountain would have done, but although God was mighty, he was not cold and hard. So he chose something that could love and communicate, show kindness and creativity, and be capable of faithfulness as well as justice and mercy. God chose human beings.

The prototype was Adam. God scratched together minerals from the dust of the ground, formed clay, and when all the body parts were functional, he breathed life into him.

Not surprisingly, Adam was highly impressed with the magnificence of the world in which he found himself. But he might have been lonely had God not introduced him to prototype number two, Eve, who was similar to Adam yet with some attractive differences. They were as thrilled with each other as men and women have been ever since.

"Go to it," said God. "Make babies." As if they needed telling!

That was the first command God ever issued, and since then, the thrill of obedience has multiplied the reflection of God's image by a few billion. Families! Somehow it took a family to adequately reflect one very mystifying aspect of who God is. He was always one, no question about that, yet he often presented himself as three. Even way back in the beginning, God had the habit of discussing everything with himself. "Let us do this … let us do that …" Yes, families. Man, woman, and – surprise! the baby.

So there they were in paradise. Food grew on trees, and there were no laws or taxes. Nevertheless, there were such things as right and wrong, good and evil, although in the early days, no such concepts ever wrinkled the brows of Adam and Eve. Yet among the myriad of trees, a couple were singled out for particular attention. "Life" and "Good-or-Bad" were their odd names: life and moral choice flourishing side by side. God had hung a warning sign on the Good-or-Bad tree: "Do not eat or you will die!" Not difficult to understand, but Adam and Eve nor anyone they knew had ever experienced death, so its threat was not too daunting a deterrent. While there were unlimited choices available to them, they couldn't shake the suspicion that stolen fruit just might taste the sweetest.

"Psst!" hissed a voice while Eve was contemplating the taboo fruit. "I hear God won't let you eat fruit."

"Well, that's not exactly true," Eve countered. "We may eat any fruit we want – except from this one tree. Apparently, it would be bad for us."

"Nonsense!" said a snake, gliding out of the bushes. "God hates competition. He wants a monopoly on defining good and evil. If you eat this fruit, lady, far from dying, you will become as smart as God, capable of making your own choices between right and wrong. Go ahead! Exercise your right to freedom of choice."

There was no denying that this was an attractive proposition. The fruit looked good, smelled good, and, yes, it tasted good. And sure enough, Eve didn't drop dead after she'd taken a bite. So she gave some to Adam, testifying that she was living proof that the snake had told the truth.

Then a strange thing occurred, an indefinable, not-yet-experienced sensation, a pain that seemed to hurt in a place they didn't know they had. Later, as they learned to define it, they called it "shame." At that time, they were both buck-naked and had never given it a second thought. But with this new sensation came the urge to hide from each other. The fig tree with its shady leaves offered a temporary solution.

Till then, Adam and Eve had never had any difficulty relating to God. Religion hadn't been invented, so they had simply enjoyed God's company, talking with him as he showed them round his creation.

"Where are you?" called the voice that spoke the world into being.

Clutching a sprig of leaves in front of them, Adam and Eve emerged shame-faced from the bushes. "We felt afraid of you because we were naked. So we hid."

"Who told you that you were naked? Have you eaten from the tree I warned you not to touch?"

Adam made a lame attempt to squirm out of the responsibility. "It wasn't my fault, God. It was you who gave me Eve, and it was she who gave me the fruit."

"Well, don't look at me," spluttered Eve. "It was a wretched snake who tricked me into it." And so the buck was passed from hand to hand.

That was the beginning of trouble in paradise, the start of alienation between man and his Creator and between humans and the world around them. Poisoned fangs, thorns, and thistles marred relationships. The joy of parenthood was tarnished by the pain of childbirth. Even the mud that clung to the soles of Adam's and Eve's feet seemed to taunt them: "One day soon you will be just like us – dirt and dust!"

Perhaps the Life tree might have reversed the fatal consequences of its next-door neighbour, Good-or-Bad, but before the idea could occur to Adam and Eve, God placed an impenetrable barrier between them and the tree of Life, protecting them from an eternity of regret. Yet the loss of the Life tree left humans with a certain homesickness as they groped to rediscover the secret of immortality.

So there was the human race in its infancy, living in a stunningly beautiful creation, instinctively preferring good over evil, yet falling for evil again and again, dressed in furs and leather at the expense of the animals that were slaughtered to cover human shame.

Adam and Eve had a couple of kids. They may have had others, but they don't merit a mention in the story. Cain arrived first, and when Adam and Eve figured out how that happened, along came little brother Abel.

Farming was the only profession in those days. Abel raised livestock while Cain chose horticulture. For some reason, as indefinable as these things often are, this caused friction between the two brothers, and a growing sensation, the very opposite of brotherly love, took root in Cain's heart.

"What's wrong with you, Cain?" asked God. "Be very careful! A fiend is crouching at your door like a wild animal ready to spring. You must control it before it controls you."

Just how many wars might have been avoided had Cain discovered that secret? At the time, it didn't seem important, just a domestic squabble. But it ended with Abel in a pool of blood in the vegetable garden, and when Cain tried to rouse him, there was no response.

"Where is Abel?" God asked that evening.

"How should I know?" Cain sulked. "Am I supposed to be responsible for my brother?"

"What have you done, Cain? Don't you hear it? Your brother's blood is calling from the ground for justice. And justice it shall have. From now on, you will live as a fugitive, alienated from my company, from the ground you till, and from your fellow man."

So Cain left home, taking with him a wife (presumably one of his unnamed sisters, as there wasn't a lot of choice available).

Meanwhile, Eve had another son, Seth, and it is through his family line that the story continues, as the image of God is handed down from parents to children through ten generations. The only significance attached to most of those generations is longevity. Enoch, however, though he lived a comparatively short life, stands out from the rest as one who walked in very close company with his Creator. Then one day his intimate walk with God took him further, right through the barrier between time and eternity – an enviable way to pass on.

A man called Job lived a life of contrasts around this time. Job was an individual who stood out for his obedience to God. Far from receiving preferential treatment, all the horrors that plague the human race chose Job as the object of their spite: bereavement, financial ruin, and to cap it all, pain and sickness. Even with the aid of supposedly wise counsellors, Job could not figure out why this had befallen him. Why? Finally, God himself explained. Job was asking the wrong questions. "Why?" or "How?" were not important. "Who?" Ah! That was a question worth answering. Who is ultimately in control even when the sky is falling? Restoration did bring something close to a "happily ever after" conclusion to Job's story. However, Job represents the kind of suffering about which humans have ever since been asking the wrong question: "Why?"

Seth sired an impressive family. Thanks to the family's tendency towards long life, Seth lived to see the birth of his great-great-great-great-great-grandson and narrowly missed by a mere fourteen years the birth of his most famous descendent, Noah. When Noah was born, the whole family, all seven surviving generations, recognised that this kid had promise. They pinned their hopes on him as some kind of deliverer. And deliverance was just what the world needed in those days, for between Cain's fugitive family and Seth's long-lived offspring, the human race was doing its best to destroy God's creation.

The sons of God (whoever they might have been, for the story is fuzzy on the issue) took a shine to human girls. The resulting offspring were hybrids, giants, and super-humans, who perhaps gave rise to legends that survived for generations. But what seems to have troubled God the most was not so much the obvious outward perversions as the hidden tendency of the human heart to do evil. He came to the point where he even regretted having made humans because of the pain and the hurt they inflicted on one another. He determined to wipe the slate clean. And that's when Noah received his call.

"Noah," said God. "I am planning to send a devastating flood, which will wash clean the face of the earth. So build a barge."

God gave Noah a blueprint for a vessel large enough to house Noah with his wife and children, plus a fair-sized zoo. It's not difficult to imagine the ridicule that the poor man suffered as he built a boat, hundreds of miles from the ocean. But the laughter stopped abruptly when the rain started. Mating couples of birds, animals, and reptiles had come wandering out of the jungle and were uncomplainingly herded into the barge. When they were all safe inside, the door banged shut and down came the rain. Bad weather persisted for the better part of six months till the mountains turned to islands and the islands gave place to a flat horizon.

Then one day the sun came out. Eager for news of the rest of the world, Noah released a raven that never came back. So he tried a dove, thinking that its natural homing instincts might make it a better choice. True enough, back it came, and after its second excursion, it returned with an olive leaf in its beak and won itself the distinction of becoming the symbol of peace and hope, for the leaf was fresh plucked from a tree. There had to be dry ground somewhere.

The barge eventually grounded on a sand bar that dried out to become an island, which a subsequent drop in water level revealed to be a mountain in what would later be identified as Turkey. The joy of being released from the barge after nearly a year of confinement precipitated a celebration barbecue. For a moment, a rain cloud threatened spoil the event, but as a rainbow appeared between heaven and earth, God spoke: "I will never again flood the earth. Whenever there is a rainbow, it will remind you of this promise."

So the story has a second start, history repeating itself. Once again there is one family: Noah, his wife, and their three sons, Shem, Ham, and Japheth, together with their wives. Before them, a fresh new world. But with monotonous predictability, one son turns bad; not murder this time, just disrespect.

Noah got blind drunk and made a spectacle of himself, sprawled naked on his bed. Ham spotted him and ran to call his brothers. "Hey guys, want to the see the old man with his pants down?" But the necessity to honour father and mother, however imperfect they may prove to be, had instinctively been passed down the consciences of the generations with the knowledge of Good-or-Bad. Averting their eyes, Shem and Japheth covered their father with a blanket. Love has always covered a multitude of sins.

It seems that the attitude of a youngster towards his parents sets a course for life. Next morning, his attitude soured by a hangover, Noah predicted that Ham and his descendants would always be the underdogs, servants to the rest of the family.

To these three brothers fell the daunting responsibility of repopulating the world. Ham's descendants, determined to live down Noah's curse, resolved to accomplish something important. It had to be tangible, highly visible, durable, and impressive. A city with impregnable walls for protection, magnificent buildings, and a tower that would reach to the sky!

"Ah!" they said, deeply impressed with their own handiwork. "This will make a name for us! Underdogs? Servants? Nonsense!"

But God, knowing that technological advance would one day endanger the survival of the human race, resolved to slow their progress. *"Passez moi une brique, s'il vous plait!"* a bricklayer said to his mate, high on a scaffold atop the half-finished tower.

"What are you babbling about?"

And foreign language was born. A simple ploy, but one that has effectively slowed man's capacity to cooperate for the common good ever since. And that's how the city got its name: "Babel" or "Babylon," as it became, a city destined to be the theatre where the brotherly tension between Ham and Shem would reach a climax a millennium or so later.

2

The Promise

Shem followed the family tradition of living a long time. So he might have been excused for regarding the birth of his great-great-great-great-great-great-great-grandson Abram as but one more family birthday to remember. The baby was born way off in Ur, on the Euphrates River, close to the Persian Gulf.

When Abram was still a lad, his uncle died, leaving to Abram's father Terah the responsibility to adopt his two little daughters, Iscar and Milcah. Abram loved his new little sister Iscar, since she was just as cute as a button. He called her "Princess"; "Sara." But when she grew into a stunning young woman, he married her without hesitation, conforming to the demands of custom that he should marry his oldest girl cousin.

"My Princess," he called her; *Sarai*. His younger brother Nahor also did the socially expected thing and married the other sister, Milcah. They might have all lived happily ever after had not their third brother died, leaving to Abram the responsibility of adopting his orphaned son, a brat named Lot.

So that was the shape of the family when Terah announced that they were moving to Canaan. The whole family upped sticks and headed north along the trade route beside the Euphrates River. They were about halfway to their objective when Terah experienced a midlife crisis. He lost sight of his goal and settled down for the rest of his days in Haran in the region of Paddan Aram, some four hundred miles north of Canaan.

The first seventy-five years of Abram's life were of little significance. But everything was about to change. He heard a voice that seemed to resonate enough authority to create a universe: "Leave home and go to a land I will show you. There I will make you into a great nation. And I will bless you and through you I will bless all people on earth." Such a promise was difficult to resist.

Taking Sarai and his nephew Lot, together with his wife and two baby daughters, Abram set out on a new adventure. He was looking for a life, one defined, not by walls and high towers, as was Babel, but simply by the words of God's promise.

As is often the case, the farther you travel, the higher the anticipation, the greater the anticlimax when you actually arrive. "This is it! To your offspring I will give this land," said the voice.

There was an oak tree by a dried-up streambed in a famine-blighted valley between two unimpressive hills. Shechem. Abram rolled together some boulders and built an altar as a way of thanking God, but his gratitude was a little thin. There was nothing for them to eat, and sparse pasture for their flocks. Instead of putting down roots, they travelled farther south, through the Negev desert; before they knew it, they had walked clear out the other end of Canaan and into Egypt.

They had to admit that Egypt was far more impressive, with its recently constructed pyramids and mighty flowing Nile River. Pharaoh, king of Egypt, had an eye for the women, and Sarai's beauty didn't escape his notice. Fearing for his life, Abram introduced her as his sister. But when the half-truth was discovered, Pharaoh sent Abram packing back to Canaan.

So there they all were, back in the land that God had promised. Grazing was limited and patience was stretched thin between Abram's herdsmen and those of Lot. "This land won't support both of us living so close," Abram told his nephew. "We must part company. You choose where you want to go, and I will head in the opposite direction." Way below them in a deep valley threaded the Jordan River, with its green-pastured banks and the thriving cities of Sodom and Gomorrah. No-brainer! Off went Lot with his wife and daughters, flocks, and herds. Abram watched him go with a twinge of regret.

Then God spoke again: "As far as you can see in any direction will one day be yours. And as numerous as the grains of sand beneath your feet will be your descendants. Go walk through it and know that everywhere you tread is yours to inherit."

Lot's choice turned out to be not altogether a happy one. Property was expensive and taxes were high. Nevertheless, there was a ready market for his meat in the nearby cities, and before long, Lot was an accepted member of the chamber of commerce, a pillar of society. But being a pillar in a society that is quaking with fear of its neighbours and is rotten with perversion is of dubious worth. As if to underscore this conclusion, an allied army from the neighbouring territory swept in one day and walked through Sodom and Gomorrah's undisciplined defences. Lot and his entire family, together with the rest of the population, were taken off as prisoners of war to become slave labour for their new masters.

When news of the raid reached Abram, he led a small detachment of servants and neighbours in a daring night attack to rescue Lot and his fellow citizens.

After they all got back to Sodom, the town council elected Lot to join their number since it was his uncle Abram who had saved the day. Lot was given a fine residence in the city and was held in high esteem.

In contrast, Abram's progress was limited. Yes, he walked the length and breadth of the land in anticipation of ownership. From time to time, he would even reach down to scoop up a handful of sand, counting the grains to get a notion of how large a family he might expect. Yet in reality, he remained homeless and childless. He had nothing to call his own except the fading memory of what God had promised.

One beautiful clear night, the voice came once again: "Abram, I myself am your reward, even more than the promises I gave you."

"Yes, I have been waiting for an opportunity to ask you about those promises," Abram replied. "I recall something about owning land and children as numerous as the dust beneath my feet."

"Get your nose out of the dust, Abram, and look up." There in the velvet night sky sparkled myriad tiny specks of light, billions of light years beyond his reach. "Can you count the stars? What I have in mind for you is as high above mere children of dust as the stars are high above the grains of sand beneath your feet."

A peace stole over Abram, a reassurance in his inner being on which he could rest. The God who made such extravagant promises would most certainly honour them. Abram believed God.

That night, Abram had a dream about his offspring (a nightmare, more accurately). A black darkness crept over his soul, and from a great way off in the future, he heard the cries of his children in slavery, imprisoned, choking as they suffocated on the poison gas of hatred and jealousy.

But next morning, the sky was clear and there were many children to conceive. But the end of the month revealed no change in Sarai's condition. Months turned into years, and patience stretched into frustration.

"God helps those who help themselves," Sarai said one morning. "It's time we took positive action to give God a helping hand." So that night, at his wife's suggestion, Abram slept in the embrace of Hagar, Sarai's Egyptian servant girl.

The tension between servant and mistress because of Hagar's subsequent pregnancy made life in Abram's household almost intolerable, but the birth of Ishmael did much to cheer everyone. It proved but a temporary alleviation of hostilities, and ultimately, the only way for peace to be restored was for Hagar and Ishmael to leave home. But the tension has continued ever since, much as does the tension between peaceful trust in God's promises and man's striving to make things happen by his own efforts.

One morning, Abram was sitting in his tent door. Three strangers approached. First glance had them pegged as ordinary nomads, but as they drew closer, a strange stillness stole over the world, as though all creation was holding its breath in the presence of its Maker.

Over a hastily prepared meal, Abram listened to what God had to say: "I am here to spell out to you the terms of a three-way covenant between you, your wife Sarai, and myself.

"Here is my part of the agreement. I am the Lord God Almighty. I will make you very fruitful, and you will be the father of nations, the father of kings. To your family I will give this land. The scope of what I am promising is infinite, will last forever, and will be for the blessing of all people everywhere.

"Here is your part of the agreement. First, your name is now changed from Abram to Abraham: *the father of many*. As a perpetual reminder that my promises are not achieved by human strength, and in particular that my promise to you of many children will not be realised by natural descent, nor human decision, nor a husband's will, you and all your male descendants are to be circumcised. By symbolically cutting off the foreskin of your penis, you will be reminded every time you set out to sire children that it is not your male potency that brings forth children, but rather the fulfilment of my promise.

"Here is Sarai's part of the agreement. She will henceforth be called Sarah: *the mother of nations*. This time next year, she will have a son."

Abraham couldn't hide a smile at the thought of himself, a hundred-year-old father, and Sarah, who was eavesdropping in the next tent, couldn't suppress a giggle.

"*Laughter*: that will be your son's name – *Isaac*.

"And now the bad news," God continued, turning to his two companions. "Since I have entered into covenant with Abraham, I think we should tell him why I brought you two along." God shared that an outcry had reached heaven against the corruption and extreme wickedness of Sodom and Gomorrah. "I am sending my two companions to see first-hand if things are as bad as we hear."

With that, the two turned and set off in the direction of Sodom. Abraham however remained standing before God. Risking his displeasure, Abraham set about pleading for mercy, arguing that to destroy those cities might put at risk a handful of innocents, who, he argued, must surely be amongst the residents of Sodom.

Meanwhile, two fine-looking young men arrived at the city gates of Sodom. Recognising them as no ordinary men, Lot sprang forward and invited them to stay in his home rather than sleep rough in the streets, as they clearly intended. But their arrival had not been missed by lustful eyes. Later on that evening, a crowd of drunken men came down the street and banged on Lot's door. "Don't be selfish, Lot. Bring your visitors out so we can get *acquainted*!"

Lot refused.

"Who in the world do you think you are? You are an immigrant; would you impose your outmoded standards on us? Your prejudice is narrow-minded in the extreme."

"So it's just as bad as we have heard," the two visitors said to Lot as a strange disorientation crept over the angry crowd. "We will destroy this city, so you and your family had better get out quickly."

Lot decided to sleep on it. Things always look better in the morning. But they didn't. He told his wife and daughters to pack, but when he called on their two fiancés: "You've got to be joking!" they jeered. "Leave town? Never!"

The two visitors grabbed Lot and his women and dragged them all out of the city towards the mountains. "Run for your lives, and whatever you do, don't turn back!"

But it was a beautiful day, and the sense of unreality persisted. Lot's wife dragged her feet and whinged. After a while, she stopped altogether, then turned and set off back down the road they had just travelled. It may have been a trick of the light, but after a few steps, she appeared to freeze to the spot, crystallising into a hideous statue. The rest of the family fled. The sky grew black, then fire and brimstone rained on those perverted cities.

Abraham was one hundred years old and Sarah past ninety when the image of God was reproduced in little Isaac. Joyful laughter rippled all around. That young boy was the apple of his parents' eyes. To Sarah, he was the fulfilment of a life of dreaming. Prolonged disappointment had given way to what she now enjoyed. And Abraham may even have begun to forget that his real reward was not so much the promise, as it was the promise-giver himself.

One day when Isaac was a teenager, that unearthly stillness stole over the grove of trees where Abraham was sitting in the shade. "Abraham, take your son Isaac, whom you love so much, and go to a mountain in the land of Moriah, which I will show you."

"Yes," Abraham enthusiastically agreed. "And what shall we do when we get there?"

"You will sacrifice him as a burnt offering in clear demonstration that it is I, and I alone, who am your reward."

Perhaps Abraham argued that Isaac was the heir through whom the promises were to be fulfilled, so how could he sacrifice what God had promised? Should he obey God's command or trust his promises? It must have dawned on him that in order to find the courage to obey, he would have to learn to trust God's ability to keep his promises, even to raise the dead, should push come to shove.

As they set off next morning, perhaps Abraham might have been excused if he had hidden from Sarah the ultimate purpose of the expedition. After a couple of days' hike, they saw a mountain in the distance. "That's the place," God nudged him. They climbed the mountain, Isaac carrying a pile of wood and Abraham the knife, a coil of rope, and a flint.

"Haven't we forgotten something?" asked Isaac. "Shouldn't there be a lamb or something?"

"Only God can provide the ultimate sacrifice so his promises can be fulfilled."

It says a lot for Isaac's faith in his father that he permitted a doddery old man of one hundred-and-something to bind him hand and foot and to lay him on a pile of firewood. And it says a lot for Abraham's faith in God that he raised the knife over his son's horrified body. With clenched teeth he was just beginning the down stroke ...

"Stop!" ordered the voice. "Now I know for certain where your priorities lie. And I will most certainly fulfil all I have promised."

Oh, the relief as Abraham used the knife, not to kill, but to cut the ropes to free his son. Father and son hugged and wept. Eventually they became conscious of the distressed bleating of a ram tangled up in a bramble bush. God *had* provided the sacrifice.

Isaac grew into a fine young man. The only cloud in his sky was the death of his dear mother, Sarah. The two had been unusually close, and he felt her loss keenly. To mark her passing, Abraham made his first real estate purchase: a field with a cave, near the city of Hebron, and there Abraham buried his wife, his half sister, his beloved Princess, Sarah.

But there was no consoling Isaac. "He needs a wife," Abraham remarked. Surely not a wife from among the descendants of Ham who inhabited that region, so he dispatched his servant to seek out the family of his long lost brother and sister-in-law, Nahor and Milcah, way up north in Paddan Aram.

Some weeks later, Isaac was out walking in the fields, grieving for his mother. In the distance, he saw a camel train approaching. As it came closer, his eyes were drawn to a beautiful young lady, riding one of the camels. His heart skipped a beat. Conscious of his gaze, the girl covered her face. Rebecca, it transpired, was the granddaughter of Abraham's brother Nahor, and by miraculous coincidence, Abraham's servant had gone straight to her.

The two were married. Isaac's mourning was over.

A few years later, Abraham's time came to await only the resurrection for the fulfilment of all the good things that God had promised him. Isaac, together with his half brother Ishmael, laid the old man next to Sarah, in the cave he owned near Hebron.

Rebecca inherited from her family the same beauty as had her mother-in-law, Sarah. Isaac inherited the same foolish notions of how to survive while married to a beautiful wife, as had his father, Abraham. He passed the word that Rebecca was his sister. But when they were seen kissing, the neighbours were torn between branding Isaac and Rebecca as incestuous or as liars.

To further upset the community, Isaac sunk a couple of wells without first checking into who owned the water rights. So he was forced to pull up his tent pegs and move to a friendlier neighbourhood, where he finally accessed water he could call his own. There God spoke to him: "I will make your descendants as numerous as the stars in the sky and will give them this land, and through your offspring all nations on earth will be blessed." Isaac called the place "Beersheba" *Well of the Oath*.

Not only did Rebecca inherit her mother-in-law's fine looks, she also followed her example by proving slow to conceive babies. For twenty long years, she waited with a growing appreciation for the frustrations that Abraham and Sarah must have endured. Then one night, as they were heading off to bed, the significance of his circumcision dawned on Isaac. "Of course! Children are the product of God's promise, not my testosterone." So he prayed that God would, by his own power, fulfil his promise and give them children.

The pregnancy that soon followed was not as enjoyable as Rebecca had anticipated. It appeared that the two children in her womb were having a wrestling match. "Why is this happening to me?" she moaned. The explanation given was that there were two nations within her, who would always be at war.

The first twin to see the light of day was hairy as a toilet brush. So they called him Esau: *hairy.* Hanging onto his heel, as though to express resentment at not being the first out, was anything but an identical twin. Jacob, *the deceitful heel grabber,* came out smooth as a hard-boiled egg.

Not only were the two different in appearance, they also were poles apart in their interests. Esau was an outdoorsman who loved to hunt, while Jacob was more the stay-at-home, contemplative type. From earliest years he was obsessed with a sense of destiny, fascinated by the promises that God had given their father and grandfather. Jacob's greatest regret was that he had been born a few seconds too late to be the oldest son, in line to inherit the promises.

In contrast, Esau seemed to be more interested in a full belly than being the father of a multitude and a blessing to the whole world. So one hungry day after a hunting expedition, he traded his birthright for a bowl of the stew that Jacob had just finished cooking. Esau didn't care much about the purity of the family line. He had a romp with a couple of no-account local girls, revelling in the pleasure of immediate sexual release, but giving no thought to the consequences. When he saw how upset his parents were, he sought to legitimise his folly by marrying them both.

3

The Fugitive

Time passed and Isaac turned one hundred, blind and bedridden. He called his favourite son to his side: "Esau, before I die I want to give you a father's blessing. So go, hunt down a deer, and let's eat first." Food was Esau's undoing. He had lost his birthright to Jacob's stew, and now he was about to lose his father's blessing for his mother's goulash. Rebecca had overheard the conversation between father and son, so she immediately had sent Jacob, her favourite, for a goat, which she cunningly prepared just the way Isaac liked it, masking the difference between deer and goat with universal ketchup. By the time Esau returned, the meal was finished and the blessing was all done. That wretched smooth-skinned heel grabber had tricked him out of his birthright *and* his blessing.

It was the potential of being murdered by his twin brother that leant urgency to Jacob's decision to leave home in search of a wife. "These local girls simply won't do, Father. I'd like to go to Mother's family in Paddan Aram, in the hope of finding a suitable cousin." The disaster of Esau's marriages leant credibility to Jacob's suggestion, so off he set with his parents' blessing.

Now leaving home means quite an adjustment for a young man, and setting out, as he was, with little more than a sketchy map drawn by his grandfather's superannuated servant did little to bolster his confidence. His first night of independence was spent sleeping rough, an activity for which Esau would have been better suited. A stone for a pillow didn't help much, but it was a dream that made the night memorable. He saw a stairway to heaven, bustling with angels coming and going. Right at the very top was God, who introduced himself as "the Lord, the God of your grandfather Abraham and your father Isaac. To you I renew my promise that I will give you this land on which you are lying. And you will have descendants as numerous as the dust that forms your mattress. In fact all people on earth will be blessed through your offspring."

So it was with a fresh spring in his step that Jacob set off next morning. The promises were no longer just a tradition passed down two generations, the rights to which he had conned from both his father and his brother. These promises now were his personally, guaranteed directly by God himself.

Rachel was a shepherdess. Perhaps it was the uncanny resemblance to his mother that caused it to be love at first sight. There before him, surrounded by a flock of bleating thirsty sheep, was a paragon of beauty. But when he discovered that she was his cousin, the daughter of Laban, his mother Rebecca's brother, Jacob stole a kiss and made a fool of himself by weeping with emotion.

Uncle Laban was, however, a different kettle of fish. In fact, the relationship between him and Jacob over the following twenty years proved to be a battle of wits that stretched Jacob's heel-grabbing talents to the very limit.

"Just because you are my nephew doesn't mean you can live here rent free," Laban explained. "If you want to marry my daughter, you will have to work for her." Seven years of hard labour fled by, but when Jacob awoke on the first morning of his honeymoon, he was shocked to see that the head on the pillow beside him was not that of his beloved Rachel. It was saggy-eyed Leah, her older sister.

"Oh, didn't you know that it's a custom in this neck of the woods that the older daughter must be married before the younger?" Laban rationalised. Mercifully for Jacob, in those days anti-bigamy laws hadn't been enacted, but another seven years' hard labour was the price of Rachel's hand in marriage.

Having babies seems to have been something of a competition between the two sisters, for over the following thirteen years, they were responsible between them for the births of eleven sons and a daughter. When either wife went through a period of barrenness, she would send a servant girl as a surrogate. But no matter how they arrived, those eleven sons, plus another to be born later, would turn out to be significant: Reuben, Simeon, Levi, Judah, Issachar, Zebulun, Dan, Naphtali, Gad, Asher, Joseph, and Benjamin. Jacob's deftness as a prolific breeder was inherited by each of his sons, who sired a tribe apiece.

Rearing a large family doesn't come cheap, and Jacob was feeling the pinch financially. Uncle Laban, however, was prospering through his nephew's proficiency as a farmer. So a deal was struck to share future additions to the flock. All perfect specimens would be retained by Laban while Jacob undertook to take only those that were blemished. At the commencement of the agreement, Laban took the precaution of removing from the flock all the existing animals that had even a hint of a smudge on its fleece, so the chance of his pure flock producing anything off white was slim. Yet from that day forward, almost every lamb born was flawed.

Resentment grew like a house on fire, and eventually Jacob left home without so much as a by-your-leave to his father-in-law. Laban was furious at the news that his daughters, grandchildren, and most of his fortune had simply walked away. So he gave chase and would no doubt have done Jacob a mischief had not God warned him to be nice. Consequently, an agreement was struck, and the two families parted company amicably, Laban to his depleted ranch in Paddan Aram, and Jacob with his wives and children, flocks, and herds back to the land of promise.

There was, of course, one major fly in the sweet smelling ointment of the homecoming: brother Esau. The likelihood was that twenty years of Jacob's absence would have done little to make Esau's heart grow fonder.

Jacob took the initiative by sending messengers to prepare the way with a carefully worded letter. They returned with the unwelcome news that Esau was headed in their direction with a small army of four hundred men. Horrified, Jacob devised a plan to soften Esau up with progressive waves of generosity. Separated by a mile or so each, he dispatched significant herds of camels, cattle, donkeys, sheep, and goats. Following the animals were herds of people carefully arranged in ascending order of importance. First went the servant girls and their children, then Leah and her brood, followed by Rachel with her boys, finally Jacob's favourite: Joseph.

As they all crossed the river into the promised land, cluster-by-cluster, Jacob himself lingered behind. This could well be his last day on earth, he surmised. To this point, he had survived by trickery. He had wrestled with his brother and won the birthright. He had inveigled a blessing from his unwitting father. Most recently, he had wrested from his uncle two daughters and a fortune in livestock. Would his luck hold, or did the promises of God offer more solid grounds for confidence in the future?

While Jacob turned these questions over in his mind, a figure loomed out of the gathering darkness and knocked him flat. Perhaps he thought at first it was Esau, but whoever it might be, Jacob scrambled to his feet and lunged back at his opponent. Before long, the two were locked in combat that lasted the best part of the night. By the time the sky was streaked with the first sign of dawn, it became apparent that neither would prevail. The stranger put a move on Jacob that wrenched his hip in excruciating agony, then made as though he would wriggle away. All Jacob could do was to hang on to his opponent's ankle for all he was worth. "Heel grabber" he had been named, and now it seemed that grabbing this heel was Jacob's last hope. He was clinging to the promises by a thread.

"Let me go, for dawn is coming," the stranger panted.

"No!" Jacob said through clenched teeth. "I will not let you go till you have blessed me."

"All right," said the man. "What's your name?"

"Jacob!"

"Your name will no longer be 'Jacob': *the heel grabber* but 'Israel': *one who struggles with God.* You have not only successfully wrestled with man for the blessing, but now you have wrestled with God for his blessing."

Jacob immediately released his grip on the man's ankle, rolled over, and sat up. With a growing sense of terror, he looked at his opponent, who was sitting silhouetted against the dawn sky. "So what is *your* name?" Jacob whispered.

"Do you have to ask? So here is the blessing for which you have fought.

To you I will give this land and you will have descendants as numerous as the grains of its sand. And your descendent will be the means of blessing all mankind."

The sun rose and the stranger was gone, and if it weren't for his limp, Jacob might have wondered if it had all been a dream.

Any residual animosity that Esau might have felt towards Jacob melted in the face of such generosity. The brothers hugged, and Jacob introduced his family.

"But what are all these animals for?"

"My gift to you, brother," said Jacob.

"I couldn't possibly accept them!": the standard token refusal.

"No, really! I want you to have them."

"But why?"

"Because to see the smile on the face of my brother whom I love is like seeing the face of God." Not that Jacob had seen the face of God, just his silhouette against the dawn sky. Yet how can a man say he loves God, who he has not seen, if he doesn't love his brother, who he has?

Esau returned to his fortress home in Mount Seir, and Jacob settled in Shechem, the same place where grandfather Abraham had first set foot in the promised land. The great oak was still flourishing, and the two hills were clothed with spring grass – no famine this time. It occurred to Jacob that since his grandfather had been driven from this valley by thirst, he might be smart to dig a well. Of course, there would be little sense in digging a well on somebody else's land, so he purchased a few acres from the mayor of Shechem. He might not own the whole country, but this, at least, would be a start.

He dug his well and drank from it himself, as did also his sons and his flocks and herds. He rolled together a few scattered boulders, likely the same ones that Abraham had previously used for the same purpose, and built an altar in honour of the "God of Israel."

Home, sweet home!

But the sweetness of home has an unfortunate proclivity to turn sour, especially when full of teenage boys.

Though the genes that produced the family's fine looks had skipped poor Leah, nevertheless those of her grandmother and great-grandmother saw to it that Dinah, Jacob's daughter, was a beauty. The mayor of Shechem had a much-loved son, after whom he had named the town, or perhaps it was the other way round. Either way, Shechem was a spoiled young man, accustomed to getting his own way, thanks to Daddy. Dazzled by Dinah's beauty, this pampered pimpernel, who had never been denied, raped her. Anxious to make an honest woman of her, he ran to his father for help. "Get her for me, Daddy! I must have her."

Dinah had arrived home dishevelled and distraught. The news that their sister had been violated inflamed in her brothers a desire for vengeance. "We will only consider giving her in marriage," they responded to the mayor's proposal, "if you, your son, and all the other men in the entire community of Shechem submit to circumcision."

The old man must indeed have been a mayor confident of the next election, for he managed to persuade every male to submit to the painful indignity. The first few days were the worst, and doubtless there were many absentees at work while the men stayed home to nurse their injured manhood. And it was while they were thus indisposed that every one of them died by the swords of Simeon and Levi, two of Dinah's brothers. They plundered the town and went home smug in the knowledge that their sister had been avenged.

"What have you done?" Jacob roared. "You have brought shame on the whole family and made us odious to the population of the entire land."

"He should not have raped our sister," they sulked.

"We'll have to move, you know. Can't stay here now."

Amongst the spoils from the city were a number of idols, sculptures, and statuettes the local inhabitants had ignorantly worshipped as divine. "We are not taking those things with us," said Jacob. "Bring them to me."

A pile of distorted notions of what God must look like was made beside the great oak. Jacob dug a hole amongst its roots and covered them over.

So once again, the family left the Shechem valley, driven away, not by thirst, as in the time of Abraham, but now by shame.

With no land to call home, Jacob and his family wandered south, eventually pitching tents for the night in the place that Jacob recognised as his first campsite after he had left his parents' home years previously. There was the same uncomfortable rock he had used for a pillow. It dawned on Jacob, as he dozed off to sleep with his head resting on the same rock, that God's promises to him had proved rock solid, and now here he was, back home. And that night, God spoke to Jacob once again, restating the promise of family and home. In gratitude, Jacob got up early next morning and built the rock into an altar. "I will call this place Bethel, because it really must be the house of God."

From there they travelled on south, past the flat-topped mountain where his father Isaac had narrowly escaped being sacrificed, on towards Bethlehem. When they were in sight of the village, Rachel, who was very pregnant, felt her waters break. Neither inn nor stable was yet available, so there by the roadside Rachel suffered the terminal agony of childbirth. If only Eve …

With her dying breath, she named the baby boy "Benoni": *son of my trouble.* "That won't do," said Jacob said after she had died, and in his grief he renamed the child "Benjamin": *son of my right hand*, in memory of Rachel, his first love.

And so Jacob eventually came back to his childhood home near Hebron. Against all odds, father Isaac was still very much alive, and it would be a further fifty years before Esau and Jacob would stand side by side at the family tomb in the cave near Hebron, to lay the old man to rest.

From there, the brothers parted company. Esau founded a nation – the Edomites – and then faded into the shadows of one who lived only for the present, with no thought of what God might have in mind for tomorrow. So the story continues, not with the children of Isaac – who would then have included Esau – but with the twelve children of Jacob: the children of Israel.

One might surmise that being the product of such amazing promises, these young people ought to aspire to something resembling sainthood. Quite the opposite was the case, however. A dozen boys, the progeny of one father, but four mothers, was the seedbed of intense sibling rivalry.

---- **4** ----

The Slave

To Joseph, the eldest son of Jacob's first love Rachel, fell the dubious privilege of being Father's favourite. Tales out of school on his siblings' shortcomings won him brownie points from his dad, along with a multicoloured cloak, but didn't do much to boost his ratings with his brothers. Notions of future greatness, fuelled by vivid dreams that one day the whole family would pay him homage, didn't do his popularity much good either.

Matters finally came to a head when Joseph's ten older brothers were away from home, pasturing their flocks on the hills up north. Concerned for their well-being, Jacob dispatched Joseph to see how they were doing. They were supposed to be on the old family property at Shechem, where they still owned a few acres. However, when Joseph arrived, there was no sign of them. But Shechem was a magic place for Joseph, alive with childhood memories. He doubtless took a drink from Dad's well and may have rested in the shade of the old oak tree with the guilty secret still hidden beneath its roots. Memories of his dear mother must have filled his thoughts. It was a happy moment, one that remained fixed in his memory, for it was the last few minutes of innocent childhood he would ever know.

"Have you seen a group of shepherds?" he enquired of a stranger, who directed him to Dothan.

"Here comes the dreamer!" scowled one of the brothers as they spotted the unmistakable colours of his wretched cloak, hiking towards them over the hills. "Let's kill the little brat and put an end to his dreams."

"That's a little harsh," suggested Reuben, who, as the oldest, retained a trace of family loyalty. "Let's drop him down this dry well shaft and let nature do the rest." Reuben had a notion of returning to rescue him later.

"We could always make some money out of him," suggested Judah, expressing the first hint of that family's enduring disposition towards financial acumen. So they sold him to a group of slave traders who were on their way to Egypt. The distinctive coat was ripped, dipped in goat's blood, then presented to Jacob, who sprang to the anticipated (but erroneous) conclusion that Joseph had been the victim of a wild animal attack. The old man was inconsolable. As time went by, shame replaced the jealousy his sons had previously felt.

Judah, in fact, felt so bad that he left home. Following his uncle Esau's example, he married a local girl, a descendent of the cursed Ham. The girl gave birth to three sons and then died. The eldest son married a wife named Tamar, then he followed his mother to the grave. According to the local custom, Judah's second son inherited his brother's widow, but thanks to cunning use of contraception, he avoided the inconvenience of babies. Then he also followed the family proclivity to die young. The youngest brother was Tamar's only remaining hope, but currently he was still too young to appreciate the birds and the bees.

"Return to your father's home, Tamar," Judah said in exasperation, "and I will call you when the little lad is grown." Years passed, and it became clear to Tamar that her infant husband-to-be was not to be. It may have been simply a woman's desire to be a mother, but perhaps it was the possibility of obtaining even a small slice of the promises of God that made Tamar determined to conceive children from Judah's family. She disguised herself as a prostitute and, hiding her face with a veil, seduced her father-in-law, accepting his signet ring in pledge for the goat, which was agreed as fair payment for services rendered. The ring was never actually recovered by Judah, as no prostitute could subsequently be found to accept the goat.

Apparently out of the blue, Tamar became pregnant, but when news of this disgrace reached Judah, he was outraged, and ignorant of his part in the affair, he determined that she should be burned to death. While on death row, Tamar sent a package to the self-righteous Judah, with a note attached: "The father of my child is the owner of the enclosed ring. Recognise it?"

Judah was mortified. "She is more righteous than I," he exclaimed, remembering his broken promises to Tamar. Tamar was spared and gave birth to twins. One of them, Perez, proved to be the most significant member of the fourth generation since Abraham.

Meanwhile, down in Egypt, things were going surprisingly well for Joseph. The traders had sold him to an influential man named Potiphar, a high-ranking member of Pharaoh's staff. So reliable did he prove himself to be that Joseph was soon promoted to manager of Potiphar's entire household.

Mrs Potiphar, however, posed a problem. Attracted by Joseph's fine physique and good looks, she attempted to seduce him and then screamed "Rape!" when he refused her advances. The whole experience was a little like Snakes and Ladders, for just as Joseph had made it up a few ladder rungs, he found himself at the bottom of a snake, in jail. But there is always another ladder, and before long, Joseph was in charge of the smooth operation of the entire penitentiary. Of course, he was still a prisoner, but the governor saw to it that he had the best cell on the block.

The monotony of prison life was interrupted one day by the unexpected arrival of a couple of celebrities: Pharaoh's butler and his pastry chef. Both had fallen foul of their master and were experiencing the sharp end of his displeasure.

One morning, they both came to breakfast looking a little off colour. "What's the matter with you two?" asked Joseph.

"I had a most unusually vivid dream," said the butler.

"Well, so did I," agreed his colleague.

"I have some experience with dreams," said Joseph. "Tell me what you dreamt."

"I was standing by a vine with three magnificent clusters of grapes. I squeezed their juice into Pharaoh's cup and gave it to my master."

"Well, don't look so glum," said Joseph. "That's simple. The three clusters mean three days. You'll be back in your old job by the weekend."

"Sounds good to me," the chef said, perking up. "In my dream I was walking along with three trays on my head containing my very finest Danish pastries. Trouble was, the birds kept swooping down to steal them."

"Are you sure you want to hear this?" said Joseph. "You have just three days left to live." Then he turned to the butler. "When your dream is fulfilled, you won't forget to put in a good word for me, will you?"

But he did.

Two years went by, long depressing years of confinement and frustration. Then Pharaoh himself had a disturbed night. Consult with the experts as he might, he could not find anyone who would interpret his dreams for him. The butler, whose privileged position enabled him to overhear his master's conversations, recalled his fellow inmate during his regrettable days of imprisonment. Joseph was summoned from prison.

"I hear you can interpret dreams," Pharaoh said hopefully.

"Actually no," retorted Joseph. "I can't. But God can. Tell me what you dreamt, and I'll ask him."

"Well, it was like this," Pharaoh said, slightly self-consciously. "Seven fat healthy cows came walking up out of the Nile River, closely followed by seven of the most scrawny specimens I have ever seen. For some reason, the skinny cows devoured the fat ones. My second dream was similar, but this time it was corn, rather than cows. Have you any idea what these dreams mean?"

"The two dreams have one and the same interpretation. The repetition simply serves to underscore the importance and imminence of what they represent. God is warning you that you are about to experience seven years of bumper crops, immediately followed by seven years of severe famine."

"What are we to do?" the troubled young king asked.

"Seems simple enough to me. Put into immediate effect a 20 percent tax, payable in grain. Store it in special granaries against the seven years of shortage."

"Capital plan!" agreed Pharaoh, who, with the typical impetuosity of youth, made Joseph his prime minister in charge of the whole operation. He was given a fine house, a beautiful wife, and impressive transportation.

At the end of seven years, his newly constructed granaries were overflowing with grain. He was not the most popular of prime ministers, but then he was responsible for the greatest tax hike in living memory. But the following year, they changed their tune when the harvest failed, and when their resources were exhausted at the end of year two, they came to Joseph, caps in hand.

―――――――――――

The famine was almost universal, with devastating effects as far away as Hebron. All Jacob's remaining eleven sons had now returned to live at home, as sons are wont to do when the economy turns sour. Word reached them that there was corn in Egypt. Ten of the eleven brothers set off in search of food, the eleventh, Benjamin, being too precious to be spared.

Joseph heard their rough Hebrew tongue the moment they entered the warehouse. There they all were, twenty years older. They hadn't changed much, while in contrast, Joseph had changed beyond recognition. During those years, Joseph had only used his native Hebrew when praying or muttering to himself. Now dressed in Egyptian finery, ever the smart dresser, he presented an imposing presence.

"So you have come to spy out the weaknesses in our national defence, have you?" the man addressed them, speaking with unexpected harshness through an interpreter.

"No sir, we are here to purchase food for our families."

"You don't seriously expect me to believe that, do you?"

"It's the truth! What else can we say?"

"So where are you from?"

"From a town called Hebron in Canaan. We are all sons of one father."

"Just the ten of you?"

"No. We have another younger brother, and one who is no more."

Seeing them all kneeling before him gave Joseph a sense of déjà vu, a memory of a long ago dream. "A likely story," he snapped. So off they all were sent to cool their heels in jail for three days.

"I'll give you a chance to prove your story," the prime minister said when next they were brought before him. "Go home and fetch this little brother you speak of, then I'll know you are telling the truth. For now, you can buy such supplies as you need, but don't even think of coming back without your kid brother."

On reaching home, they were mystified to discover that the silver they had paid was hidden in their sacks of grain. "Better give Egypt a wide birth!" they resolved.

But the famine persisted. "We can't go back without Benjamin," they insisted when Jacob suggested a return to Egypt. "The man will condemn us for espionage, and you'll never see any of us again." Jacob's empty stomach won the argument, and all eleven brothers set off for Egypt.

"Perhaps he won't remember us," they postulated, but he did. He had been looking out for them every day since they had left. And there was his little brother, Ben, son of his own dear mother, Rachael. Joseph was hard pressed to fight back the tears. Yet he maintained his distance and concealed his identity.

Perhaps, they thought, it was to compensate for having falsely accused them on their previous visit that the brothers found themselves invited to lunch by the premier of Egypt. But as they waited for the great man to arrive, doubts disturbed their peace. "We'll all be in prison before the day ends. You'll see."

But when Joseph eventually showed and took his place, their fears soon gave way to delight, as an opulent feast was laid out before them. For some reason, young Benjamin received considerably larger portions than did any of the others. When it was time to leave, the brothers returned to the warehouse to collect their sacks of grain. Little did they know that concealed in each sack was the silver they had paid, but in Benjamin's sack was the prime minister's favourite silver cup.

That evening as they sat round the campfire, their relief at being on the way home with the family still intact was profound. But their peace was short lived, as out of the shadows emerged Egyptian soldiers. "Why have you abused our master's hospitality by stealing his silver?" demanded the one in charge.

"We most certainly have not," Judah responded. "If you find any stolen property amongst our stuff, we will all return as slaves and the thief will be put to death."

"My master would not be so unjust as to go that far. No, the culprit alone will return as his slave, while the rest of you will be free to go."

They were mortified to discover the offending object in Benjamin's sack. So back they all went to Egypt – all of them, not just Benjamin, the whole family acting with a self-sacrificial loyalty that twenty years previously would have been anathema to them.

"Didn't it occur to you," boomed the prime minister when they arrived, "that a man like me would be capable of knowing your very thoughts? How did you imagine that you could deceive me?"

They felt naked and exposed. Innocent as they were of stealing a mere cup, they were guilty beyond question of selling Benjamin's older brother into slavery. And now Benjamin would suffer the same fate. Was he just pretending, or did the premier really know the truth?

For Joseph, however, the question was more complex. Had his brothers changed over the past twenty years, or would they still be prepared to sell out their kid brother, leaving him as a slave in Egypt while they went on their callous way?

Judah stepped forward. "My lord, don't be angry, but if this my brother does not return home, our father will die of grief. I myself guaranteed his safe return with my life. So please, accept me as his substitute, your slave, but let my brother go home."

It was at that moment that the stern face of the prime minister crumpled. Joseph lost it. Tears spilled down his cheeks, and he wept uncontrollably. The brothers shuffled uncomfortably, as guys always do in those circumstances. The other Egyptians all withdrew from the room, and the eleven brothers were left alone with an inexplicably inconsolable premier. Then he spoke for the first time in Hebrew. "I am Joseph, your brother, whom you sold into slavery." The silence was intense. "How is Dad?"

"Very well, thank you," they replied mechanically. Then Joseph went over to his little brother and enveloped Benjamin in his arms, and the two hugged and wept for a long time, a process that was repeated ten more times as each brother in turn received the same treatment. "And now," Joseph said, pulling himself together, "you mustn't think badly of yourselves. For though you may have had dubious motivation, God's intention was a wonderful plan to save the whole family. He merely sent me ahead to make the necessary preparations for your arrival. This famine is going to continue for the next several years. So go back home and get your wives and children, and of course, our father, and bring them all back to Egypt, where I will make it my business to see the whole family generously provided for."

News of this reunion reached Pharaoh, who sent along chariots to transport the women and children and a specially padded one for Jacob.

Jacob was stunned, unable to take it in when first he heard the news. It was the chariots that convinced him.

And that's how it came about that the children of Israel, some seventy persons in all, set out for Egypt, driven by famine, as had been their great-grandfather Abraham over two hundred years before. They had conspired to sell their brother into slavery, and though God used their unkindness for their salvation, it was nevertheless into four hundred years of slavery they were all unwittingly headed.

A nagging regret dogged Jacob's footsteps as he travelled past the southernmost border of the land of promise. Was he right to leave?

Their route led them through Beersheba, where Jacob's father Isaac had dug his well. Jacob recalled how as a child he had watched his father build an altar in that place and how moved his dad had been when God had spoken, reiterating the same promises that he had previously given to Abraham.

Jacob made camp for the night by the well, and with the help of his sons, rebuilt his father's altar. As he offered a sacrifice, he passed on to the next two generations the story of the promises that God had made and how they all were the fulfilment of what had been spoken. And that night, Jacob had another vision of God: "Do not be afraid to go down to Egypt, for I will make you into a great nation there. I will go down to Egypt with you, and I will surely bring you back again."

When they arrived in Egypt, Joseph introduced his father to Pharaoh. "How old are you?" asked the young king.

"One hundred and thirty."

Pharaoh looked incredulous.

"But that's quite young compared to many of my forebears." Then the old man, with the authority of the Creator himself, blessed the man many regarded as the most powerful king on earth.

So the whole family lived out their days in Goshen, in the district of Rameses, where the grass, watered by the Nile, was always green.

It was there on his deathbed that Jacob blessed his sons. The words he uttered, it must be admitted, were a mixed bag, some unworthy of being described as a blessing. However, for Joseph there was reserved something special: "You are the prince among your brothers because of the hand of the Mighty One, who blesses you with the blessings of the heavens above." Then placing his hands on Joseph's two sons, Ephraim and Manasseh, he promoted them a generation, elevating them to be blessed as though they were his own sons. For that reason, there never was a tribe of Joseph, but rather the two tribes named after his sons, Ephraim and Manasseh. One further gift for Joseph remained: "I will to you the parcel of land I bought near Shechem, where I dug the well by the old oak tree. You will return to that land some day."

For some strange reason that maybe even Jacob himself didn't fully appreciate, the most striking blessing was given to Judah, the father of Perez (the illegitimate son of Tamar). "The sceptre and the right to rule will always be held by Judah, until he comes to whom belongs the allegiance of all nations." Nobody had much idea what that meant, but history wasn't written yet.

Having delivered his final words, the old man lay down on his bed and breathed his last. In accordance with his will, his body was embalmed in a manner for which the Egyptians were famous. The whole family took one last excursion back to Hebron, where they laid his mummified remains in the cave near the family homestead. Perhaps Jacob had secretly hoped that the obligation to bury him in the promised land might have served as an occasion for his family to stay there. However, they didn't linger but returned to Egypt, where through subsequent generations they would find themselves increasingly enslaved by a life of ease and plenty.

Years later on his own deathbed, Joseph gave instruction to his family. He did not want to be buried in the family tomb in Hebron, but rather he chose to be laid to rest in the parcel of land that his father had specifically willed to him. There was a stream and an old oak tree that he used to climb as a child. There were the stones his great-grandfather had used for an altar to worship God. A well was close by, dug by his father, who had given him a drink from its cool water. And that was where he had last played with his mother just a few days before she died giving birth to his little brother Ben. To Joseph, that was indeed the land of promise, for it was there that God had assured Abraham that he was home.

5

The Deliverance

The decline was gradual, from honoured guests, to tolerated neighbours, to feared rivals, to subjugated slaves. As the memory of Joseph's significant role in their national history faded, the Egyptians began to wonder who these foreigners were who lived among them as a distinct society. The fact that they were shepherds, a despised profession in that land, was a strike against them, but their habit of breeding like rabbits was a positive threat. Their number had grown from the original seventy refugees to several hundred thousand, and the population explosion showed little sign of slowing.

The Egyptian authorities resolved to turn a nuisance into an asset and declared all Hebrews to be slaves. Yet the more they were suppressed, the more they multiplied. "What would happen if they rose up in rebellion and took sides with our enemies?"

Birth control being unreliable in those days, the Egyptians resorted to abortion, or something very close to it. They first demanded that Hebrew midwives snuff out the lives of all male babies at birth, but when something akin to the Hippocratic oath prevented the midwives from obeying, the Egyptian authorities made a universal law that all Hebrew male babies were to be thrown into the Nile. If the blood of Able cried out to God from the field for justice, then the outrage of thousands of drowned little boys made the Nile run red.

The anguish that was felt in the household of Amram and Jochebed when their baby was born a boy was typical of that experienced in almost every home. Should they throw him into the Nile themselves or wait till the Egyptian authorities came and threw him in? The decision was a compromise. Yes, they would put him in the Nile, but no, they would not *throw* him. So they circumcised him, as God's covenant with Abraham required, placed him in a waterproof basked, and launched him to his destiny. Little Aaron, who was three years old and had been born before the pernicious law was enacted, was still too young to appreciate what was happening, but Miriam, his older sister, could not take her eyes from the little craft as it floated down stream. She followed it till it caught in some reeds near the riverbank, and then she sat down under a tree to keep watch.

As coincidence would have it, a young lady of some importance chose that precise spot to take a dip. *She must be some kind of princess,* Miriam thought, for she was surrounded by quite the entourage. Then the baby started to cry. "Keep quiet for your life," Miriam mouthed silently. But the important lady had heard and waded over to where the basket was bobbing in the reeds. Tenderly, she lifted out the little fellow, laid him over her shoulder, and patted his back as she waded to shore. As the seriousness of the discovery dawned, an intense discussion took place between the princess and her attendants. Clearly they were torn between compliance with the law and response to maternal instincts. Miriam stepped forward. "Excuse me, miss, but would you like me to find a nanny who could take care of the baby for you?" How could she refuse? So the baby's own mother was hired as his wet nurse and nanny by no less a celebrity than Pharaoh's own daughter, who named the baby "Moses."

That's how it came about that Moses was raised in Pharaoh's palace as an Egyptian.

The family history, the story of Abraham, Isaac, and Jacob, had been passed down now through several generations, but the God who had given them such extravagant promises seemed to have forgotten them (or lost interest). It was hundreds of years since anyone had heard from him, and while the legend gave some hope to the enslaved people, nobody cared much whether it was actually true or not.

Forty years passed, and Moses was enjoying the privileged life of a prince of Egypt. But he never could forget his Hebrew roots. Sheltered as he was in his palatial surroundings, he resolved to have a look for himself to see how the other half lived. He was appalled when he observed the harsh circumstances under which the Hebrews were being forced to live and the cruel regime that subjugated them in slavery. His anger boiled over when he came upon an Egyptian abusing a Hebrew slave. Moses gave expression to his feelings with his fists till the bloodied Egyptian lay still on the ground. Moses couldn't find a pulse. He straightened up, panting, and looked around. The Hebrew had fled and no one appeared to be looking, so Moses quickly scooped a shallow grave in the sand and buried the corpse.

Next day, Moses took another walk about. He came upon a Hebrew who was intent on punching out one of his fellows. "Who made you our judge?" the man sneered as Moses intervened. "I suppose you are going to kill me like you killed that Egyptian yesterday!"

So the truth was known! As the gravity of his situation dawned upon him, Moses had little alternative but to run. So he fled and kept going till the desert swallowed him up and he was so lost that he doubted his pursuers would ever find him. He felt lonely and disoriented in a foreign land. Things took a turn for the better when Jethro, a local sheep farmer, showed him unusual kindness and hospitality, to the extent of giving him his daughter to keep him company. Zipporah became his wife, and nine months later, Gershom was born. Moses tried his best to explain to his wife the benefits of circumcision, but to her it seemed so barbaric that she talked him out of it.

Bit by bit over the following forty years, Moses adapted from a prince of Egypt to a stuttering old shepherd in a desert landscape. Then one day, he noticed an unusual phenomenon: a bush that appeared to have flames coming from it, yet was itself not incinerated. *Well, you see something new every day,* Moses thought as he walked over to examine it. Then an awe-inspiring stillness crept over the landscape, and a voice that hadn't been heard in four hundred years spoke: "That's near enough! Moses, take your shoes off. You are standing on holy ground."

"Who's there?" gasped Moses.

"The God of your fathers, Abraham, Isaac, and Jacob. I am aware of the misery of my people in Egypt and have come to rescue them and take them back to the land I promised to give them. I am sending you to Pharaoh to demand their release."

"Why me? Who am I to go to Pharaoh?"

"Who you are is not important. But what is important is that I will be with you. And you will bring the people here to worship me on this mountain."

"Suppose the people ask who sent me. What do I say? What's your name?"

"My name is who I am, who I was, and who I always will be. Just tell them, 'I AM, the God of Abraham, Isaac, and Jacob' sent you."

"But what if they don't believe me?"

"Throw down your shepherd's staff!"

Moses did, recoiling in horror as the staff became a snake.

"Now grab it by the tail!"

Not a smart idea, Moses thought to himself, but perhaps less dangerous than disobeying the voice. The snake vanished, and a staff was all that remained in his hand.

"Now put your hand in your inside pocket." When he pulled it out, his hand was rotten with leprosy, but much to his relief, a return to the pocket had the reverse effect.

"Now if they still don't believe you, pour a bucket of water from the Nile on the ground, and it will turn to blood, like that of all those Hebrew babies they are guilty of drowning."

"One more problem," stammered Moses. "You ssssee, I'm not much of a ttttalker, always had a bbbit of a ssspeach imppediment. Wouldn't you be sssssmart to pppick someone else?"

It was clear that the voice was getting a little exasperated. "Just who exactly do you imagine made your mouth in the first place? But if you are really that worried, you can take your brother Aaron with you to be your spokesman."

So Moses put his wife on a donkey, and together with his son Gershom, they headed for Egypt. As he plodded along, he thought back on what God had just said to him: "When you return to Egypt, I will harden Pharaoh's heart so that he will not let the people go. Then say to Pharaoh, 'This is what the Lord says: Israel is my firstborn son, but you refused to let him go; so I will kill your firstborn son.'"

And there was Gershom, Moses' own firstborn son. Moses recalled his negligence in failing to circumcise the lad, the sign of the covenant of trust that God would fulfil his promises by his own power, not through man's ability. Moses was aware that he had done his human best to strike a blow for the freedom of his fellow Hebrews and had lamentably failed. He had wound up a fugitive for his pains. If he was now to succeed in his new mission, nothing less than a major intervention by God himself would suffice.

Moses' feet began to drag. They were not the feet of a man who brings good news of freedom, for they were stained with the blood of a man whose life he had taken. His feet grew leaden. He was too old and weak, too sinful for the task. That night, he fell deathly sick and cried out in fear of the God who would insist, "Not by might, nor by power, but by my Spirit."

"Circumcise the boy, or I am a dead man," he croaked to Zipporah by his bedside. Quick as a flash, she did the deed and threw the bloody foreskin at Moses' feet. The fever passed, and in the morning, Moses set off like a man released from a burden. God had washed away the guilt of his indiscretions in Egypt. Now it no longer depended on him. God himself would do the miracle.

What a welcome sight: Aaron was walking down the road to meet him. Aaron listened to Moses' story and readily agreed to help. They called together the Hebrew elders and explained their mission, confirming their story with the magic snake stick. Gradually, it dawned on the assembly that God had in reality heard their cry for help, and they worshipped him.

Pharaoh, however, proved to be no such pushover. "Who is this God you speak of, that I should obey him? I will not let you go! Idle hands find mischief. You people haven't enough to do, and that's why you come up with these foolish religious notions." He ordered the taskmasters to increase the pressure.

"All your talk about freedom is only making things worse," the people complained. No matter how Moses insisted that it was not his idea, but God's, the Hebrews would have none of it. So Moses and Aaron felt caught between a rock and a hard place, when they returned to a stubborn Pharaoh to represent a people who didn't want to be represented. Yet so clear was their mission from God that they went, nonetheless. The amazing staff-turning-into-a-snake routine went over like a lead balloon, for Pharaoh's sorcerers could perform that same trick just as well. The fact that Moses' snake swallowed their snakes did little to increase the applause. So Moses was understandably apprehensive about the outcome of turning a bucket of Nile water into blood. But when the whole river turned to blood, even Moses was surprised.

"Just a red tide!" Pharaoh explained. From the polluted waters emerged frogs, thousands of them. Those slippery little fellows hopped their way everywhere, down the streets, into the palace, through to the kitchen, into the cookie jars, up to the bedrooms, and under the covers. At Pharaoh's insistence, Moses prayed, so the frogs died and were piled in putrefying heaps. Next came swarms of gnats like smoke that got into people's eyes, went up their noses, and irritated their skin. Close on their heels were flies that buzzed and bit and suffocated. Even Pharaoh's sorcerers had to admit that this was powerful magic. The plagues, however, were not universal, for there were no flies on the Hebrews.

"Okay," said Pharaoh. "You can go, but just don't go very far."

"No deal!"

Next day, all Egyptian livestock was dead in the fields, and the following day, boils blossomed on everyone's skin, like barnacles on a boat's bottom. Yet still Pharaoh would not give an inch.

"You haven't seen anything yet," Moses assured him as the sky grew black and hail stones as big as hen's eggs devastated the land, breaking tree branches and killing anyone and anything unfortunate enough to be caught outdoors.

"Enough already!" shouted Pharaoh. "So I was wrong. Stop the storm, and I will let your people go. Do what you have to. Just leave the women and children at home."

So next it was locusts that blackened the sky and stripped every green leaf and blade of grass in the land, except in Goshen, where the Hebrews lived.

Still no movement. So the sun declined to shine for three days, and a darkness as thick as tar suffocated the land.

"On your way," rasped Pharaoh, clutching a lantern with a hand that shook. "Yes and take the women and children with you. Just leave your belongings behind."

"Not on!" said Moses.

"Then get out of my sight," snarled Pharaoh, "for if ever I set eyes on you again, I swear I will kill you."

"If that's how you choose to play it, then so be it. But this is what God says: 'Israel is my firstborn son, and I told you, "Let my son go, so he may worship me." But you refused to let him go; so I will kill your firstborn son.' By this time tomorrow, you and all your officials will be begging us to leave."

White with rage, Moses turned on his heel and left, slamming the door behind him.

The events of that night have become part of the tradition of the descendants of Israel. They packed all their possessions in anticipation of a hasty departure. At God's instruction, they ate bread made without yeast. Each family slaughtered a lamb, which they roasted and ate, taking care that no bones were broken. Some of the lamb's blood was smeared on the doorposts and lintel of each home. Then they waited to see what would happen.

About midnight, lights started flickering on in the homes of their Egyptian neighbours, and gradually wails of anguish filled the streets. Not a family escaped bereavement. Perhaps it was one of the same angels who had visited Sodom who that night brought death to a people whose hearts refused to acknowledge and obey God, their Creator. But when he saw the blood of the lamb on the doorposts of the Hebrew homes, he passed over, a deliverance celebrated by that name to this day.

6

The Law

By dawn the next day, there was no suggestion of an escape, but rather a mass exodus of over a million people. They were urged on by their Egyptian neighbours, who pressed on them gold and silver and provisions for their journey, if only they would just go and bring this misery to an end. Four hundred and thirty years had passed since the first Hebrew slave had been sold in an Egyptian market. Now finally out of slavery, they walked towards freedom, driving their flocks and herds, camels and donkeys, dragging their grandparents and babies. They remembered to take with them the casket containing a mummy, the remains of Joseph, who was still to be buried in Shechem.

To follow the clearly established trade route would have had them over the border and into the land of promise inside a month, but instead they turned north, to find themselves confined in a peninsula of land surrounded on three sides by water. Did they fancy a holiday by the sea, or were they lost? Whatever the reason, it seems God had a method for their madness: "Lest they get discouraged by the battles ahead and turn back to Egypt." "Burning their boats" or "blowing their bridges" was perhaps what he had in mind.

But Pharaoh's take on it was that the Hebrews were hopelessly lost in the desert and hadn't the slightest idea of the way to their precious land of promise. On consideration, the loss of a million slaves would make a significant dent in his national economy, but now here they were, his to reclaim. Pharaoh led his army in determined pursuit. As evening came, he saw them, caught between him and the water, with no place to run. But before he could reach them, an impenetrable fog bank rolled in from the sea. So he pitched camp for the night, confident that there was no way they could get away.

Meanwhile, the sight of the advancing Egyptian army had caused panic in the Hebrew camp. "Was there insufficient space in Egyptian cemeteries that you had to drag us out here to bury us in the desert?" they wailed at Moses. Up till that point, they had never actually seen Moses in action. There was no mistaking the series of plagues that had precipitated their release, but the connection between those events and Moses himself was tenuous.

"Don't be afraid," Moses urged. "This is a good place for us to be, for we are shut up to a miracle. Stand firm and watch carefully to witness the rescue that God is about to achieve on our behalf." So saying, he pointed his staff out over the water, towards the town of Baal Zephon on the shore opposite. "Let's roll!"

It may have been foggy where the Egyptian army was camped, but for the Hebrews, it was a brilliant moonlit night. In the semi-darkness, they observed a most extraordinary thing. The waters of the bay appeared to be swept back by a strong wind that suddenly howled out of the desert behind them. One moment there was water; the next, there was a causeway to the far shore. Forward they surged, and before dawn the entire population had crossed over.

In the morning, the Egyptians were mystified to see the Hebrew camp deserted. Then they spotted the causeway and immediately gave chase. The wind still blew, flattening the water and pushing it aside. But halfway across, there was suddenly an eerie silence, and before the Egyptians could turn to run, walls of water were rushing at them from both sides. The path that had been release to the Hebrews proved annihilation to their enemies. And that was the last the Hebrews ever saw of their slave masters. That day, trust in God and confidence in Moses' leadership took a giant step forward. Old Miriam, Moses' sister, leading a group of beach-combing women with tambourines, marched up and down the shore, singing a somewhat macabre song of worship: "Sing to the Lord, for he is very great. Horses and riders all drowned in the sea!"

A family camping trip requires careful planning and adequate provisioning. But over a million people, leaving home with a few hours' notice, walking into a desert, led by a senior citizen with a stutter? Irresponsibility! At least that was the conclusion of the majority when their water bottles ran dry on the third day. Water was to be their recurrent challenge. First, the only water they could find was contaminated. God led Moses to a bush whose properties purified the water. The oasis with the twelve springs was a welcome break. But they couldn't stay there indefinitely, and their next campsite at Rephidim offered no water at all – contaminated or otherwise. "Take your shepherd's staff and strike that rock over there," God ordered. And out gushed a torrent of pure, clear water, sufficient for the needs of a million thirsty people.

Then there were over three million square meals to be provided each day. The sandwiches were all gone in short order. The chickens quit laying because of the disruption of moving, so it was chicken soup for a few days. Sheep and goats provided a couple of weeks of stew. Then what? Discontent rumbled from a million empty bellies. "At least we had enough to eat back in Egypt! We're all going to starve to death out here."

Next morning when the dew was still sparkling on the tent flaps, the ground was covered with … "Well, what is it?" That's how it got its name: "Manna." "What's-its-name." You could eat it raw, boiled, baked, grilled, however you fancied. But all the essential nutrients for a balanced diet were all present in good old What's-its-name.

God promised to give them each day their daily bread, but some didn't believe him. Despite God's specific instructions that they were not to store it over night, some sought to lay aside a secret stash, just in case God might fail to provide next day. But in the morning, the stench of their maggot-infested reserve made the secret hard to keep! "But on Fridays you may gather twice as much, and it won't rot overnight, so you can sleep in on Saturday morning and enjoy a day of rest in celebration of God's faithful provision for another week." Whatever possessed some of them to decline so attractive a celebration of so generous a gift? But workaholism and lack of faith have always been a destructive combination.

Some of the local inhabitants were offended at a million gypsies in their back yard, and an army of Amalekites attacked. A young man named Joshua led the defence and didn't do too well, till it occurred to someone that just as God provided each day their daily bread, he might also have a handle on delivering them from evil. Moses went up on a hill overlooking Rephidim, where the battle was raging. As he held up his hands in an attitude of prayer, Joshua's troops began to prevail, but as Moses' aching arms fell to his sides, the Amalekites scored a few points. It was quite clear that there was a direct correlation between Moses' persistence in prayer and what was actually happening on the ground. So a couple of the lads held up Moses' drooping arms, and the value of two or three joining hands in prayer was recognised.

Relationship was a major challenge. A million people, and many of them cousins, were bound to step on each other's toes from time to time. The line-up for justice stretched round the block, and there was only Moses to arbitrate in each domestic dispute.

"This pressure will kill you," pronounced Moses' father-in-law, Jethro. "Delegation is the way to go." So Moses established a four-tier justice system while acting personally as a one-man supreme court for the really difficult cases.

So there they were, a logistician's nightmare, yet doing very nicely, thank you. God provided everything. He personally guided them, leading the way as a cloud during the daytime and as a flame at night. He gave them food, water, protection, and justice. What more could they want?

Three months to the day since leaving Egypt, they arrived at the foot of an imposing mountain. Moses recognised it as the same mountain where God had spoken to him through the burning bush. Leaving the expedition in the valley, Moses hiked to the top. And there God spoke once again.

"My intention is to make these people my own unique, treasured possession. But I need to know if they will worship me and if they will obey what I tell them to do." So Moses went down to get their assurance that their intention was most definitely to do everything that God would command. Back up the mountain went Moses with the positive response. "Go down again and consecrate the people, for I am about to give you all my instructions." Down he went.

But the third hike up the mountain was one that neither Moses nor anyone else would ever forget. For suddenly the mountain seemed to erupt like a volcano. Fire and smoke belched forth, thunder rumbled, and from somewhere there was an ear-splitting fanfare of blaring trumpets.

"Go back down and tell the people not even to think of setting foot on the mountain, let alone attempting to come up." So down he went again. But the whole crowd was so terrified by the noise and smoke that they hardly needed telling. The awesome reality of the presence of the God they had come to worship gripped them in a holy terror.

Trembling with fear, Moses returned up the mountain yet again. This time God delivered to him ten commands, ten timeless words.

"Treat me as your first and greatest priority. Don't make or worship idols. Don't abuse my name. Celebrate the seventh day of the week as a holiday, a holy day of rest. Respect your parents. Don't murder. Don't commit adultery. Don't steal. Don't lie. Don't covet what doesn't belong to you." That much God delivered to Moses engraved on two slabs of rock.

Then followed some very practical instructions which covered such issues as employment, personal injury, property, social responsibility, equality of justice for all, annual holidays, hygiene, and diet. Moses wrote all these in a book and then returned to the people and read them every word.

"We will do everything the Lord has said. We will obey!" they agreed, and genuinely meant it at the time. Twelve altars were constructed, one for each tribe. Bulls were sacrificed, their blood being sprinkled on the people as token of their agreement with the covenant and all that was written in Moses' book.

Next day, seventy of the chief men of the people accompanied Moses part way up the mountain and saw first-hand a glimpse of the glory of God. Then Moses, taking Joshua his young assistant with him, headed to the top of the mountain, leaving Aaron in command of the people left in the valley. This time, God gave a blueprint for a mobile place of worship. Everything was to be portable and was described in meticulous detail: the tent, the perimeter fence, the altar, the furnishings, even the priest's clothing. The centrepiece was the ark, a gold-clad chest that was designed to house the rock slabs on which God had engraved the ten commands. On its lid there would be perched two awe-inspiring gold angels whose wings would touch overhead, providing a covering for a kind of throne, a representation of God's mercy and grace. The significance was doubtless that while the rock slabs would always stand in testimony *against* offenders, the mercy throne above would represent God's grace *towards* offenders.

It was as God handed to Moses the two engraved rock slabs that this principle of mercy covering law was put to a severe test.

Moses had been gone for six weeks. The people were restless. It wasn't difficult to imagine that some mischief must have befallen their leader. That mountain didn't look a safe place for an old man. "So here we are, up a creek without a paddle. We have no leader, no idea what God is really like, and no clue where to find this land of promise. What we need is some kind of a flag, a national symbol to hold us together."

They took their idea to Aaron and then gave him a sack of gold trinkets for him to work with. The finished product was a clay model of a young bull, covered with a veneer of the gold they had all contributed. It glittered in the sunlight. It dazzled them with its apparent virility and strength. They had each contributed something to it and thereby derived a sense of ownership. "My gold ring is in there somewhere!"

People were loud in their appreciation of Aaron's creativity. "This must be the god that delivered us from the Egyptians and led us here," suggested one admirer, taking too far his adulation of Aaron's handiwork.

"Hold on a moment," protested Aaron. "That's not it at all. This is just a national emblem. God is the one who brought us here, and tomorrow we will set aside time to worship him."

So next day, they all turned out for the worship service. But somehow God seemed extra invisible that day, less real, perhaps even irrelevant. True, the mountain still quaked, but by now they had grown accustomed to it and no longer feared the one who shook the mountain. As soon as the worship service was done, they turned to the marvel which they themselves had created: the golden bull calf. Their admiration flared into adulation, and before you could repeat the second commandment, the whole nation was worshipping the image. Their behaviour soon reflected their belief, for man is born to mirror. The glory of God the Creator, reflected in faithful family life, was traded for a man-made metal animal, mirrored in behaviour beneath that of any bull, gold or otherwise.

Up the mountain, God interrupted his dictation to Moses. "Your people have become corrupt. Go down." The sight that confronted Moses caused him to seethe with anger. He flung down and smashed the rock slabs containing the commands, then stormed through the revellers and pushed over the calf, which shattered in the fire. But still the people danced. It was plain that they were running wild, way out of control. He had to get their attention.

"Who is on God's side?" he yelled. A gang of men from Moses' own tribe, the Levites, ran over. "Grab your swords and restore order!" Three thousand people lay dead before the rule of law was re-established. Now he had their attention.

"What have you done, Aaron?"

"The people gave me gold trinkets, which I melted in the fire, and out came this calf." Well, perhaps there was a small grain of truth in what he said, but then there often is in the origins of deviant religion.

Moses took a rock and pounded the calf to powder. Then he made soup of it, mixing it with water in a big pot. "Now drink it!" he roared at the people and stood by till it was all gone. Presumably the idea was that when it reached the other end of their alimentary canals, the people would be able to look back and boast that it was "all their own work," proudly worshipping their own excrement. Such is the folly of those who venerate their own accomplishments.

With a red face, Moses went back up the mountain to face the God who had thundered, "Don't make or worship idols!"

"This is a stubborn people," God began. "Now get out of my way so I may destroy them. I will start afresh with you as the father of a new nation, and all the promises will be channelled through you."

But Moses stood his ground. "Then what would become of your reputation? 'God brought these people out of Egypt into the desert only to annihilate them!' Why, you would become the laughingstock of the whole world. And what of your promises to Abraham, Isaac, and Jacob? Are you a promise breaker? No, God! If you are going to blot out these people, then blot me out first. Destroy them? Over my dead body!" Extreme intercession.

"Very well," said God. "I will keep my promises. Go ahead! Lead these people up to the land, and I will send an angel to help you conquer the people now living there. But I won't come with you, for if this kind of thing happens again, I might not be able to restrain my anger. But Moses," God concluded, "I am very pleased with you."

"Then come with us! We would rather be here with you in the desert than in the land of promise with only your angel for company."

"It's okay, Moses. My presence will go with you. Be at peace."

"Then let me see you," blurted Moses, desperate for reassurance.

"If you saw my face, you would die. But nevertheless I will pass in front of you with my hand over your face till I am past. Then you may see my back. And as I pass, I will proclaim my name, so that while you may not *see* who I am, you may *hear* who I am." Faith has always been born from what the ears hear, rather than what the eyes see.

Next morning early, there was Moses, waiting expectantly in a cave, high on the mountain. As the sun rose, a bright mist obscured the view, and a voice proclaimed, "The Lord, the compassionate and gracious God, slow to get angry, overflowing with love and faithfulness, forgiving wickedness, rebellion, and sin. Yet he is not so unjust as to leave guilt unpunished, but will let subsequent generations experience the consequences of the misdeeds of their fathers." Then the mist cleared …

God gave Moses a replacement copy of the ten commands and again reassured him that he would accompany them on their journey, as originally promised.

When Moses came down the mountain, this time he was amazed at the reaction of the people. They looked at him as though seeing a ghost and then fled. "What gives?" Moses enquired of Aaron.

"It's your face, brother. It's shining!" So to avoid giving little children bad dreams, Moses took to wearing a veil.

The months that followed were filled with God-inspired creativity. The mobile place of worship, the "tabernacle," as it became known, was constructed under the supervision of Bezalel, an artist from the tribe of Judah. Stung as they were by their recent mistake of contributing their trinkets to the golden calf, they were only too glad to contribute to the right cause. The outpouring of generosity was a thing of beauty. By the first anniversary of their exodus from Egypt, the tabernacle was complete. When every last detail was in its place, the cloud that had guided them by day, the flame that had led them at night, moved into the tent, filling the whole tabernacle with the glory of God.

Much was made of the ordination of Aaron and his four sons as the first generation of priests. As a reward for having stood with Moses on the day of the riot during the golden calf incident, the men of the tribe of Levi were set apart as tabernacle assistants. But that wasn't the only reason: "Because I spared Israel's firstborn while I killed those of Egypt," said God, "therefore all Israel owes me their firstborn sons. By way of proxy, I accept the Levites and from now on assign them to serve me in my tabernacle."

While the instructions of how they were to perform their duties were somewhat stringent, those for the priests were exigent. Two of Aaron's sons made the fatal mistake of deviating from the book when offering incense. The fire flared from their incense burners, and they were scorched to death on the spot. Be sure the remaining brothers were careful how they led worship from then on.

However, jealousy tends to make light of caution. Korah, a Levite, had aspirations of becoming a priest. Together with a couple of buddies, Dathan and Abiram, he incited 250 other priest-wannabes to protest against Moses' insistence of Aaron's monopoly. "Why do you set yourself up, Moses, as superior to the rest of us? What gives you the sole right to appoint your own family to the plum jobs? Everyone is holy, so everyone should have equal opportunity to be priests."

"Then don't let me stand in your way," retorted Moses. "By all means bring incense burners and offer incense. Let's all meet tomorrow morning, and we'll see how God accepts your worship."

So next morning, Korah was there with his 250 supporters, but since the gathering had been at Moses' suggestion, Dathan and Abiram refused to attend. They weren't going to be pushed around any longer by Moses, the dictator who had dragged them from a land of security with false promises of milk and honey.

Moses, who was the epitome of meekness – anything but a dictator – was deeply offended. Followed by a crowd, he went off to confront the two absentees. And there they were, defiantly squatting in their tents, refusing even to come out to meet him. Moses turned to the crowd, who were uncertain what to think in the face of this potential vote of no confidence in his leadership. "Stand clear of their tents! If these people die of old age, then God didn't call me!"

The ground beneath their feet shook, then split open. Dathan and Abiram, together with their families, tents, and all their possessions, simply disappeared into the abyss. The crowd screamed and scattered. Meanwhile, the fire in the incense burners held by the 250 would-be priests suddenly flared and consumed those who held them.

Shock stunned the whole camp that night, but by next day, dismay had given place to anger. "You have murdered God's people," they accused Moses and Aaron, as though the two leaders had themselves somehow perpetrated the appalling disasters of the previous day.

Then the glory of God glowed red in the tabernacle, and a voice thundered, "Moses and Aaron, stand clear of the people, for I am about to annihilate them!" Instead of running, the two brothers threw themselves down in an attitude of prayer. Even so, death started to sweep across the crowd like fire over a stubble field.

"Quick!" shouted Moses to Aaron. "Take your incense burner, and offer incense in the prescribed manner, with fire from the altar."

Aaron hurried, horror driven, into the middle of the assembly to the very place where the wave of death was to break next. There he took his stand in defiance of the angel of death. "Over my dead body!" he roared through clenched teeth. And the plague stopped. Aaron was left standing between the living and the dead. Intercession: the duty of the true priest.

They were all profoundly shaken by the experience, but in case any question remained over exactly which tribe he had chosen as priests, God commanded them all to lay before the ark one representative staff from each tribe. Aaron's staff would represent the Levites. When the people approached the ark first thing the following morning, there were the twelve staffs, but the one belonging to Aaron was alive. During the night it had sprouted, budded, blossomed, and produced fruit, a crop of almonds.

"Now you keep that staff by the ark as a sign to the rebellious," said God.

Those were days of swift and tough justice. It seems that God was setting precedents to stress that he meant exactly what he said and intended to be obeyed by priests, Levites, and regular lay people alike. For example, two men got into a fight, and in his rage, one of them blasphemed God's name. Command number three was violated. Everyone who had heard the blasphemy was required to gather round to place a hand on the man's head, then stand back to stone the offender to death.

Another man was found gathering firewood on the Sabbath day. Command number four. He also was stoned to death.

Yes, there was not the slightest doubt that God meant it when he said, "Don't take my name in vain," and "Keep the Sabbath as a holy day of rest." These were not values to be assessed or negotiated, but absolutes with life-or-death consequences.

Six weeks after the tabernacle was first set up, the cloud lifted from the tent and moved to its accustomed place at the head of the column, ready to lead the Israelis forward. Camp was struck, and in careful order they set out, tribe by tribe. And that was the pattern they adopted as they proceeded during the days that followed. When they arrived in a location where they were to stay for more than an overnight stop, the cloud returned to the tabernacle. Then when it was time to move on, it moved to the head of the column.

It's easy to overlook God's provision in normal circumstances and give credit to nature, but in the daily life of the Israelis, "mother nature" could claim little credit for the miracles of constant provision. One might suppose that this obvious direct dependence on God for everything – water, food, protection, and direction – might have fostered in the Israelis a more grateful attitude towards their benefactor. But such was not the case. The people complained about the inconvenience of living as nomads. They moaned about the food: "Back in Egypt, we could eat meat and fish and a salad bar of vegetables. Now all we get is this 'What's-its-name.' Manna, manna, manna. We're sick to death of manna." It started with a few malcontents but quickly spread till everyone was grousing. "Give us some meat, Moses!"

"I'll give them meat!" God responded when Moses passed on their complaint. "Not just for a day or two, but for a whole month till the meat comes out of their noses!"

Moses, the pragmatist, reminded God of the sheer impossibility of providing meat for so many people for thirty days straight.

"Just watch!" God responded, and that night millions of quail, migrating north from the Gulf of Aqaba, settled round the camp, their tiny wings exhausted from their long flight. Next morning, it was simply a matter of picking them up. There was more meat than could be carried, a superabundance. A few million birds were plucked and gutted – no refrigeration, nothing but heat and flies. The stench was unimaginable, and the meat stuck in their throats. Severe sickness resulted, and many died. "You shall not covet!" God had said, and the cemetery where they buried the resulting dead was ever after called "Kibroth Hattaavah": *Graves of Coveting*. They had craved that which their circumstances would not stand. They had whinged till they had their way. Simple lack of hygiene killed them. Command number ten.

But human beings are slow learners, and the menu continued to cause malcontents to gripe. Grumbling poisons gratitude, and a plague of venomous snakes slithered from the dust. Many died a painful death before they made the equation between their toxic words against God, and the snakes that bit their ankles. It had been a snake in the original paradise that first libelled God with misleading Adam and Eve, and now only trusting God's true promises could reverse the damage.

"We have sinned, Moses," they confessed. "Pray for us!"

Moses made a bronze replica of a snake and nailed it to a pole in the middle of the camp. "If anyone is snake bitten, let him simply look at this bronze snake and he will live." God's punishment was always trumped by his mercy.

7

The Doubt

Perhaps the greatest insult that the Israelis delivered to God in those days was their scepticism of his promise to give them a land to call home.

Their travels had brought them to within a couple of weeks' leisurely walk from the border of the territory to which they were headed, and excitement was mounting. Moses dispatched twelve men, a representative from each tribe, to travel ahead to spy out the land. The men were gone for six weeks: forty days to be precise, for this number turned out to be significant.

The whole nation gathered round to hear their news when they returned. "What was it like?" they clamoured.

"Well, taste for yourselves," they responded, still staggering under the weight of the fruit they had brought back with them.

"So tell us about it!"

"Well, we have good news and bad news. It's no exaggeration to say that the land is rich in milk and honey. But the problem is that it is occupied land. There are people living there, many people, huge people – giants, in fact. The cities are impregnable. And the wilderness is so hostile that people who go there never get out alive."

"What are you saying?"

"That it would be suicide to attempt to invade that land!"

Shock swept through the crowd.

Evidently they were not unanimous, for two of the twelve, Joshua and Caleb, objected fiercely. "Listen up! We should go immediately to take possession of the land. God is giving it to us. Of course we can do it! Piece of cake."

"Get real," retorted the majority of the spies. "Some of the people we saw were so big that by comparison we felt like grasshoppers." The story grew better and better, unimpeded by the truth.

The crowd dispersed, and all evening long, little groups gathered around campfires. "We should have stayed in Egypt. Better slaves than dead. We should elect a new leader and head back right away."

Next morning, there was a general assembly, and Moses invited Joshua and Caleb to speak. "The land God has promised to give us is exceedingly good. It is God himself who will lead us there and protect us. The resistance of the people who live there is gone, but God is with us. Don't fear, and don't rebel against God. Let's go!"

But the "Nays" outweighed the "Yeas." In fact, it grew ugly to the point that they threatened to stone Moses, Joshua, and Caleb, whose only crime was affirming the good news of God's sure promise.

Had it not been for the terrifying appearance of the glory of God, the story might have ended right there. A voice thundered, "How long will these people treat me with contempt and refuse to believe? Moses, get away from them, for I am about to destroy them all, but I will start a new nation out of your descendants, greater and stronger than these people."

"But God," Moses protested, "then the Egyptians and the inhabitants of this land will conclude that you were not able to keep your promises, so were forced to kill us all in the desert. And what of your nature? I was given to understand that you were slow to anger, abounding in love, quick to forgive sin and rebellion. And we have seen the truth of that ever since we left Egypt. Were we mistaken?"

Once again, Moses had acted rightly; instead of distancing himself from the rebellious people, he identified as one of them, putting himself in the firing line of God's anger.

"Very well. I forgive them. I will keep my promise, but I will skip a generation. I will wait till all those now over twenty are dead. They have seen all the miracles I performed to bring them out of Egypt, yet still they refuse to trust me. So we will wait forty years, a year for each day they spied out the land I promised them – promises they declined to believe. Then, when the children and teens are grown up, they can lead the way into their inheritance."

The ten pessimistic spies immediately fell sick and died. "It's the plague!" someone shouted. The people ran for cover. But next day, they sent a delegation to Moses. "We were wrong. Forgive us! We will go up to the land of promise, after all."

"Too late, I'm afraid. For if you were to attempt to do that now, you would do so in disobedience to God's orders. You would be defeated." But many of them went anyway and were never heard of again.

So the Israelis turned south, back towards the Red Sea. What might have been a few months in the wilderness turned into years. Miriam died and was buried in Kadesh. She had faithfully watched over Moses ever since he was a baby in the basket on the Nile. The grief of her loss may have contributed to Moses' emotions becoming brittle, for once again the people complained about lack of water.

"Call an assembly," God said to Moses and Aaron. "Take Aaron's staff, the one that sprouted almonds, then in the hearing of the whole assembly, speak to that rock over there, commanding it to pour out water."

But when the people gathered, they started again: "We are going to die of thirst in this terrible place. We were better off in Egypt."

For one fatal moment, Moses lost it. He lifted the staff, and instead of speaking to the rock as God had instructed him, he vented his frustration on it, striking it twice. Certainly water gushed out, and the people's thirst was satisfied.

But God was not pleased. He had had a special reason for commanding Moses to speak to the rock, not to hit it. "Moses, you and Aaron didn't trust me enough to honour me as holy. I am the Rock. You may speak to me, but not club me; ask of me, but not demand. Therefore, you will not be permitted to lead the people into the land."

Not long after, Aaron died while on a mountaintop. His son, Eleazar, became high priest in his place. Aaron wasn't the only one to die; in fact, the mortality rate rose steeply, and soon a whole generation was all but extinct. Those who had been children when they left Egypt were now mature, the oldest of them pushing sixty.

It was around that time that the fiery cloud of God's presence started to lead the people north, in the general direction of the land of promise. There was a well-established trade route, and a few merchants passing that way might have excited little interest. But a million and a half people posed a major threat to the nations who lived along the way. The king of the Edomites, the descendants of Esau, refused unequivocally to permit them to set foot on his turf. Despite protestations that they were long-lost brothers, Edom was adamant and backed it up by massing his army on his southern border. So they were obliged to take the long way round, over difficult terrain.

The king of Arad was next to object. He made the mistake of actually attacking Israel, who soundly defeated him and destroyed his cities. King Sihon, ruler of the Amorites, suffered a similar fate, as did King Og of Bashan.

These victories opened the way right to the very doorstep of the land of promise. They pitched camp on a level plateau above the Jordan River, facing across to a fortified city they identified as Jericho. However, they were still occupying Moabite soil, and their leader, a stubborn monarch named Balak, took a dim view of all these foreigners camping in his back yard. He was smart enough not to attack by force, choosing rather to enlist the help of the spirit world. He sent for a powerful medium named Balaam to come and hex these intruders.

At first, Balaam refused the summons, but he could not resist the hefty bribe that was offered for a really potent curse and eventually set out on his donkey. It seems the beast was smarter than its owner, for it saw what Balaam was blind to: an angel barring the way. The dumb ass bolted in terror, squashing Balaam's leg against a wall. Finally, it simply lay down and played dead. Balaam was furious and beat the animal mercilessly. So incensed was he that he failed to notice the incongruity of it when the donkey spoke: "Why are you beating me, your faithful old donkey? Have I ever let you down before?"

Then Balaam saw the angel. "Lucky for you that the donkey stopped when it did, otherwise you would be dead! But go ahead for now, but be very careful that you speak only what God permits you to speak."

So Balaam came to King Balak, who took him up three different mountains, giving Balaam a variety of vantage points from which to view the huge encampment in the valley below. Balaam was overawed by the wonder of Israel, and all he could do was to utter blessing after blessing.

Balak was about to send him home in disgust when a crafty look came over the old wizard's face. "Though I may not be permitted to curse your enemies, there is another strategy that might just work ..."

It was a simple but deadly plan that nearly succeeded where sorcery had failed. The women of Midian simply used their bodies to allure Israeli men, first to their beds and then to worship their gods and on into witchcraft. An epidemic of promiscuity broke out among the people that spread like forest fire.

Moses called an assembly of leaders, who wept with him in frustration and shame. He was in the very process of delivering his instructions on what was to be done when one young stud from the tribe of Simeon walked by the tabernacle with a scantily dressed Midianite woman on his arm. With no compunction, he took her to his tent and, without so much as closing the flap, proceeded to have his way with her in full view of all who passed. Quick as a flash, Phinehas, Aaron's grandson, grabbed a spear and drove it right through the copulating couple and into the ground. The epidemic was nailed right there, but not before twenty-four thousand were dead. Rebellion was like witchcraft: difficult to distinguish the one from the other.

But the Israelis were stung by the strategy of Midianite seduction, so they put together an army of twelve thousand men, who routed the Midianites. After the battle was over, they found a donkey standing beside a wizened old corpse. Balaam!

So the demise of Midian left huge, depopulated territories on the east bank of the Jordan. It seemed a crime to the tribes of Reuben, Gad, and Manasseh that such fine grazing land should lie fallow when they had flocks and herds hungry for pasture. At first, Moses was outraged when he heard their request to have their share of the inheritance allotted to them in land that fell short of the land of promise. This move might discourage the other tribes, as had the disastrous report from the spies forty years earlier. But he was persuaded when the men of these three tribes promised to lead the attack across the Jordan and only return home when the conquest was complete. So it was agreed.

So there they all were, their journey through the wilderness complete. The land of promise was just over the river. Memories of the report brought by the spies lingered. In so much as they had talked of fortified cities, they were unquestionably right. Staring them in the face was Jericho, with impregnable walls and daunting fortifications. The people strained their eyes to see if they could see giants moving amongst the trees on the far bank.

Moses and Eleazar, Aaron's successor as high priest, organised a census. This was the second since leaving Egypt. A couple of interesting statistics showed up when the number crunchers had finished their work. First, there were only three people over sixty: Moses, who was twice that age, and Joshua and Caleb, the two faithful spies, both octogenarians. The other interesting observation was that the total number was almost unchanged over the forty-year period. The numbers of the tribe of Simeon had tanked, over 60 percent down, perhaps as a result of having borne the brunt of the recent epidemic during the Midianite seduction affair. But to compensate, other tribes had made significant gains, notably Manasseh, who had grown a whopping 65 percent.

Realising that his days were numbered, Moses called a general assembly. Everyone gathered in a natural amphitheatre overlooking the land God had promised them. Moses stood on a rock. Behind him flowed the Jordan River, and beyond that, the harsh red mountains that rose from the fertile valley. Over a million people hung on every word the old man had to say.

"I want to remind you today that you are a unique people. Never in history has a whole nation heard the voice of God speaking directly to them. And never has a people so dramatically been rescued from slavery. You are unique in having experienced the direct leading, provision, and protection of God over the past forty-year period. God did it all so that you would know beyond doubt that he, and he alone, is God. He didn't choose you because there was anything special about you, but simply because he loves you. And he loves you because he loves you and you must love him too, with all your heart: body, mind, and soul. You will demonstrate the reality of your love by obeying all his commands.

"God is about to lead you into the land that he promised to give to Abraham, Isaac, and Jacob. He will drive out the depraved inhabitants who presently live there. Be sure to destroy every vestige of their corrupt religious practices. And in no circumstances are you to get drawn into their ways or beliefs. To that end, do not permit your children to intermarry with them, for in no time you will be making child sacrifices and be into black magic and be calling on the dead to be your spirit guides.

"One day, God will raise up from among you a special prophet. Him you must obey.

"When you are happily settled in your new homes and God has fulfilled all that he has promised, be very careful that you don't grow complacent and forget God. Should you ever wander from his ways, you will be cursed every which way. But so long as you walk close to him, you will be blessed beyond your wildest imaginings."

Then he raised his arms to heaven and said, in a voice that crackled like a desert storm, "I call heaven and earth as my witnesses. I have this day set before you life and death; blessing and curse. So choose life! Love and obey the Lord your God, for he is your life."

There was a long silence. Then he continued in a gentler tone, "I am 120 years old and am not permitted to lead you into the land of promise." Turning to Joshua: "Joshua here will be your leader from now on." Then laying his hands on Joshua's shoulders: "Be strong and courageous, for you must lead this people into the land. God himself goes before you and will be with you; he will never leave you nor forsake you. Do not be afraid; do not be discouraged."

Moses' job was complete, the job he did his best to decline that day when the bush had glowed with God's glory. There never was a prophet like him who spoke to God face to face and who performed such spectacular miracles.

God led him up nearby Mount Pisgah and from that vantage point showed Moses the land he had promised.

It was there in the land of Moab that Moses died. The funeral was a private affair, with only God in attendance. No one ever found the grave.

---8---

The Homecoming

It had been five hundred years since Abraham first heard the promise, and for all those generations, it had remained just words, like seeds long dormant in the ground. For the past forty years, they had been living as nomads in no-man's land, anticipating the day when they would walk onto promised soil. Now, finally, the day had come.

"Every place you set your feet will be yours," God assured Joshua, as the mantle of leadership settled on his shoulders. But Joshua was terrified. "Don't be fearful or discouraged. Be strong and audacious. I will be right there with you. The Book of the Law will be your handbook. It will show you how to be successful."

A couple of strong swimmers crossed the river one night, and the next morning, the two spies walked bold as brass through the main gates of Jericho. The city was in no imminent danger of being attacked. The swollen river would see to that for the immediate future. So no one challenged Salmon and his buddy, but that didn't mean their arrival had gone unnoticed. Two strangers wandering round the city were unlikely to escape the attention of local eyes everywhere they went.

But neither was a pretty young woman likely to escape the attention of the two Israeli men. They followed her home, doubtless with the intention of checking out local culture, and were delighted when she invited them in. It gradually dawned on them that their hostess was a professional at that game, who had spotted them long before they had noticed her.

"Your presence in Jericho is no secret, you know, fellows. I'm betting the police are on their way, even as we speak." A pounding on the door confirmed her words. So the game was up before it had even started. "Quick," she hissed. "Up here." She led the way to the flat roof, where she was drying flax. "Lie flat!"

Before they could protest, she had buried them under the bundles of stalks. They heard her retreating footsteps as she ran down stairs to open the door. Would she betray them? They had no choice but to wait and see. They heard distant muffled voices filtering through the stems, but then there was silence. They waited for what seemed like a long time, and then she was back. "It's safe to come out now," she said, shifting the flax. "I told them that you had paid me a quick visit, then took off, who knows where." That was an easy story to be believed. Men didn't usually stay long in the prostitute's house.

"Now you fellows, listen up," she said earnestly as she set food and drink before them. "I have no doubt that God is going to give you this whole land. We may have our local idols, but your God is God of heaven and earth. I want you to swear that neither I nor my family will suffer any harm when you come back with your army to capture this city. Swear it, and I will help you escape."

"Fair enough," they agreed. "But when we come back, be sure that all your family is here with you in your house. And clearly display this scarlet cord in the window that faces out over the wall of the city, so we will recognise and respect your house. Oh, and what's your name?"

"Rahab." They shook on the agreement, and there may have been the beginnings of a romantic attachment, for when the subsequent battle was all done, Salmon would return to make her his wife.

Her house being built right into the city wall, Rahab let them climb down a rope to freedom. When they made it back to Joshua, they were able to bring the encouraging report that the people whose cities were so well fortified and forbidding were in reality as terrified as children.

So next day, they moved the entire camp to the brink of the Jordan. The river was swollen by the spring rains, spilling over its banks. The question that was in everyone's mind was how could they get across the churning maelstrom of foaming water? Nevertheless, very early in the morning, a couple of days later, they struck camp. The Levites, carrying the Ark of the Covenant, were at the head of the column. Undeterred by the current plucking at their legs, they waded straight into the river. Sheer madness! Any moment they and the ark would be swept away, and the whole advance ignominiously stopped before it was started.

But for some inexplicable reason, the water got no deeper. No matter how far the Levites walked into the river, the water remained ankle deep. The raging current ceased to rage. It dwindled to a stream, then a trickle, then puddled into pools, and finally was as dry as a creek bed in a drought. The Levites stood, dry shod, in the middle of the riverbed, and the whole nation crossed over. They were led by an army of forty thousand, drawn from the men of the tribes of Reuben, Gad, and Manasseh, exactly as agreed.

Now, for the first time since Jacob had left for Egypt 450 years previously, the children of Israel stood on the land of promise.

When they were all safe across, twelve men, one from each tribe, were ordered to go back down to the riverbed to pick up twelve boulders. The last to leave the river were the Levites carrying the ark and the very moment they set foot on dry ground, the waters of the river resumed their flood levels, cutting off their line of retreat. They had arrived! They were committed! There was no turning back. This was it.

That evening as they settled into their new base camp, they built a cairn with the boulders from the riverbed so that if any subsequent generation should ever forget their grand entrance to the land of promise, the stones would serve as a reminder. The place became known as "Gilgal."

That night, God spoke to Joshua. He reminded him that the sign of the covenant to which Abraham had agreed six hundred years before had been ignored. For the past forty years, no one had been circumcised. Here they were, out on a limb, totally dependent on God's miraculous intervention, and if ever circumcision had significance, then surely it was now. Next day, all the men were circumcised. *This is madness!* they must have thought, as the following week, the entire army was in too much discomfort so much as to sneeze. "We are totally at the mercy of our enemies!"

"Not so!" said Joshua and Caleb, the only two healthy males in the camp. "We are, as always, at the mercy of God, by whose grace we are this day as numberless as the grains of sand beneath our feet."

Their arrival in the land of promise coincided with the fortieth anniversary of the night the destroying angel had passed over their homes in Egypt while killing the Egyptian firstborn. So as the army was in no fit state to do much else, they celebrated the Passover.

The land of milk and honey also offered an abundant supply of fruit and vegetables. For the first time in forty years, the Israelis enjoyed a change of diet. And that was the last day that manna was ever seen.

Joshua was still working on his self-confidence, transitioning from his role of second fiddle to Moses to fearless leader. Repeatedly in those early days, God had to urge him to be strong and courageous, reassuring him that he would never be far away.

Joshua went out one night on his own to reconnoitre his first big challenge: Jericho, the fortress city. The indestructible walls stood black and menacing against the starry sky. How could they ever get in there? He had seen those walls forty years before and had done his best then to reassure his fellow spies that their threat was but an illusion. But now they seemed very real. And were there really giants crouching in the darkness?

Suddenly, a slight movement caught his eye. Someone was standing but a few paces away, tall and terrifying.

"Declare yourself!" barked General Joshua, hiding his fear behind military brusqueness. "Are you for us or for our enemies?"

"Neither," was the unexpected reply. "I am Commander of the armies of the Lord."

Joshua buckled at the knees and fell face down.

"What are your orders, sir?" he stammered.

"You can start by removing your boots. This is holy ground!"

"Fear God and you will then have nothing else to fear," felt like a good line for a song. That dark night, a reckless, daring confidence was born in Joshua. "Be strong and courageous, for God will be with you wherever you go!" Jericho? A pushover!

The instructions that the commander gave to Joshua were unusual, to say the very least. Siege works were not to be an option. "Have the men march round the city once a day for six days. No talking, but blow the bugles continuously. Take the ark with you, carried by the priests. On the seventh day, it will be seven circuits. When you take the city, burn it and slaughter the inhabitants. Everything that breathes must die. Everything that burns must burn. The gold, silver, and bronze, however, are to be gathered as an offering to the Lord. In future, the men can keep what plunder they find, but this is the first conquest, and the loot is first fruits to the Lord."

And so it fell out.

Jericho residents were nonplussed. The disciplined silence of the marching men contrasted with the menacing wail of the bugles. The tramping boots seemed to shake the foundations of their security. After a week of this, the residents of Jericho were just beginning to relax when the routine changed, and after the first time round, the soldiers kept going. By the seventh circuit, the city was completely encircled by silent marching men. Then the bugles changed their tune to one long scream, and a nerve-jarring war cry rose from the men. Ornaments rattled on the shelves, and pictures fell from the walls. The ground rumbled deep down, and masonry began to fall from the ceilings. Then everything broke loose, and the roof caved in. The noise of falling stones, the screams of terrified people, the smoke of fire, and the dust of destruction.

To the Israeli army outside, on the perimeter road that circled the walls, the sight was awe-inspiring. One minute the walls stood strong and defiant, the next they became blurred, indistinct, as they crumbled to rubble and dust. Jericho's protection really *was* an illusion. The only section of the wall that remained intact had a length of scarlet cord dangling incongruously from a small window. Then every Israeli found himself in the front row of the advance, from all sides at once. There was no resistance. Everything that breathed, breathed no more. Everything that could burn, burnt.

In the turmoil of the battle, disoriented by the horror of it all: the stench of death, and the dust of destruction, one Israeli lost his sense of perspective.

Achan was ransacking a fine house in what must have been an upmarket district of town. The resident family, whom he had found huddled in a corner, were all bloody corpses, and the house was beginning to burn nicely. Then, through the smoke, there before Achan was the open safe, spilling out a fortune in silver and gold, enough to set him and his family up for life. No one was there to see, and surely God wouldn't miss a handful of cash. And in any case, in the context of such violent horror, what did a few less coins in the offering amount to? So he grabbed the loot, wrapping it up in a fine-looking cloak, and hurried back to his tent before anyone would notice.

That night, there were celebrations. What they had feared for forty years had turned out to be a cakewalk. A handful of scrapes and bruises, but no real casualties to talk of.

So what was the next step? Joshua resolved to drive a wedge into the middle of the land by heading up into the mountains directly west of Jericho. This would discourage any kind of united resistance. There was a town named Ai, a name that implied that the place was already a ruin, so without so much as a by-your-leave from the commander-in-chief of the armies of the Lord, Joshua sent spies to reconnoitre. The celebrations were still going on when they returned. It seemed that Ai was indeed a bit of a dump, but a fortified dump nevertheless. "But compared to Jericho's defences, a good sneeze should take care of those walls. No need to stop the party. Just send a couple of thousand of the lads up there, and they should be back by supper time."

To be on the safe side, three thousand men went and were indeed back that same evening, but bleeding and dispirited. And when they called the roll, thirty-six men were missing.

Fear spread through the camp like dysentery. Clothes were torn in frustration, and dust flung into the air.

"So what's this about, God?" Joshua accused, pounding his fists on the ground. "If only we had been content to stay in the wilderness on the other side of Jordan. Word of this defeat will get out, you know, and our name will be mud. The natives will join forces and wipe us out of existence. And that's not going to do your reputation any good, either."

"Get up and stand to attention when I'm talking to you," God replied.

"There is sin in the camp. One of your men has taken home something that I said was to be destroyed. So now your whole army is in jeopardy till he and all his family are no more." God gave instructions on how the guilty party was to be identified.

Next day, everyone was called out on parade: an impressive sight, twelve squares with banners for each tribe. Achan was not pleased to be dragged from the warmth of his bed so early in the morning. His head ached after the celebrations of the previous night. After all, he had more to celebrate than anyone else. He was rich, and nobody knew it.

He took his place amongst the ranks of Judah. Joshua was explaining that there was sin in the camp and that it was necessary to identify the culprit. No fear of his being singled out from a line-up of over a million! But it was annoying that the other eleven tribes were quickly dismissed, leaving Judah alone to face the accusing eyes of the general. No one went back to their tents; they all hung around to see what would happen. After all, everyone loves a who-done-it.

Achan was still but one in a hundred thousand. No immediate cause for concern. The tribe was organised along family lines, clans, families, and households. The Zerahite clan was next identified. For the first time, Achan felt a twinge of disquiet, one that broke into a cold sweat when Zimri was chosen. Zimri was Achan's grandfather. From there it was inevitable. Carmi, Achan's dad, was singled out, and finally, from among his brothers, Achan. So there he stood, with a million accusing pairs of eyes upon him.

"What have you done?" Joshua asked.

Well, there was no sense in hiding it. "You'll find some gold and silver and clothing hidden under the ground sheet in my tent." Half an hour later, there it all was, in a pathetic little heap on a flat rock. Achan stood by, shame faced. Set for life, was he? The whole army joined in stoning him and his family. Destruction! Then they burned the corpses and heaped stones over the ashes. Trouble! *The Valley of Trouble*, that terrible place was forever called.

Morale was low. "Don't be discouraged!" God commanded Joshua once again, as he gave him specific instructions on exactly how Ai was to be taken. "This time, the men can keep the plunder for themselves."

There was no marching round the city, no bugles blaring, just cunning. A company of men snuck round the back of the city and hid in a ravine. Joshua marched the main army in a full frontal attack on the city gates and then, feigning defeat, fled in apparent disarray. The king of Ai led his entire defending force in delighted pursuit, unaware that a hostile force was sneaking out of the bushes and in through the still wide-open gates. It may have been the smell of smoke that finally got their attention, but too late. They were trapped. Nowhere to run. Nowhere to hide. No one escaped. The last to die was the king himself, hanging from a tree.

A few days later, a dishevelled group of travellers wandered into the Israeli camp at Gilgal. Apparently, they had come from a distant land to make a treaty with Israel. Apologising for their appearance, they insisted that when they had left home, their clothes and provisions had been fresh. "Travel's a curse!" they explained, showing their mouldy provisions. Flattered by the thought that distant lands had not only heard of them but wanted to make friends, Joshua shook hands and signed a treaty. He might have been smart to have asked God first, because three days later, the truth came out. The travellers were from Gibeon, a city just to the south of Ai.

"Kill them!" someone shouted.

"Not so," said Joshua. "We can't break our word."

"But they lied to us."

"If we want the Lord's favour, we must be trustworthy, just as he is. But ... [perhaps as an afterthought] ... I suppose there's no harm in using them as slave labour?"

The capitulation of Gibeon disturbed the king of Jerusalem, a near neighbour, a mile or so further to the south. "King" is perhaps an exaggeration, for Adoni-Zedek was little more than a town mayor. But to say he was a king sounded more impressive. What troubled him was that Gibeon was a sizable city, with a fierce reputation for being mighty warriors. If Gibeon had gone under, what hope for the rest of them? So Adoni-Zedek shared his concerns with some of his cronies, and four other kings from neighbouring cities in the southern half of the land united their fighting men to form one formidable army. They marched on Gibeon, bent on destroying the turncoats.

A runner was dispatched from Gibeon to Joshua in Gilgal, to beg for help from their new allies. It would have been so easy for Israel to do nothing, to simply allow Adoni-Zedek to do what their oath had prevented them from doing. But, as it turned out, this was a divine appointment that would save Isreal a lot of time and trouble, one big battle being much more efficient that a string of small ones. God gave the operation the thumbs up, and the Israelis marched all night up the rugged trail from the Jordan Valley to Gibeon, high in the mountains between the ruins of Ai and Jerusalem.

Adoni-Zedek and his allies were caught completely by surprise. Panic threw them into confusion. Many died, but even more fled south towards home. The skies turned black, and hail the size of goose eggs added to the slaughter. The five kings sought refuge in a cave, a short-lived reprieve, since someone saw them go in and kept them there, prisoners on death row till the executioner would arrive.

The day wore thin, and it looked like many of the allied soldiers would escape under a cloak of darkness. "Let the time stand still!" Joshua cried out in a thunderous voice. And the sun stayed where it was till the killing was all done. Daylight saving.

That decisive battle secured the southern half of the land: the hill country, the Negev, the western foothills, and the mountain slopes. There was some mopping up to do, pockets of resistance, but that was all part of the process of taking possession of the territory, securing and settling the towns and garrisons.

One might imagine that the kings of the northern territory should have learned by the mistakes of their southern neighbours, yet not one of them suggested peace talks or negotiations. It was King Jabin of Hazor, capital city of the north, who took the initiative. He rallied the support of a plethora of kings from far and wide, Lebanon south to Galilee, the Great Sea to beyond the Jordan. They arrived at a secret rendezvous high up in the mountains, just west of Hazor. Their army covered the mountain slopes like trees in the forest. The commanders of the cavalry didn't think much of the location, complaining that their horses and chariots would be useless in the steep terrain. But doubtless their fears were calmed with promises that this was just to be the meeting place and battle would not be joined till they were well positioned on the flatter ground near Hazor.

But a secret meeting place, when attended by hundreds of thousands of noisy soldiers hauling heavy equipment, quickly ceases to be a *secret* meeting place. Joshua had scouts in the mountains, looking down on the northern allies.

"They have horses and chariots," they reported breathlessly to Joshua.

"Some trust in chariots and some in horses, but we trust in the name of the Lord our God," Joshua replied calmly, mindful of the time he and his fellow spies had reported to Moses what they had first seen of the land forty years back.

"Don't be afraid of them," the Lord assured Joshua. "By this time tomorrow, they will all be dead."

And so it turned out. The Israelis mounted a surprise attack before Jabin and his allies were organised. Thousands were killed in the confusion. The rest fled north, up through the mountains, desperately trying to stay alive. Their relentless pursuers hacked them down all the way up into the snows of the Lebanon mountains.

"Let's keep the horses and chariots. They could be useful," someone suggested. But Joshua did as God had told him: hamstrung the horses and used the chariots for firewood.

All that remained in that region was to take possession of the towns. They made an example of Hazor and burned it to the ground, but there was no sense in unnecessary destruction, so other cities were kept intact. But that is more than can be said of the population. Every man, woman, and child was slaughtered.

So the promised land was under Israeli control. That's not to say that there were no survivors. There were groups hidden away in remote and inaccessible areas, notably the Philistines, comparatively recent immigrant invaders from the island of Crete. They hung on for generations.

What followed might have been contentious: the dividing up of the turf between the tribes. Only the Levites would get no specific territory, since they were set apart to be scattered throughout the land to minister to the spiritual needs of the other eleven tribes. Negotiations might have been heated. Who would get the waterfront lots along the Mediterranean coast? Who would have the fertile Jordan Valley? They agreed to leave the allocation to God, and when they had divided up the map into unequal parcels, they rolled the dice, trusting God to let the lines fall where he chose.

Caleb, Joshua's fellow spy from way back, now eighty-five, insisted that Hebron was his inheritance. "Moses promised that land to me!"

"Whatever do you want that place for? It's steep terrain, and Hebron is a heavily fortified city, garrisoned by giants."

"But that's the point," Caleb insisted. "It was giants, impregnable fortifications, and impossible terrain that made the people fear when our fellow spies brought them a negative report. I want to prove them wrong."

"But you are an old man."

"I am still as strong and fit as ever I was. Besides, I want the next generation to learn to carry on the family tradition."

So the old man led the attack on Hebron, killing off the defending giants and securing not only the city, but the traditional family tomb where Abraham, Isaac, and Jacob were buried: the cave of Machpelah.

The fortress of Debir was further up in the hills, and doubtless Caleb could have done the job himself, but instead he involved the next generation. "Whoever takes Debir gets my daughter Acsah as the prize." Othniel, Caleb's nephew, had long loved his cousin, so he won the prize. When the wedding gifts were being opened, there were the title deeds to Debir and a huge chunk of desert real estate to go with it.

"Thanks, Dad," said Acsah, "but desert land is of no value without water." So Caleb extended the property lines to include "the Upper and the Lower Springs."

However, other members of the same tribe of Judah were not so successful. Jerusalem was an impregnable fortress, perched on top of inaccessible cliffs. A group of stubborn and determined Jebusites hunkered down there and stayed put. "Forget it," the Israelis conceded, and they did forget it, for four centuries.

Ephraim and Manasseh, being prolific breeders, had multiplied more than the average, so they demanded more land. "That's fine," Joshua agreed, "but you have to take and clear it yourselves." This was no simple task, since the valleys were defended by warlike Canaanites, with state-of-the-art iron chariots, and the dense forests were inhabited by fierce mountain people. But they rose to the challenge. And it was there where the mountains gave way to the plains in the west that Joshua himself settled in a town named Timnath Serah.

Throughout the country, certain cities were designated "Cities of Refuge." These were safe houses to which people guilty of manslaughter could run for protection, safe from the vengeful relatives of their accidental victims.

Also scattered throughout the tribes were forty-eight cities, which together with the surrounding farmland became the homes of the tribe of Levi. That way, they would be on hand to care for the spiritual needs of the whole nation, exercising their ministry in every corner of the land.

So there they were, home and dry. The land was taken; the people were settled into their new homes; the promises of God had proved true.

Joshua summoned the leaders of the tribes of Reuben, Gad, and Manasseh. "You fellows have been as good as your word. You promised Moses on the day he allocated you territory east of Jordan that you would not stay home, but would lead the attack in the land of promise. Mission accomplished! You are now free to return home and join your families." So they set off with vast herds and truckloads of booty.

When they reached the Jordan River, which separated their lands from those of their brother tribes, they paused to build a replica of the altar of the Lord that was in the tabernacle, back in Shiloh. "This will serve to remind our kids where our spiritual roots are. And perhaps it will also remind our fellow Israelis that we are still part of the family – separated by the river, yes, but united under God."

Good intentions can sometimes be misunderstood. Rumours flashed round the land. "Those guys from the tribes of Reuben, Gad, and Manasseh have turned traitor. No sooner are they over the Jordan and they have started a new religion, built a pagan altar to God-knows-who! Get your swords!"

Mercifully cool heads prevailed, and a delegation of leaders preceded the angry mob. Understanding dawned. Peace restored.

Some years later, Joshua called a national assembly at Shechem. Hundreds of thousands arrived in the valley where Abraham had first pitched his tent on promised soil, seven hundred years earlier. Six tribes stood on the arid slopes of Mount Ebal, while the other six massed on the fertile side of Mount Gerizim. There in the valley between them was a scattered mound of moss-covered stones that Abraham himself had gathered as his first altar to God. And by it wound a stream that had dried up during that hot summer, forcing Abraham to migrate further south to Egypt. There was the well that Jacob had dug a couple of generations later, as a precaution against drought. And there was the ancient oak tree whose roots hid the guilty secret of the murderous sons of Jacob, whose names their tribes still bore. This valley was land promised to Joseph by his father Jacob, many generations back, down in Egypt.

The first item on the agenda for the national assembly was therefore a funeral. For the past fifty years, they had been hauling with them a four-hundred-year-old mummy, the remains of Joseph. There he was finally laid to rest, and with him were buried the last vestiges of their years of slavery.

Next Joshua supervised the reconstruction of Abraham's altar, on which they offered sacrifices to God. Now they were home, dead centre on the very ground where God had promised Abraham: "To you and to your descendants I will give this land." A large flat-faced rock stood like a huge tomb stone, right next to the green oak tree, death and life side by side. On the face of the stone, Joshua instructed a mason to engrave the non-negotiable ten commands.

Joshua had them boost him up onto the rock to address the assembly. He stood there, leaning on his staff, face blackened by the sun, skin wrinkled with age, wispy white hair blowing in the wind. A great silence settled throughout the valley.

"I set before you this day, life and death; blessing and cursing. Choose life!" Turning to those on the lifeless slopes of Mount Ebal, Joshua recited a horrifying catalogue of woes that would befall those who might ever dare to disregard the law of God. There was shocked silence when he finished. Then turning to those on the lush green slopes of Mount Gerizim, he promised a plethora of blessings that beggared the imagination. "All these will be the inheritance of those who obey these commands!"

Then from either side of the valley echoed the thunderous agreement of a million voices, promising obedience.

When the echoes had died away to silence: "Your forefathers worshiped so-called gods in the land beyond the Euphrates. The Egyptians worshipped the gods of the Nile. The inhabitants of this land worshipped all manner of deities. But it was the Lord God who brought you miraculously to this place. Choose then today whom you will serve, but I and my family will serve the Lord." Again – thunderous agreement.

"But no!" Joshua countered as the roar once again died away to stillness. "You cannot say you will serve the Lord and then later change your minds."

"We will never change our minds. We are determined to serve the Lord."

"You will hold each other accountable for this decision?"

"Absolutely!"

"Then destroy the idols and so called 'art' that you have among your plunder. And turn your hearts fully to the Lord."

"Yes!" they bellowed. "We will serve the Lord our God and obey him completely."

When the echoes of their determination had faded and silence again settled in that valley of decision, Joshua spoke one last time, standing on the stone that spelled out the absolutes of God's standards, there in the shade of the oak tree of life: "This stone has heard your words and will forever stand as witness to your promise."

From there, they all drifted back in a thousand directions to start a whole new life as a nation in their own homes, on their own farms, in their own towns, tribe by tribe, living proof that God keeps his promises.

Not long after, Joshua died and was buried on his farm in Timnath Serah.

9

The Anarchy

With Joshua dead and the nation dispersed into tribal states, the people lacked a focused leader. It was left to the individual to do as he saw fit with his inheritance. Abraham, Isaac, and Jacob were shadowy figures buried in half a millennium of history. Moses was long gone, and even Joshua was a fading memory. So to Israel, this was a new era in a strange culture. Fascinating expressions of faith were evident everywhere they looked. These objects of worship were solid and tangible. They looked good on the shelf, first as ornaments, then as talismans which, when believed, became expressions of faith – petition in tough times and praise when life was good. And the local people were interesting. The girls were sexy and the guys were hunks, and before you could say "Who's your father?" the purity of the family blood line was contaminated, and mixed race marriages confused the identity of who should be honoured as god.

God was not pleased, and trouble multiplied. But whenever things got rough, a memory would stir and the Israelis would cry out to the God about whom their grandparents had told them, the Lord who had delivered them from the Egyptians back in the last century. Then the Lord would be sorry for them, for he hated to see them suffer. His solution was always the same. He would raise up a man, a man who would lead them, a deliverer. "Judges" these leaders were termed. Othniel was the first. Caleb, the aged spy, had taught him well, challenging his nephew to defeat the giants in Debir. Othniel called Israel to arms and defeated the king of Aram, who had been making their life a misery.

But as predictable as taxes, the next generation was back to their old ways, and trouble followed, this time in the form of the Moabites.

King Eglon led his force across the Jordan and captured what had been Israel's first prize: Jericho. From there, he harassed the Israelis, imposing punitive taxes on all who wanted to stay alive. For eighteen years, Eglon grew fat at Israel's expense. Then one year at tax time, Ehud, a lefty from the tribe of Benjamin, led a delegation to deliver the tax money to Eglon at his palace in Jericho. Security searched Ehud for weapons but missed the dagger he had concealed where a right-handed man would not expect it to be.

When the money was delivered into Eglon's greedy hands, Ehud whispered, "I have a secret message from God to deliver – for your ears only." Intrigued, Eglon dismissed his servants. As soon as they were alone, Ehud pulled out his concealed weapon and plunged it into Eglon's vast stomach, where it disappeared, enveloped in years of greed. Quick as a flash, Ehud locked the door and made his escape down the latrine and out through the sewage system. By the time the king's servants had found a spare key and plucked up the courage to interrupt what they had taken to be Eglon's private time in the washroom, Ehud was long gone and was raising an army to kick the Moabites back across the Jordan, where they belonged.

Peace at last, eighty years of peace, enforced by a judge named Shamgar. But as soon as that generation was dead, history repeated itself, and once again Israel's misconduct led to their downfall. This time their tormentor was Jabin, a Canaanite king in the north whose army was commanded by Sisera. Sisera was a ruthless cavalryman, who boasted nine hundred state-of-the-art iron chariots. For twenty years, life was misery for the wretched Israelis. Then they remembered to pray.

Honest leaders were in short supply in those days, but the brightest light around was a wise woman named Deborah. To her, people would come to air their grievances and to seek her wisdom under a palm tree on a hilltop near Bethel. Clearly something had to be done about Jabin, and since male initiative was lacking, Deborah took it upon herself to commission a man to take action. "Barak, the Lord commands you to raise an army of ten thousand and march them up to the top of Mount Tabor." Sounded doable, but Barak needed reassurance.

"I'll only go if you'll come with me, Deborah."

"Very well, but since you have requested a woman to hold your hand, to a woman will go the credit for the victory."

Sisera and his armoured divisions massed in the plain at the foot of Mount Tabor while Barak looked down from his lofty vantage point. The mountain was impossible terrain for Sisera's chariots, while the plain was ideal. So long as he stayed on the mountain, Barak would be safe, but to descend to the plain would be suicide. When he hesitated, Deborah urged him, "Go on! Today the Lord has delivered Sisera into your hands." It sure didn't look promising, but how could he refuse a woman?

Perhaps the rainy season was Barak's salvation, and perhaps the flat ground was too soft for chariot wheels, but for whatever reason, Sisera abandoned his ride to flee on foot through the mud. He ran till he was utterly spent. Then he noticed a settlement of nomads with a woman crouching in a tent door.

"Come in, my lord," she beckoned. "Don't be afraid."

"Spare me a drink," Sisera panted, "and don't let anyone know that I am in here."

Exhaustion overcame the defeated general, who sank into a deep sleep. The woman quietly took a hammer and spike and nailed his head to the floor. He never woke up. Legends and ballads are made of such heroism, and a song was written in celebration of the event.

Next it was the turn of the Midianites to chastise Israel. These fierce desert people swarmed up from the south and east, and for years, they made it their business to impoverish the land, stealing livestock and destroying crops. They were led by two ruthless warlords, Zebah and Zalmunna. Israel begged the Lord for help ...

Gideon was little more than a boy when these two thugs came to the family farm in Ophrah. He saw the glint of sadism in their eyes as they hacked a couple of his brothers to death. The memory haunted him into adult life, so little wonder that when he was called to be the next judge, Gideon was hiding in a wine press, secretly threshing wheat for fear the Midianites might put him to a similar fate. He glanced up to ensure he was alone and, to his horror, saw someone sitting just a few feet away, leaning against a tree, gazing into the distance.

"God be with you, mighty warrior!" the stranger said, without getting up.

"Nice thought," Gideon retorted. "But what good would that do? Seems he's lost his touch. Whatever happened to the good old days, when he rescued Israel from Egyptian slavery? Now he has abandoned us to Midian supremacy."

The stranger turned and looked Gideon in the eyes. "So go and do something about it. Save Israel from Midian. I am sending you."

"Me, save Israel? Dream on! I am a nobody!"

"I will be with you, so you can't lose."

Gideon invited the stranger to stay for a meal, but when he laid the food out on a rock, fire flared up and consumed the food as though it were an offering. When Gideon swung round to look at the stranger, he had vanished.

"I am a dead man! I have seen an angel."

To save Israel was a grand ideal. But where should he start?

"Start at home," came the answer that same evening. "Clean house and get rid of all trace of idolatry."

So that night, Gideon hacked down the family idol and demolished its altar. He rebuilt a new altar to the Lord and then went to the barn and slaughtered his father's best bull, which he sacrificed to the Lord.

Next morning, there was trouble. "Whoever is responsible for this desecration must die," community leaders demanded.

"If Baal is a real god, he can defend his own honour without your help," Joash, Gideon's father, responded, jumping in to rescue his son. Further argument was eclipsed by news that the Midianites were advanceing.

At that moment, the Spirit of God came on Gideon. He blew a call to arms on a ram's horn, and to his amazement, thousands responded. Gideon was terrified.

He couldn't sleep that night, so, kneeling beside his bed, he prayed,

"God, I need a sign that you really are with me. Nothing dramatic. How about this fleece I am kneeling on being soaked with dew in the morning, and all the ground around it bone dry?"

In the morning, he jumped out of bed and squelch! The fleece was soaking. One more step coated his now wet feet with dry dust.

But perhaps that was a natural phenomenon? "Other way round tomorrow, God. Dry fleece and wet ground! Then I'll know it's you. Okay?"

Next day, his bleary feet hit a warm dry fleece, but his next step sank up to the ankles in mud.

There being no further combinations of wet and dry, Gideon was forced to concede that God really was with him.

"But so that you will be quite clear that it is simply *because* I am with you that you will have the victory, reduce the size of your army," God instructed him.

Gideon announced that anyone who was afraid was free to go home. Since they were already hopelessly outnumbered by Midianites, it was no surprise that two-thirds of the volunteers upped sticks and left. Gideon must have been tempted to leave with them, but he stayed, along with ten thousand others.

"Still too many!" said God. "Take them to the river for a drink." Nine thousand seven hundred sank their faces in the water to drink, oblivious of the proximity of hostile troops. Three hundred lifted the water to their vigilant faces and drank from cupped hands. They were the chosen ones.

So there they were, just three hundred, bivouacked in the hills, and a menacing hoard of enemy marauders in the valley below. Another sleepless night.

God encouraged Gideon. "Go down and attack. But if you are afraid to go down, then just do it. Go down. Then you will find the courage you need to go down." So he went down – great cure for the faint of heart.

He crept into the camp and overheard a conversation between two Midianites. One was recounting to the other a nightmare that had just woken him. Apparently, he had dreamed that a loaf of bread had rolled down the hill and knocked over a tent. "It's an omen," his friend cried. "We are finished!"

"Get up!" Gideon yelled when he got back to his camp. "God has given them to us on a plate."

His plan could hardly be called "a plan of attack." He spread his men around the Midianites in three companies, each man armed with only a bugle and flaming torch hidden under a clay pitcher. Then on his command, they all smashed the pitchers and blew the bugles and shouted, "The sword of the Lord and Gideon!" The sound of smashing jars, yelling men, and blaring bugles woke the sleeping Midianites. As they stumbled out of their tents, the hills were full of lights and war cries. In the darkness, it was impossible to tell friend from foe, but since all their foes were in reality safe up in the hills, they set to slaughtering one another. Survivors fled for their lives. The three hundred gave chase and were soon joined by thousands of other willing volunteers who slaughtered stragglers all the way to the Jordan River. But it was the original three hundred who pursued the survivors deep into enemy territory.

They finally caught up with the Midianite warlords, Zebah and Zalmunna, still in command of a not inconsiderable army of fifteen thousand. Thinking they were safe home, they were less vigilant than prudence should have demanded. Without a moment's hesitation, Gideon attacked. The slaughter was complete, with the bonus of capturing the two leaders alive.

"Do you recall years ago when you came to a farm in Ophrah, near Tabor?" Gideon asked them.

An evil look came over their faces. "Yes, and we cut down to size some of those arrogant young weasels who lived there."

"Those were my brothers." Gideon took a sword and ended years of sleepless nights and fear-filled dreams.

But Gideon's retirement was not the success it perhaps could have been. The plunder from the battle made him a rich man, but riches can be a curse if misused, and even worse if worshipped. He married several wives and sired seventy sons, plus one illegitimate kid, Abimelech, through a flutter on the side with a young servant girl..

Abimelech was a mistake right from the start. As soon as Gideon was dead, he murdered his seventy brothers and set himself up as king. What popularity he may have initially enjoyed was short lived. Civil unrest grew to rebellion, till finally Abimelech and his band of thugs forced thousands of his fellow citizens to take refuge in the temple they had built to honour Baal. Abimelech simply burned it down over their heads, a fail-safe way to crush opposition. He might have extended his reign of terror further had not a woman thrown a rock over the city wall and cracked his skull.

Issachar was the next judge, then Jair, who, with the help of his thirty sons, travelled around the country on thirty donkeys, dispensing peripatetic justice.

Yet the Israelis continued to do what seemed right in their own eyes and started to follow the fashions of morality and religion celebrated by the people who lived around them. Trouble followed as night follows day, and soon the Ammonites were making incursions into Israeli territory on the east bank of the Jordan. Predictably, they cried to the Lord for help.

"No!" said the Lord. "You have made your bed; go lie in it. Perhaps your new gods will deliver you."

"You are right," they whined. "We have sinned and do deserve punishment. But please rescue us anyway, just this once." They made a show of serving the Lord, and since he loved them so dearly, he gave them Jephthah for a judge, the illegitimate son of a prostitute, who had rallied round himself a band of outlaws.

So it was to Jephthah that the elders of Israel sent asking for help. With considerable reluctance he responded to the summons, and leaving his wife and much-loved daughter he headed east over the Jordan, to confront the Ammonite threat.

Perhaps it was an unhappy childhood, or more likely his rejection by his own father, that left Jephthah with little understanding of the unconditional nature of God's love. He thought it necessary to solicit God's favour with extravagant promises. "If you give me victory, God, then I vow that whatever or whoever is first out of my front door to greet me when I get home victorious, I will offer to you as a sacrifice." It was a gamble, but in all likelihood it would be the family dog.

Yet, when the victory was won, it was his beloved little daughter who was looking out of the window for his safe return and ran happily out to hug him. Now what was he to do? Would it be more honourable to break his vow to God or to murder his child? He chose the latter. Little wonder sceptics despise religious fanatics.

The next there was Ibzan of Benjamin, Elon from the tribe of Zebulon, and Abdon of Manasseh, but despite these judges, the national confusion in which everyone did what was right in his own eyes grew worse. Forty more years of disobedience brought the wrath of God down on their heads, this time through the Philistines. So next it was from the tribe of Dan that the deliverer arose. But deliverance was slow in coming, since the new judge was not even born when the people started to pray to the Lord for help. To further slow the process, the chosen parents were incapable of child bearing. But not long after the first prayer meeting for national deliverance, a stranger approached a certain Mrs Manoah and informed her that she would give birth in the near future. Her husband was sceptical when she got home with her unlikely tale and desired to hear the same prediction from the horse's mouth. So next week, the same visitor was back, and this time Manoah himself heard that his future son would grow up to be Israel's deliverer. He was to be set apart for God's holy purpose, drinking no alcohol and never shaving his head.

Manoah asked the stranger's name.

"Why do you ask my name? It is beyond understanding."

They invited him to stay for a meal, name or no name. When the food was served, the stranger just disappeared, somehow caught up in the flame of the cooking fire.

"We have seen God!" they screamed, anticipating imminent death. But they didn't die, and the baby boy was born as promised and never had a hair cut or so much as touched a grape. "Samson," they called him. Knowing he was special, his doting parents spoiled little Sam rotten. He grew into a handsome young man, with eye-catching physique and unheard-of strength. "One day he will deliver Israel from the Philistines," they whispered smugly to one another.

So they must have been devastated when the young man announced his intention to marry a Philistine girl. "We thought he would destroy them, not marry them!" But since he had always had his way, his parents set off to meet the proposed in-laws. Samson followed them a couple of hours later – an unfortunate delay, since a young lion chose to ambush the lone traveller, springing onto his back. Samson merely shook it off and wrung the beast's neck, then continued nonchalantly on his way.

The girl proved very much to his liking, and an agreement was struck between the families; the wedding date set. En route to the wedding a week or so later, Samson noticed the rotting carcass of the lion he had killed. Some bees had made their home in the rib cage, and Samson scooped out a handful of their honey.

That night, they held a stag party for Samson, attended by thirty local Philistine lads. "I have a riddle for you," said Samson during the speeches. "If you can guess it by the time I am back from my honeymoon, I will give you each a new suit. But if not, you each give me one. Okay," they agreed. "So here's the riddle: 'Out of the eater comes something to eat. Out of the strong comes something that's sweet.'"

In vain they strove to guess the meaning, baffled by his poetry. Eventually they cheated. They went to the bride: "We didn't come to your party to be ridiculed. Find out the answer to the riddle or we'll burn your house with you and your family in it."

That ruined the honeymoon. The girl sulked, cried, and begged, and eventually Samson told all. Samson was furious when the young Philistine men solved his puzzle, so he walked to a nearby Philistine town, murdered thirty men, and took their clothes. "Here's your reward," he said, dumping the bloodied garments before his "friends." Then, abandoning his bride, he went back home.

But later on that summer, when the harvest was ready for cutting, Samson's testosterone demanded expression, so he headed back to reclaim his bride.

"I thought you had left her for good," explained her father. "So I gave her to your best man. But I do have another daughter ..."

Samson was furious. So started a cycle of tit-for-tat violence that escalated as each side, blaming the other, sought vengeance. Samson set fire to the Philistine fields, burning the harvest. The locals blamed the girl's father for upsetting Samson, so they burned his house with the whole family in it.

"You killed my wife!" Samson roared and single-handedly killed half the neighbourhood. He stamped off in a rage and withdrew to a cave near

Bethlehem. An angry Philistines mob of a few thousand pursued him. "We only want Samson," they told the terrified local Israelis.

"We don't want no trouble," the locals stammered. "Why don't you let us arrest him for you?" So it was three thousand of his own countrymen that approached Samson in his cave and tactfully explained the situation.

"Fine," agreed Samson. "You can take me. Just promise that you won't kill me." They bound his arms and led him to the Philistines. But as soon as he saw them, he snapped the ropes, grabbed the only weapon within reach – a donkey's jawbone – and slaughtered a thousand men.

His prowess with the jawbone having been witnessed by the local delegates, Samson was recognised as the new deliverer of Israel, so they made him judge.

For twenty years, the fear of Samson kept the Philistines at bay. But Samson had one outstanding weakness: women. He couldn't keep his hands off them. One evening, he spotted a Philistine prostitute and spent the night with her. But he was not the only one doing the spotting that evening. The hairy man, built like a mountain, was not difficult to pick out of a crowd. Thinking they had him trapped, the city officials locked the city gates, planning to take him at first light. But in the middle of the night, Samson got up to head for home. Finding the city gates locked, he simply hoisted them onto his shoulders, posts and all, and walked out of town.

Then there was Delilah. Samson was fascinated by this Philistine beauty and returned to her embrace night after night. The Philistines offered her a fortune to find out the secret of his great strength. So that night when Samson was laying on his back in her bed, she seductively whispered in his ear, "Let me tie you down! But it's no fun unless you really are at my mercy. How can I do that so you can't escape?" He told her to use leather thongs. Later when he had dozed off to sleep, she tested him. "The Philistines are coming!" she shouted. Of course, he jumped up, snapping his bonds like burnt string.

"Just kidding!" But Samson rather enjoyed the game, so on subsequent nights, he led her to use different kinds of restraint, each with the same predictable result.

"You don't love me!" she moaned. "You don't play fair. If you won't trust me with your secrets, how can you expect me to believe that you really do love me?"

Such was Samson's infatuation with the woman that he made the fatal mistake of divulging to her that the secret of his strength was in his hair. "Shave my head and I'll be weak as a kitten." She did and he was.

"The Philistines are coming!" Up jumped the bald man, only to be easily overpowered by enemies who had been hiding in the closet. They took him to the same town whose gates he had recently destroyed. There they put out his eyes and set him to hard labour in the dungeon.

Their enemy subdued, many Philistine leaders came to town for a celebration. They gathered in the great temple of Dagon, their god to whom they unwisely gave all the credit for having brought down Samson. The impressive structure was packed with people, both in the main hall and upstairs in the gallery: thousands of Philistines jammed in, shoulder to shoulder.

"Bring him out!" they demanded. "Let's see what he can lift!"

And there he stood, hair half grown, restrained between the two massive pillars that supported the upper structure of the building. "God, give me strength," Samson prayed for perhaps the first time in his life. And God did. Samson flexed his muscles, and the crowd roared approval. But their shouts soon turned to screams when the pillars started to crack, and then to disintegrate, bringing the whole structure down. In his death, Samson killed more Philistines than he had in his whole life.

The absence of a king left the people doing what was right in their own eyes, with little notion of morality and only a distorted memory of the faith they had inherited through Moses and Joshua. With judges like Samson to help them discern right from wrong, little wonder they were somewhat inept when it came to moral choices.

It was in this moral vacuum that a group of men from the tribe of Dan set out to seek suitable real estate to call home. They were discontent with the land God had allotted them and surmised they might do better up north. En route, they encountered a young Levite who was ministering at a privately owned shrine housing a smorgasbord of pagan idols. The Danites sensed that some kind of religious dimension to their quest might prove helpful, so they commandeered the Levite, taking his idols along for luck. They finally came to a suitable city to call home. It was situated at the foot of a snow-peaked mountain and was plentifully supplied by a spring of fresh water. So they slaughtered the inhabitants and renamed it "Dan," after the founder of their tribe.

And that's how the north was won. Everyone doing what was right in his own eyes. In fact, this absence of a moral compass almost wiped out a complete tribe.

It started with a simple domestic matter. A Levite who lived up in the hills of the territory allotted to Ephraim had taken a concubine who proved unfaithful. She, fearing the consequences, fled back to her father's home in Bethlehem. A few months later, the Levite came looking for his lost love and, delighted to find her at home, persuaded her that he meant her no harm and would she please come back to him.

Her father was overjoyed so wined and dined the Levite for several days, only releasing him to leave on his journey home in the afternoon of the fifth day.

Prejudice prevented him from stopping for the night in Jerusalem, which at that time was still inhabited by foreigners, so they travelled on through Benjamite territory as far as Gibeah, arriving too late to find a room for the night. They were preparing to camp in the city square when an old man, a native of the same part of the country as the Levite, came by and begged them not to stay in the streets: "Come home with me. It's not safe out here."

Once inside the old man's house, they were just settling down to the evening meal when there came a banging on the door and the sounds of a mob outside.

"Hey, old man! Don't be selfish. Send your guest out here so we can have our way with him also." The old guy did his best to persuade them otherwise, but they were not going to be put off. So the Levite pushed his run-away concubine out the door and bolted it behind her. After that he got some sleep. But that's more than can be said for the wretched girl.

In the morning, her blood-soaked body was lying on the doorstep, raped to death. When he had had his breakfast, the Levite slung the body over his donkey and headed for home. There he dismembered her, slicing her into twelve sections, and then sent one bloody parcel to the elders of each of the twelve tribes, with a covering letter outlining the crime. The gruesome forensic evidence leant both credence and horror to the story, so four hundred thousand armed men responded to the call for vengeance, massing in Mizpah, just five miles up the road from Gibeah.

"So what happened?" they asked, hungry for the gory details. The Levite told his story.

"So what is your verdict? What shall we do?" someone shouted. They rose to their feet to a man and, waving their swords, vowed death to the men of Gibeah. Only the tribe of Benjamin was not represented that day, for blood being thicker than water, they were rallying to the defence of their fellow Benjamites in Gibeah.

Next day, the four hundred thousand Israelis faced twenty-six thousand, six hundred Benjamites. The men of Benjamin had a tendency to left-handedness, as the unfortunate king Eglon had discovered to his cost years earlier. Along with that characteristic came the gift of accuracy with a sling and stone. They were famed to be able to nail a hare on the run. It may well have been this acumen that gave them the edge against overwhelming numbers, so when the tally was taken at the end of the day, twenty-two thousand Israelis were dead. Next day, the Israelis pressed their attack a second time; this time the Benjamites felled a further eighteen thousand.

Israel withdrew to Bethel to lick their wounds and to pray for God's help. Forty thousand casualties! Ten percent of their number dead! "God help us," they wept, and God assured them that he would.

Encouraged by this, they laid plans for a third attack. It had worked in Joshua's now-legendary siege of Ai, so they staged the old "ring the bell and run away" trick. Israel's main force feigned retreat and began to withdraw from Gibeah's city gate. The Benjamites streamed out in confident pursuit, whirring their slings, but forgetting to close the gate behind them. As soon as they had gone, a concealed force of Israelis snuck in behind them and torched the city. Smelling smoke, the Benjamites glanced back and then found themselves facing two fronts. They panicked, and what followed was a blood bath. Twenty-six thousand Benjamites were slaughtered, and a mere six hundred men escaped to take refuge in a natural fortress, the Rock of Rimmon. There they stayed holed up for four months while the Israelis finished the job they had started. They burned and looted Benjamite towns, killing all the inhabitants, men, women, and children, vowing that they would never give their daughters in marriage to any Benjamite who might seek a replacement wife.

But when it was all done, they began to feel victor's remorse. They had all but annihilated an entire tribe. Yes, there were still six hundred men holed up, but their wives were dead and the other Israelis had vowed not to give their daughters to any dirty Benjamite.

"We have to do something, or the tribe of Benjamin will become extinct. But where can we find wives for the survivors?" they wondered. Then a something-less-than-romantic solution suggested itself: "There is no one here from Jabesh Gilead, is there?" There wasn't. "Since they didn't come to fight with us, they deserve to die. And, of course, the women from that city are not restricted, since none of their men joined us in the vow, so those women are free to marry Benjamites." Two birds with one stone!

So off they set to the obscure town in the territory over the Jordan in the region allotted to Gad. They killed all the men, women, and children, preserving only the teenage girls who were still virgin. Then they offered the beleaguered Benjamites at the Rock of Rimmon peace terms, with a promise of four hundred young virgins to sweeten the deal. Nervously at first, the Benjamites filtered out to be met with their repentant brothers from the other eleven tribes. "Sorry we couldn't find you a wife each, but from here on you'll have to do your own courting. But here's a suggestion ..." My, but those fellows really were romantics.

The plan was simple. There was an annual festival being held the following week in Shiloh. Part of the celebration was a parade of young girls, all dressed in their fine dresses, dancing and singing. To everyone's surprise, out of the trees sprang two hundred Benjamites, who grabbed a girl each and carried her off home. And that's how the tribe was saved.

Yes, in those days Israel had no king, and everyone did what was right in his own eyes.

---------- **10** ----------

The Nexus

Into the leadership void stepped Eli. From his seat at the entrance to the tabernacle in Shiloh, he exercised the joint roles of priest and judge.

On the domestic scene, life for Eli was a disaster. His two sons, Hophni and Phinehas, were rogues. They made a habit of stealing the best meat from the pilgrims who had come to offer sacrifices to the Lord, even taking it by force if objections were raised. To compound their crimes, they fooled around with the cleaning ladies in the tabernacle. Despite grim warnings delivered to him by men of God, Eli proved unable, or perhaps unwilling, to rein in his wayward sons. Maybe he enjoyed the meat his sons shared with him?

It was there one day, sitting in his chair by the door to the tabernacle, that Eli noticed a woman behaving in a bizarre fashion. She was clearly in a state of great agitation, her mouth moving soundlessly and her arms gesticulating. "Lady, lay off the booze, won't you?"

The woman was shocked. "Oh no, my lord. I am not drunk. I am in great anguish of soul. I'm praying." Turned out her name was Hannah, the childless wife of one Elkanah. She longed for children more than words could express, so the anguished petition was bubbling soundlessly from her heart.

Perhaps to cover his embarrassment over his faux pas, Eli blessed her. "The Lord will grant you your request," he concluded confidently.

And indeed he did, for nine months later, a baby boy was born to her: Samuel. Hannah stayed home and weaned the child, and then the following year, at the time of their annual pilgrimage, Hannah and Elkanah took the child along with them to Shiloh. Approaching Eli in his customary seat, Hannah reintroduced herself. "I am the woman you thought was drunk. And here is the answer to my prayer. In gratitude to the Lord, I am here to present this boy to him for life-long service." Augmenting the presentation with two sides of beef and a skin of wine, they steered young Samuel toward the uncertain arms of Eli.

So it was in the tabernacle that Samuel lived from then on, surrounded by the precious relics of the years of wandering in the wilderness. Most significant of all was the ark of the covenant, containing the two slabs of rock on which were inscribed the ten commands. It was next to the ark that Samuel made his bed at night, and he doubtless watched the shadows from the lamp dancing on the canopy over his head and glimpsed the light winking in the reflection from the gold of the two cherubim, towering protectively over his place of rest. He would listen to the breeze flapping the fabric of the tabernacle or the noise of the rats scurrying about their business. But there is something about the sound of your own name that stands out from the clutter of other sounds, that grabs the attention, that makes it personal, imperative. One night, Samuel was woken by that sound. He jumped up and went to see what Eli wanted.

"It wasn't me who called you, lad. Go back to bed!" He did so and was just dozing off when a second time he heard his name. Once again, Eli denied having called. A third time the summons roused him, and caught between reluctance to upset Eli further, and unwillingness to fail to respond to his call, Samuel returned.

"It really wasn't me, but perhaps it was God who called you. If it happens again, then ask him what he wants."

It is unlikely that Samuel went back to sleep; he lay in the darkness with his ears tingling in expectation and his heart beating in apprehension.

Suddenly from the darkness, but very close this time: "Samuel, Samuel." The lad jumped up. "Yes, Lord, I am listening."

In the morning, Samuel went quietly about his business till Eli called him. "So did you hear the voice again? What did he say?" Samuel hesitated. "Listen, Samuel, if you don't tell me, then God may strike you dead" – powerful incentive to talk.

"Well, he talked about doing something that would make the ears of all who hear of it tingle."

"Anything more specific?"

It must have been hard for the lad to pass on the message. "He said that he is very displeased with the behaviour of Hophni and Phinehas, and with your failure to discipline them. And he said that it would be useless for you to seek to cover it up by offering more sacrifices."

There was an awkward silence, then: "Okay," submitted Eli. "He is the Lord, so he will do as he sees fit."

That was the first of many times that the Lord spoke to Samuel, and he always took care to pass on the message he received faithfully. Soon he became widely respected as a prophet. However, nothing much changed in Eli's household.

But then, quite suddenly, everything did change.

There was war with the Philistines, and since it was not going well, the generals of Israel decided that they needed divine intervention. If they were to take the ark to the battle, then surely they could not possibly lose, since God would be bound to take care of his most treasured possession. Eli was reluctant to let it go but conceded when they agreed to allow Hophni and Phinehas to go along to care for it. He was an old man by then, nearly one hundred, and gravel blind. But he sat in his accustomed chair by the entrance to the tabernacle, listening for sounds of the ark's safe return.

At the battlefront, there was jubilation when the ark entered the Israeli camp. Not so amongst the Philistines. Fear gripped them. "These are the same gods that delivered the Israelis from the Egyptians. We are doomed. Who will deliver us?"

"Pull yourselves together," their leaders snapped. "Are you not men? So fight like men." And they fought with a strength borne of desperation, slaughtering thirty thousand Israelis. Amongst the casualties were Hophni and Phinehas, and amongst the plunder was a gold box: the ark. The Philistines had taken the ultimate prize.

News of the defeat was carried swiftly back to Eli, who was still sitting expectantly by the door of the tabernacle. "And amongst the dead are Hophni and Phinehas," panted the messenger.

"But what of the ark?" asked Eli, aghast.

"Gone. They took it."

Eli may have tried to rise, but his chair toppled and he went over backwards. He broke his brittle old neck and died in the entrance of the tabernacle.

Meanwhile, the Philistines had triumphantly carried the ark to the temple of their god, Dagon. Next morning, when they went to view their spoil, there was Dagon: fallen off his perch on the temple floor. So they heaved him back into position. But the next day, there he was again, flat on the floor, only this time, like Eli, he had broken his neck. His head had rolled to the entrance of the temple.

From that time on, things did not go well for the Philistines. Rats infested the city of Ashdod, and then tumours began to break out on many people's skin, big lumps that grew like mushrooms over night: Bubonic plague, or something like it. Eventually someone linked their troubles with the presence of the ark of the god of Israel.

"Send it away!" So they sent it to Gath. Rats followed like the Pied Piper, and in a matter of days, the Gathites sent the troublesome box on to Ekron.

"Not in my back yard," an Ekronite wailed. "Send it home where it belongs," and that was agreed. On the advice of their religious leaders, they would send along with it a box of gold replicas of the rats and tumours to appease the god of Israel. But there was still a modicum of doubt. The ark was, after all, a very valuable object, and gold rats and tumours don't come cheap. And suppose there was in fact no connection between the plagues and the ark? What a waste!

So they decided to make it difficult. They put the ark, together with the box of gold baubles, on a new cart and hitched it behind two cows that had never before been yoked. Worse: those cows had sucking calves that would be penned up at home.

"Let's see if the god of Israel really does want his ark back!" Those cows never glanced back but headed straight ahead till they reached Beth Shemesh in Israeli territory.

The Beth Shemeshites were thrilled to see the ark. Some Levites lifted it from the cart and placed it lovingly on a rock. Then they broke up the cart for firewood and sacrificed the cows in gratitude.

But some made the mistake of treating the ark with familiarity. They opened the lid for a peep inside, and seventy died. Terror spread like a brush fire, people scattering in all directions. "We are not safe so close to God's presence." So, taking a leaf out of the Philistines' book, they determined to send the ark somewhere else. That "somewhere else" turned out to be the home of Abinadab in the town of Kiriath Jearim. There on a hilltop, the ark rested for twenty years.

The Philistines continued to be a thorn in the side of the Israelis, who predictably turned to the Lord in their distress. And that was when Samuel, now a grown man, took centre stage. "If you are serious about returning to the Lord, then destroy all vestige of idolatry and join me in a solemn assembly at Mizpah."

From far and wide, they came to the hill town situated some twenty miles south of the ruins of Shiloh, the same venue they had used for the meeting to destroy the Benjamites. Together, they confessed their sin before the Lord, and Samuel sacrificed a lamb on their behalf. Unfortunately, word had reached the Philistines that the Israelis were assembling at Mizpah, so while Israel was busy worshipping, peril was knocking at the gates.

"Pray for us!" the crowd begged Samuel when they realised the danger, and he did. The sky grew black, and before they could say "Amen," there was the most violent thunderstorm anyone could remember. Rain deluged, lightning blazed, and thunder bellowed. The Philistines fled, terrified. Israelis left the prayer meeting to pursue their retreating enemies, and that was the last anyone saw of the Philistines for as long as Samuel was the presiding judge.

That event established Samuel as what would turn out to be the last judge of Israel. Since Shiloh was no more, Samuel established his base at Ramah, his parents' home. From there, he travelled round the country, judging, blessing, or prophesying as each occasion required. As the years caught up with him, he established a fixed base in Beersheba in the south and appointed his two sons as junior judges. These two young men soon caught on to the reality that people would pay good money to ensure that a ruling would be in their favour.

The Israelis were disheartened at the realisation that Samuel's sons were no better than those of Eli. History was repeating itself. They longed for a better form of government. "Why can't we have a king, like other nations?"

"Because God himself is our king," Samuel explained.

But when he told the Lord what they were asking, he was surprised to find that God supported their request. "Yes, they are rejecting me, but that's nothing unusual. Just warn them what life under a monarchy will be like."

So Samuel told the people the worst: "Any king you choose would make slaves of you. He would take your sons to fight his battles, or work in his weapons factories, or plough his fields. He would take your daughters to work in his kitchens and perfumeries. And have you ever heard of taxes? He will cream off your income at an outrageous percentage, and property tax will ultimately cost you the family farm. Then you will be sorry."

But they insisted, so Samuel sent them home, promising to give the matter his consideration.

A few days later, as Samuel was talking to the Lord about the people's request for a king, God spoke to him specifically: "About this time tomorrow, a man will come to you. You are to anoint him as king."

A feast was prepared and a table laid. Next day, Samuel was at the city gate, chatting with the elders. "That's him," nudged God. Entering the city was an impressive young man, tall and handsome.

Catching Samuel's eye, the young man walked over to him. "I am looking for the prophet who lives hereabouts."

"Well, you've found him," Samuel said. Then, to Saul's astonishment, he added, "Head on up to the community hall, up there on the hilltop, and let's eat." Saul hesitated, uncertain why he had been invited to dine with the prophet. After all, he was only seeking the man's advice over where he might find some lost donkeys. "Oh, and don't worry about those animals you have been looking for," Samuel continued. "They have been found. But now you are the one that everyone is looking for. In fact, you are the one all Israel is hankering after."

"Nobody wants me! You must have mistaken me for somebody else."

When they reached the hall, there was a banquet laid on a long table.

Saul was shown to the seat of honour at the head of the table, and a juicy steak was placed before him. Saul was more mystified then ever but gladly tucked in to a free meal. It was dark by the time it was all done, so Saul accepted Samuel's hospitality for the night.

Next morning as he was leaving, Samuel put his arm round his shoulders and walked a few steps with him. "Before you leave, I have a message for you from God."

"And what would that be?"

Instead of replying, Samuel produced from a pocket a flask of oil, which he uncorked and poured over Saul's head. Then he hugged him. "The Lord is anointing you king over Israel." Saul gasped. "If you doubt my word, then you will doubt no more by the time you reach home. Watch for these signs. As you reach the border of Benjamin, you will meet two men who will tell you that the donkeys have been found. Next you will be met by three men, one carrying three young goats, another three loaves of bread, and the third, a skin of wine. They will give you two of the loaves. Finally, when you reach your hometown of Gibeah, you will be met by a procession of prophets, playing musical instruments. The Spirit of God will come upon you. You will join them and be forever changed."

Saul turned to leave, still not knowing quite what to make of the strange words of this weirdo. "Oh, and one more thing," Samuel called after him. "Should you ever get into trouble and have need of me, then go to Gilgal and wait till I get there. You can count on me to join you there within seven days. But always remember: Do nothing till I get there and tell you what to do. Nothing! Have you got that? Do nothing till I get there." There was a strange urgency in this apparently unnecessary instruction.

And so it came about exactly as Samuel had foretold, each successive sign leaving Saul more and more stunned. But it was when the Spirit of God caught Saul up in that procession of joyful prophets that his heart was changed. There he was, in his hometown, behaving in a way that till then he would have judged bizarre at best.

"What's happened to Saul?" people were muttering. "Has he become a prophet or something? What would his father say?"

But as to what Samuel had told him about being king, Saul said not a word.

It was some days later that Samuel sent messages all over the country, summoning them to meet him back at Mizpah. They arrived with a high sense of anticipation. Would this be the time when they would get their king? Thousands of them assembled in twelve great companies, tribe by tribe.

Samuel addressed the nation: "This is what the Lord says: 'It was I who delivered you from Egypt, but now it seems you have rejected me. So present yourselves before me this day, tribe by tribe, clan by clan.'"

Representatives from each of the twelve tribes in turn filed up to Samuel, but it wasn't till Samuel was faced by the delegate from the smallest of all the tribes that he called a halt: "This one." This was the tribe that had all but been annihilated a generation previously: the tribe of Benjamin.

Then Samuel called up the clan leaders of Benjamin, and the clan of Matri was chosen. Then family heads filed up to Samuel, man by man, till Kish was selected. Kish lived in Gibeah, the town that had been at the very heart of the troubles, when every man did what was right in his own eyes, because in those days there had been no king in Israel. The sons of Kish were lined up.

But Samuel was clearly perplexed. "There is someone missing."

"He is hiding over there among the baggage."

A red-faced young man emerged, but he was nevertheless an impressive sight, eighteen inches taller than his fellows.

"Do you see this young man? This is the Lord's anointed one."

"Long live the king! Long live the king!" they chanted.

But the adulation was by no means unanimous. Some muttered their discontent: "A wretched Benjamite!"

There were no job descriptions, no protocol of expected behaviour for newly appointed kings, so Saul went home and got on with the daily chores of running the family farm. But events were soon to demand more regal action.

The Ammonites came out of hiding where they had been since the days of Judge Jephthah. They made a quick raid on Jabesh Gilead, an isolated town separated from the main Israeli landmass by the Jordan River. As in Gibeah, the population of Jabesh Gilead had been decimated during the troubles, the only survivors being the virgin teenagers who were forcibly taken as wives for the only survivors of Gibeah. There was thus a strong family bond between those two cities, miles apart though they were. Word reached Gibeah that a group of Ammonites had surrounded Jabesh Gilead and were threatening to gouge out the right eye of every man when the city was captured, if they didn't capitulate immediately.

Saul was just returning from the fields with a couple of yoked oxen. "What's the trouble?" he demanded. When he heard the news, he was furious, and in his righteous anger, he felt the call of God to action. Doubtless inspired by the story of the Levite whose concubine had been raped in that very city of Gibeah, he slaughtered the oxen and cut them up, sending a chunk to each of the tribes in Israel. And, as before, the troops assembled, three hundred and thirty thousand men. They marched all night and in the morning broke into the Ammonite camp and slaughtered them.

"Who said Saul should not rule over us?" someone asked afterwards. "They should die."

But Saul stopped them. "Not so! This is not a day to kill each other. It's a day to be grateful to God, who rescued us."

Samuel suggested that they should all go down to Gilgal, to give Saul a proper coronation. And this they did with joyful celebration and prayers for God's blessing on their new sovereign.

Gilgal was still a significant place. It was the site of the first camp that Joshua had established when they entered that land, generations previously. A memorial cairn stood there, built of the twelve stones taken from the streambed of the Jordan as they had crossed dry shod. It served as perpetual reminder of the Lord's faithfulness in bringing them safely out of Egypt and into the promised land. Samuel, sensing that the coronation of the king would suggest a good time for him to retire from his role as judge, stood by that heap of stones and made his retirement speech.

"Firstly, I ask you, have I in any way ever failed you these past years or taken unfair advantage of you in my role as judge?" Unanimous agreement that he had done a good job.

"Secondly, has God ever failed you as he brought you from Egypt, through those long years in the wilderness, then over the Jordan, where he gave us this land to be our home?" General agreement that God had never let them down. So he moved on to the most recent chapter in their history.

"I remind you that in contrast to God's faithfulness, your forefathers turned repeatedly away from following the Lord and suffered the inevitable consequences. But God rescued you by appointing a series of judges, of whom I am the last. And now you have rejected me, demanding instead a king. Well, you've got one. But just so you will remember how God feels about it, watch this." With that, he lifted his hands in prayer, and the sky turned black with clouds. A thunderstorm devastated the ripe harvest fields, flattening the crops. The celebration turned to terror.

"Pray for us or we are all dead men!" they begged. So Samuel did.

When the storm had passed, Samuel concluded his speech: "And now it is time for me to retire and leave the leadership of this people to the king. But far be it from me that I should sin against the Lord by neglecting to pray for you. I will gladly continue my role as teacher, showing you the way that is good and right. But promise me you will fear the Lord and serve him faithfully with all your heart."

11

The Failure

Saul was thirty years old when they made him king, and he ruled till he was seventy. He got married, and he and his wife raised five kids. Jonathan was the oldest, a fine lad, loved by his father and admired by all. The youngest was Michal, a cute little girl who would grow to become a beautiful woman.

It may have been a career move towards succession to the throne that caused Jonathan to join the army. But to call it an army is perhaps an exaggeration, since Saul had but three thousand fighting men. These he divided into two companies, putting the smaller, a contingent of one thousand men, under Jonathan's command.

But an army with no weapons is like a dog with no teeth.

The Philistines, who had been somewhat subdued since the days of Samuel, were now re-emerging as a thorn in Israel's side. They had made no direct attack but till this point contented themselves with sabre rattling. To ensure that the Israelis had no sabres to rattle back, the Philistines killed all the blacksmiths and confiscated everything with a sharp point. This left the Israeli army with but two swords, one stuck in Saul's belt and the other in that of Jonathan.

Much like the toothless dog, Saul could only growl his distaste for Philistines.

Young Jonathan argued that actions would speak far more eloquently than growls. So without so much as a by-your-leave from his father, he led his thousand men against a small Philistine outpost and sent them packing, with their tails between their legs. Jonathan's victory was celebrated in the Israeli camp till news reached them that, in response to his precipitous initiative, a countless hoard of Philistines, armed to the teeth, was gathering at Michmash, just down the road from Gibeah, Saul's hometown.

"Now what are we going to do?" Saul snarled at Jonathan. "You and your hot-head ideas!"

In the face of such impossible odds, they had no choice but to turn to God for help. Saul withdrew with his army to hold a religious retreat at Gilgal, his place of coronation. That was the place that Samuel had promised to come within a week, should he ever be in trouble. So Saul waited for the designated seven days, determined to obey Samuel's instructions by doing nothing till he arrived. Every day more of his terrified men deserted. By the weekend, Saul was desperate. If he didn't do something soon, there would be no one left. So Saul took it upon himself to take action. He initiated the prayers and offered a sacrifice without Samuel present. Scarcely had he pronounced the benediction, and with the smell of the sacrifice still hanging in the air, into the camp strode Samuel.

"What's going on here?" he demanded.

"Well, I waited the seven days, but you didn't show, so I had no choice but to go ahead without you."

"If only you had showed patience, then God would have established for you a permanent throne in Israel. But now God has in mind a replacement, one who will love him with his whole heart."

Samuel strode off, leaving Saul with egg on his face and his army yet more demoralised. What had started as a trickle of deserters now became a torrent.

The best method of defence being attack, Saul led his diminished force up the mountains to a face-off with the Philistines. What else could he do? He established his camp outside his hometown of Gibeah, and there he sat under a pomegranate tree, watching the Philistines a couple of miles up the valley at Michmash. They blackened the ground by their sheer numbers.

"Bring the ark of God," Saul ordered, and it was Ahijah, Eli's great-grandson, who supervised the transporting of the ark to Gibeah. But the arrival of the ark did little to boost morale, since the last time it had been used in confrontation with the Philistines, it had been captured and Israel defeated.

When Saul next counted his men, he found that they were down to a mere six hundred. In the face of such odds, what were they to do now? Attack? Hardly! Religious ceremonies have long been an attractive alternative to positive action, and it was for that course of inaction that Saul opted. Ahijah and the ark were centre stage.

But Jonathan wandered off with his bodyguard. "You know," he mused, "God is very great and nothing will prevent him from saving his people, whether with a large army or just a few men. So with God on our side, you and I must be a winning team! The Philistines don't stand a chance."

"Agreed!" said his young companion.

"Right then. Here's the plan. You see up on that cliff top, there is a garrison of Philistines. Why don't we climb up there and attack?" It may not have been the smartest of plans, but it was better than doing nothing at all.

"I am with you all the way!" agreed his buddy.

"So let's climb up to that little ledge just below the top of the cliff and declare ourselves. Then if they say, 'Come on up,' we'll take that as a sign that God has given them to us. If, however, they say, 'Wait there,' then we are in trouble, but since we are dead anyway, we have nothing to lose."

Under cover of darkness, they made their way to the base of the hill. They started their ascent up a steep scree slope, doing their best to avoid dislodging any rocks. Just before dawn, they reached the base of the cliff, directly below the Philistines. Carefully they inched up the rock face till they reached the ledge, fifty feet below the lip.

As the sun spilled over the horizon, and the Philistines were stirring from their slumbers, they heard the sound of shouting. Looking over the cliff, they saw to their amusement two young Israelis, one brandishing a sword and both yelling defiance. It was such an absurd sight that it reduced the Philistines to helpless laughter. When eventually they had recovered enough to speak, one of them yelled over the edge, "Why don't you come up here? We'll show you a thing or two."

"Right," said Jonathan. "They are ours!" and the two scaled the remainder of the cliff and pulled themselves over the lip. The Philistines watched them with amusement. But before they could say, "Good morning," one of the two sprang to his feet and, pulling from his belt 50 percent of the armoury of Israel, launched into a ferocious attack. The other followed up, clubbing and kicking and stabbing the fallen. Together, they slaughtered twenty men. The rest fled in terror, reporting that they were under attack by a fierce hoard of Israelis. Panic multiplied and Philistines ran in all directions, bumping into one another and, mistaking their fellows for the enemy, slashed with their swords in a frenzy of killing.

Meanwhile Saul, who had just woken in his camp under the pomegranate tree, became aware that something had changed in the Philistine camp. It was not the battle cry that he heard floating down the valley, but the sounds of confusion. He mustered his men, all 598 of them. "Who is missing?" he demanded. Jonathan and his bodyguard! Ahijah wanted to do something religious around the ark, but Saul was now impatient for action. "The time for talking is over. Let's be at them."

He led his men down the valley towards Michmash. As they progressed, their numbers were swollen by returning deserters. The closer they got, the clearer it became that the Philistines were in total disarray.

"I declare this day to be a fast," pronounced Saul. "No man is to eat or drink till every Philistine is dead." So the slaughter went on all day and might indeed have gone further had not the men grown faint through lack of nourishment. Only Jonathan and his sidekick still had some bounce at day's end. They had not heard about the fast, since they were not present when it had been called. Some wild honey in the woods had proved an energy booster.

"He must die!" Saul said when he learned that his fast had been ignored, but mercifully common sense asserted itself, arising from the men who insisted that since Jonathan was responsible for the day's victory, Jonathan should most certainly not die.

That day was a turning point for Saul. The Philistines retreated and gave them no more grief (for a while at least). Saul strengthened his army by conscripting many talented young warriors. To whip them into shape, he enlisted the support of his cousin, Abner, appointing him his general.

Justice is sometimes slow coming. Back in the days when Moses was leading the children of Israel from Egypt to the promised land, they had encountered a mixed reception from the peoples through whose land they sought to pass. The Amalekites had been particularly brutal in their refusal, attacking and harassing Israel throughout their journey.

In his final speech beside the Jordan, Moses had commanded, "Remember what the Amalekites did to you along the way when you came out of Egypt. So when you are settled in the land, you must blot out the memory of Amalek from the face of the earth. Do not forget!"

It was with this in mind that Samuel came to Saul. "There is an ancient wrong that you are to right. The Amalekites are to be annihilated, every man, woman, and child and all their livestock. And you are to be God's instrument to carry out this mission."

So Saul led over two hundred thousand men into the attack, inflicting almost total genocide. But it did seem to Saul a terrible waste that some of the prime livestock should be destroyed out of hand. Perhaps they should preserve a few beasts to offer as sacrifices to God? And then there was the king: Agag. Surely to show mercy would demonstrate Saul's magnanimity in victory, and to spare his life might even be the kind of loving forbearance that would please God.

When the slaughter was all finished, so pleased was Saul with his achievement that he erected a monument in his own honour, and then he led his men to Gilgal for a thanksgiving dinner. It was there that Samuel caught up with him.

"The Lord bless you!" boomed Saul, full of the bonhomie generated by pride in a job well done.

"Then what is this bleating and mooing I hear?"

"Oh, that! Those are the sheep and cattle that my men rescued and brought here to sacrifice to the Lord."

Samuel cut him short: "Hold it right there. Perhaps I should tell you what the Lord told me last night."

"I'd love to hear it."

"He reminds you that it was he who made you king and he who commissioned you to completely destroy the Amalekites."

"And that I have done, except, of course, these few animals that my men wanted to bring here to sacrifice. Oh, and there's King Agag over there. Mercy is good, don't you think?"

"Obedience is what God requires. That is what he wants, even more than sacrifices."

"But I did obey!"

"No, your arrogance is akin to idolatry, and your rebellion opens the path to witchcraft."

"Alright, so perhaps I have sinned a little, and I'm sorry. But it was not my fault. It was my men who insisted, and I had to give in to them." Samuel turned to leave. "Please don't walk away. Come back and worship with us!"

But Samuel didn't stop. Saul grabbed his cloak to detain him, but the hem ripped off in his hand. "The Lord has torn the kingdom from you this day and is giving it to someone better than you," Samuel shouted over his shoulder.

Saul was desperate. "I beg you, come back to worship with me so I won't lose face before my men."

Samuel did turn back, but instead of merely joining in the singing, he summoned King Agag and hacked him to death. "Real worship is total obedience!"

And that was the last Saul ever saw Samuel, at least while he was living. For the witchcraft to which Samuel had alluded would one day prove Saul's way to contrive one more meeting with Samuel, long after he was dead.

12

The Romance

Some years previously, there had been famine throughout the region. A man named Elimelech, together with his wife, Naomi, and their two sons, had left their parched farm in Bethlehem and travelled east over the Jordan River in search of sustenance for themselves and grazing for their livestock. They settled in the land of the Moabites, on the eastern shores of the Dead Sea. To make a bad situation worse, they hadn't been there long before Elimelech fell sick and died. Naomi was devastated, but life must go on, and as the two boys came of age, they met and married local girls, mixed marriages that might have been frowned upon had not Orpah and Ruth been so utterly charming.

For ten years, all was well, then sickness struck again, and this time both young men succumbed. So there was Naomi, widowed, both her sons dead, and two daughters-in-law to care for. She resolved to head home to Bethlehem, way up in the distant mountains on the far side of the lake.

The three widows hadn't travelled very far before Naomi realised the folly of what they were doing: "This is madness. Why would you two pretty young things stick with me? I am too old to even think about marrying again, and even if I got married today, are you really going to hang about for … how many years, waiting for me to raise sons for you to marry? Go on back to your families and your friends. I am not safe company since the Lord has evidently turned his back on me."

They clung together in a pathetic huddle, hugging and weeping. Eventually Orpah gave in. "Well, okay. I'll go, then. But I will never forget you, as long as I live."

But Ruth refused to let go. "There's no way I am going to leave you," she sobbed. "I will go wherever you go and live wherever you live. Your people will become my people and your God will be my God. I want to be buried where you are buried. May God strike me dead if I ever abandon you!" How could Naomi argue with that? So the two continued on their journey, arm in arm.

Footsore and weary, they arrived days later in Bethlehem and limped onto Elimelech's old farm. It was a tangle of weeds, and the house was a ruin.

The neighbours noticed someone on the land. "Hey! What are you doing ... Wait a moment. Are you Naomi?" The years had not been kind to her.

"Yes, but don't call me 'Naomi.' 'Mara' would be more appropriate – 'Bitter' – since the Lord has made my life a misery. I left with a husband and two sons, now they are all dead. And look at me!"

Word of her return was passed around Bethlehem. "And she has brought a young foreign woman with her, a Moabitess. She was married to one of her sons! Can you imagine that? A foreigner!" Nevertheless, there was a grudging respect for Ruth, who had stuck with her mother-in-law, even through her own bereavement.

Living off the land takes work, and their land had lain fallow for a dozen years or more. There was nothing to live on. "Let me go to someone else's land to see if I can glean some of the grains that the harvesters miss," suggested Ruth. It was the beginning of the barley harvest. So off she went to the fields around Bethlehem. There were gangs of harvesters, working shoulder to shoulder, cutting and standing the sheaves of barley. Ruth watched for a while, discerning who was the foreman. "Excuse me, sir. But might I be permitted to glean any grains that your harvesters miss? I promise not to get in the way."

"Why, certainly, miss. Go right ahead." So all morning she crawled along, scratching among the stubble for the odd grain that might have been dropped.

Around lunchtime, an important-looking man, presumably the landowner, came to check up on the progress they were making. "The Lord be with you!" he said and all the harvesters replied, "And with you too, sir," raising their caps. He went to have a chat with the foreman. Surveying the workers, his eye settled on Ruth. "Who is that young lady?" he asked.

"That's Ruth, the young Moabitess that came home with Naomi, the widow of Elimelech. She's a good worker, by the looks of her. Never stops foraging for grain."

Ruth saw the important-looking man walking over towards her. Afraid that she'd be sent away, she pretended not to notice, going on feverishly scratching among the stubble.

"Young lady," he said kindly. "You are most welcome to glean here on my land. In fact, don't even think of going elsewhere, for you will be quite safe with my servant girls, and I'll tell the men to leave you alone. Oh, and if you get thirsty, feel free to drink from those water jars over there."

Ruth was flabbergasted. "Sir, I am amazed that you would even notice me, a mere foreigner. You are so kind."

"Oh, no. It's you who are kind. I have heard all about how good you have been to your mother-in-law, leaving your own homeland and coming to join a people you knew nothing about. May the Lord richly reward you, since you have come to place yourself under his protection."

At lunchtime, they all stopped work to eat what they had brought with them. Ruth was a little embarrassed, since she alone had nothing to eat.

"Come over here!" someone shouted. She looked up to see the boss beckoning her. Nervously, she went and sat by him as invited. To her amazement, he shared his lunch with her, more than she could eat. So she slipped some of it into her pouch to take home to Naomi.

That afternoon, it seemed the harvesters became more careless, for everywhere she went, there were grains scattered all over the place, and amongst the standing sheaves there were whole heads of grain, just lying on the ground for the taking!

At knocking-off time, she gathered up her gleanings and triumphantly poured them onto the kitchen table when she got home. "And that's not all," she said, pulling from her pouch the remains of her lunch.

"Wherever did you get all that?" Naomi asked, aghast.

"I think the owner of the fields is a man named Boaz."

Naomi's jaw dropped. "Well, there's a coincidence. That man is a relative, one of our kinsman-redeemers, as a matter of fact." Since Ruth had no idea what a kinsman-redeemer was, Naomi explained. "In our culture, land is never offered on the open market. It has to stay in the family. So when someone dies, the closest relative has first option. But with it goes the obligation to raise sons to continue the family name and maintain the family inheritance. So the widow of the deceased also becomes his responsibility."

"So Boaz has first dibs on this farm and on you, Mom, as Elimelech's widow?"

"Yes and no. The land, yes, but since I am old, there is no likelihood of my bearing any more sons to carry on the family name. You, on the other hand ..."

Every day till the harvest was ended, Ruth would faithfully glean on Boaz's land. And every day, she would pretend not to notice his glances in her direction.

When the harvest was done, Boaz announced a celebration. "This could be important," Naomi told Ruth. "Have a good bath, then put on your best clothes, and wear some of this perfume that I have been keeping for just such an occasion. Then here's what you must do ..."

That afternoon, all the workers joined in tossing the barley so the wind would carry away the chaff. Then, as the sun was setting, with a huge pile of clean grain in the middle of the area of stamped-down soil that served as a threshing floor, the feast began. Everyone ate and drank their fill. Ruth watched from a distance. She watched till the feasting ended and the workers started to wander off home. But her attention was on Boaz. The fire was burning low, and she saw him move to the far side of the pile of grain. There he burrowed a bed in the grain and lay down to sleep. Soon his quiet breathing turned to rhythmic snores. Only then did she move closer, terrified that anyone would see her. She came right up to the sleeping form, curled up at his feet and lay still – petrified.

Perhaps it was a dream or maybe it was the perfume, but at some point in the night, something woke Boaz. He sat bolt upright, and there was a woman next to him. "Who's there?"

"It's Ruth, sir. Let me share your blanket, since you are a kinsman-redeemer." She held her breath. If Naomi had miscalculated, she – Ruth – would be thrown out in disgrace, a woman of loose morals.

There was a chuckle from the darkness. "Well, bless your heart! All the young men in town have noticed you. You could have had your pick, but instead you have come to me. Kindness seems to be your middle name. Now don't be nervous. But I must tell you that I am not first in line. There is a relative closer than I. First thing tomorrow, I will go and see if he wants to redeem you. But if he doesn't, as sure as the Lord lives, I will marry you, and gladly. But lie here till morning."

Just before dawn, she got up to leave before she could be recognised. "Hey Ruth!" he hissed. "Don't go home to your mother-in-law empty handed. Take this." He scooped a mound of grain into her shawl and helped her hoist it onto her back.

Naomi was up early, but perhaps she had never gone to bed, so anxious was she to find out what was happening with her plan. Then in walked a radiant Ruth, who dumped a huge mound of grain on the floor. The answer was never in doubt.

Early that morning, Boaz went and sat down in the town gate, an open area with the equivalent of a coffee shop. It was a place where the town council would meet, where business transactions would be sealed, and where legal disputes were settled. Boaz sat for a while and chatted with other elders who were passing the time of day. Then he spotted his man.

"Hey, excuse me!" he shouted. "Would you spare me a minute?" The man came over and sat down.

"I need to bring to your attention the fact that the land belonging to the late Elimelech, our mutual relative, is to be sold, so needs to be redeemed. You are the closest relative, so it's yours if you want it. If not, I'll take it."

The man brightened up at the news of this sudden windfall. "Why yes. I'll certainly take it."

Boaz's heart sank down to his boots. "But you need also to be made aware that along with the field goes the responsibility for Elimelech's family. There's his widow, Naomi, to care for. And since both her sons are also dead, you would have to marry Ruth, the Moabitess, Naomi's widowed daughter-in-law." He held his breath.

"Well, that casts a different complexion on the deal. That might in the long-term compromise my own family and their estate. So no. I won't do it. The land is yours along with the woman." So saying, he removed his shoe and handed it to Boaz, a sign to all the surrounding witnesses that the agreement was final and binding.

"So I want you all to witness my intention to purchase the land belonging to Naomi and also to marry Ruth so that the good name of Elimelech can be preserved in Bethlehem."

The surrounding elders congratulated Boaz and agreed that they were indeed witnesses. They added a special blessing addressed to Ruth: "May this woman who has come from afar add to the family of Israel as did Rachael and Leah, wives brought from afar by Jacob. And, through the children that this young woman will bear to you, may your family be blessed in the tradition of Perez, son of Judah and Tamar."

And this part of the story really does have a happy ending, for within the year, a child was born, whom they named Obed. Naomi loved and cared for that kid as though he was her own. Obed in turn married and sired a son named Jesse, who inherited the family farm in Bethlehem. There he raised eight sons, the youngest of whom was a ruddy-cheeked little fellow named David. And there they were all living when Saul had become king.

13

The Poet

Eight sons are useful when you are running a farm. The grain fields that Boaz had passed down to them required the skill and muscular hard work of the older boys, so the runt of the litter was relegated to watching the sheep. Young David probably didn't mind much, since the peace and quiet of the outdoors inspired his creativity. He was a sensitive lad who loved music. For hours, he would pick out notes on an old harp that he packed around with him as he kept a watchful eye on the flock. And he had a way with words, weaving them together, expressing ideas that matched in poetic couplets.

When he was not plucking his harp, he would work with a sling and stone. Doubtless he had heard of the skills of his cousins from the tribe of Benjamin, and he determined to share that proficiency. Many a rabbit became barbecued supper in his lonely vigils up on the hills around Bethlehem.

One day, he heard the familiar family whistle summoning him home. On arriving at the homestead in town, he was surprised to find the place full of strangers. He pushed his way in. "About time too," muttered one of his big brothers. All seven of them were there, and next to Jesse, his father, stood a stranger, an old man David had never seen before.

As the lad approached, the old man said, "Ah! This is the one." He called the lad to his side and then produced a horn, from which he removed the plug and poured the oily contents over David's head. "Young man, you will be the next king of Israel." And with that, they all sat down to eat. David found out later that the old man was a prophet named Samuel. Everyone seemed terrified of him.

To imagine that such an anointing would improve David's place in the family pecking order would be a mistake. Nothing changed. He was still the youngest, still required to watch the flock. But from then on, something imperceptibly changed in David's heart. He felt a fresh confidence, a sense of anticipation, and a consciousness of the closeness of God. It was as though the Spirit of God had become his close companion. Music and poetry came to him so vividly that he began to write it down.

Sitting on a slope one lonely evening, watching his flock graze on the pasture that spread down to a stream, a confidence stole into his heart: "*The Lord is my shepherd, so I will never need a thing...*"

Perhaps a growl disturbed his concentration, then suddenly all was pandemonium. The sheep were scattering, running for their lives, pursued by a lion, running at full stretch, seeking to pick off a straggler. Without a second thought, David launched himself in pursuit of the lion. When he got close enough, he landed a direct hit on its flank with a well-slung rock. The animal roared in fury and turned towards David, growling and snarling as it approached. Far from wanting to run, David was furious that this brute would dare to threaten his sheep. He advanced on the beast, step for step, holding his shepherd's staff out in front of him. The animal crouched and then sprang, but David was ready. The staff took the brunt of the assault, and as David sprawled to the ground with the lion on top, he grabbed it by its mane and slit its throat with his shepherd's knife. When he had stopped panting, he pushed the dead beast off and cleaned his knife on the fur. He called in his sheep, quieting them by his voice and comforting them with his presence.

Some weeks later, there was a similar attack, this time by a bear, who suffered a similar fate. David learned that confidence in the protection of God had all but banished his fears. He wrote some more. "*He who lives in the protection of the Most High, who rests in the shade of the Mighty one, will call the Lord, 'my refuge and my fortress, my God, in whom I trust.'*"

Soon he was writing new material almost every day, inspired by everything he saw and experienced. When the dry season turned the land to dust, he observed a deer lying in the shade of a shrub by the dried-up streambed. I know how that feels, he thought: *"As a deer gasps for water, so my soul longs for you, God. My soul thirsts for you, my body pines for you, as in a parched land with no water."*

It is doubtful that he had aspirations to be a professional musician, but if he had, then he would have been overjoyed when he received a summons from the royal court to be a musician to soothe the king's jangled nerves. This was but a half-time position, so he divided his days between caring for his sheep and being a harpist in the service of King Saul. It was but a ten-mile jog between Bethlehem and Gibeah, where the king made his home. On the way, he had to skirt the fortress town of Jerusalem, still stubbornly occupied by Jebusites. What a great city could be built up there! Perhaps one day ...

Urgent messengers arrived in Bethlehem, requiring every able-bodied man to rally to the king. The Philistines were coming. Jesse was too frail to go but sent his three oldest sons. David begged to be included but was told not to be silly: "Stay home and watch the sheep!" Since Saul was occupied mustering his army and had little need of a musician, David was stuck at home full time, caring for the flock, far from the action.

"Davy," his father said one evening, "tomorrow I want you to go to the front and see how your brothers are doing. Oh, and take these supplies with you. Give them to the quartermaster." He didn't need telling twice, and off he went at first light. He found the army drawn up on a bluff beside the Elah Valley. They were well dug in, having been there for six weeks already. The Philistines were similarly hunkered down on the opposite side of the valley. David delivered the supplies and then found his brothers, who were none too pleased to see him. "So who's watching the sheep, Davy? Come to watch the battle, eh, you conceited little runt?" They couldn't forgive him for the suggestion that he might some day be king.

There was a strange atmosphere amongst the troops that David could not immediately discern. Fear! That was it. Fear was paralysing the whole army. You could smell it. But why were they so afraid?

Then a great shout rang from across the valley, a war cry perhaps. Was this an attack? David ran to look and was in time to see a giant of a man striding down the slope opposite. He was indeed a terrifying sight, ten foot tall if he was an inch, and armed to kill. His voice rumbled across no-man's land. "This day I defy Israel. I challenge you to one-on-one combat. Send me your best man. If he kills me, then we Philistines will be your subjects, but if I win …"

There was silence in the ranks of Israel, each man shrinking back into his own private place of fear.

"Just who does he think he is to defy the army of Israel?" came an adolescent voice. "Is there a reward offered as an incentive for one of us to kill him?"

"Actually, the king has offered a huge reward: life exemption from taxes and the princess in marriage."

"So what are you waiting for?" asked David. Just raising the question achieved a slight shift in attitude amongst those who heard him. Was it cynicism or a spark of hope?

His brothers told him to be quiet, but David wandered away, persisting with his question. A stirring of hope rippled through the ranks. The swell reached King Saul, who was standing in his royal tent talking with Abner, his general, and wondering how to break the deadlock.

"Young man," he addressed the youth, for whom he had sent. "I hear you have been asking questions, unsettling the men." There was something familiar about the boy. One of his court musicians! That was it.

"Sir, I am willing to fight that man!" The offer from a naïve teenager was beneath contempt. "I am a shepherd from Bethlehem, where I care for my father's flock. I have recently killed both a lion and a bear that threatened my animals, and I will similarly kill that Philistine who dares to defy the armies of the living God. The God who delivered me from those predators will deliver me from that brute also."

There was something about the absolute confidence of the youth that got through to the king. And anyway, it wasn't as though others were lining up to volunteer for the job, so what had Saul to lose?

"Okay, kid. You're on."

Declining Saul's offer of armour, David took but his leather sling and shepherd's staff and set off down into the valley. A strange silence came over the troops above him on either side of the valley. What was to be made of this new development?

David might naturally have felt alone and scared: *"Even though I walk into the valley of death, I will not be afraid, for I'm not alone; you are with me; your club and your crook give me confidence."* Humming the words of his own song leant him courage.

He paused when he reached the streambed at the bottom of the valley. Carefully, he selected a handful of smooth round stones and slipped them into his pouch. Then, jumping lightly over the stream, he advanced on his enemy.

"Am I a dog that you come at me with a stick?" the giant snarled in disgust.

"You come armed with sword, spear, and javelin, but I come in the name of the Lord Almighty."

The mention of God incensed the man, and invoking the name of his own god, he called down a terrible curse on David. "Come here, you little rat! The crows will be pecking your eyes out and the foxes chewing on your bones before this day is done."

"No, actually the shoe is on the other foot. Before this day is over, I'm going to strike you down and cut off your head. And let's not disappoint those birds. They will be feasting on the carcasses of all you Philistines by nightfall."

Selecting a stone from his pouch, he tucked it into the leather pad of his sling and began to whirl the thong. In a voice that could be clearly heard by the whole Philistine force, all straining over the lip of the hill to see their champion kill the little Hebrew, he said, "Let the whole world know for certain that there is a God in Israel. It is not sword or spear that prevails. The battle is in the hands of the Lord, and it is he who will give all of you into our hands." As he spoke, the whirring of the sling increased, and at just the right moment, the stone was released, shooting straight and true to strike the giant between the eyes. Like a great cedar, he toppled to the ground, stunned. Not wasting a second, David ran forward and pulled the massive sword from Goliath's scabbard. Before the Philistine could regain control of his wits, David drove the blade through his chest. Then to make sure of his kill, he hacked off his victim's head, holding it up by the hair for all to see. He was still standing there when a wave of wildly yelling Israeli soldiers surged down the hill, past him, then up the opposite slope in pursuit of the terrified Philistines. As the sound of battle faded into the distance, David made his way back to the Israeli camp, lugging the massive Philistine head and dragging the sword that was far too big to stick in his belt. It was there that General Abner found him and brought him to the king. "And bring that head with you, kid."

"What's your name, young man?" Saul asked as David stood before him, still clutching the dripping head by the hair.

"I'm David, the son of Jesse of Bethlehem. I work part time as one of your musicians."

"Well, let's make that a full-time job from now on. I need you around."

Jonathan, Saul's son and heir to the throne, had been present when David had volunteered to fight the giant. He had heard David decline the offer of Saul's royal suit of armour, insisting that God himself would be his protection. Had it not been with this same reckless, daring confidence that he, Jonathan, and his bodyguard had attacked the Philistines at Michmash? Jonathan admired David's spirit and so was thrilled to see him return unscathed.

As soon as his father turned from David to attend to other matters, Jonathan took him by the arm and led him out of the tent. "Let's take a stroll," he suggested.

David knew full well who this was, since he had seen him in court. Now here he was, walking in the company of royalty, dressed in his simple shepherd's rags. If David felt awkward, then Jonathan didn't appear to notice. He was just impressed beyond words with David's display of trust in God. As they wandered off along the hillside, they discussed many things and found in each other kindred spirits. And that was the beginning of an enduring friendship. Since Saul had not rewarded David in any way, Jonathan took off his own cloak and threw it over David's shoulders. He buckled his own sword to David's belt.

Word of David's achievement had preceded the victorious army as they marched back to Gibeah. David walked with the prince, close behind King Saul. Crowds of people lined the street, clapping and cheering. Gradually a chant became discernible above the general hubbub. "Saul has killed thousands, but David *ten* thousands." The king was not amused.

Next day, it was business as usual, the king warming his throne and David plucking the harp. Saul was muttering. Hard to tell if he was talking to himself or praying, but it was clear that his mood was not jovial. Suddenly he jumped to his feet and hurled a javelin at David. Nimble as a deer, David dodged the shaft, which stuck quivering in the wall right above his overturned stool. David stood staring at the king in shock, ready to run should the attack be repeated. The two faced each other wordlessly for a moment, and then Saul turned and walked out, leaving David shaking like a leaf.

Next day, both Saul and David were back as though nothing had happened. "So it seems I am in your debt," Saul said, breaking the awkward silence. "I promised you my daughter in marriage, and my daughter Merab you shall have."

Jonathan was thrilled: "So you are going to be my brother-in-law!" But as time went by, it became increasingly doubtful that the promise would be kept, and when the girl was given in marriage to another, the matter was obviously closed.

But Saul had a younger daughter, Michal, a beautiful young lady who, it was said, had a serious crush on the dashing young David. Being the youngest, she was spoiled rotten, with a personality to match. "How would you like another chance to become my son-in-law?" Saul asked David, thinking that if he married the headstrong Michal, she would seriously clip his wings.

"Sir, I am but a poor man, and the bride price would be more than I could afford."

"Money is not as important to me as putting down the Philistines. How about making the price for marrying my daughter a hundred dead Philistines?" Death certificates had not been invented, and scalps had not yet come into fashion, so they settled on foreskins as proof of death. Perhaps David would be killed while raising the bride price and the marriage need never happen. But he wasn't. In fact, he returned ahead of schedule with twice the agreed number. The marriage was celebrated, and to Saul's chagrin, the couple seemed very much in love.

Saul's displeasure was further enhanced by the realisation that David was popular with everyone, loved by the crowds, adulated by his men, best friends with his son, and adored by his daughter. But the thing that stuck most in the king's throat was the realisation that even God loved him.

Saul began to hint to his commanders that it would be no bad thing if David met a premature end, killed in battle, perhaps? But Jonathan interceded on David's behalf, and the suggestion was forgotten.

But jealousy continued to gnaw at Saul's heart, and a few weeks later, when David was idly plucking his harp after returning from leading yet another successful assault on the wretched Philistines, the green-eyed monster broke loose. Grabbing his spear, Saul rushed at the little upstart, intending to pin him to the wall. But once again, David was just too quick for him. He ran home and told his bride about his father-in-law troubles.

"Then you must run for your life," Michal said. "Leave immediately. Don't wait till morning." But a peep through the curtains revealed men already watching the house.

"Quick, climb down this rope," Michal urged, dropping a cord from the bedroom window. So David left home to start the life of an outlaw.

Scarcely had he gone when there was an urgent banging on the door. "He can't come," she countered the royal summons. "He's not well." That bought her a few minutes. Quickly, she laid a dummy on the bed and threw the covers over it, leaving some goat's hair showing on the pillow.

"We are to carry him to the king in his bed, if necessary," the returning soldiers growled, pushing past her.

"Why did you try to deceive me, your own father?" Saul asked, when the deception was reported.

"But he threatened me!" wailed Michal. Who can stay angry with a youngest daughter in tears?

So where was David to turn? He daren't go to his family home in Bethlehem. Too obvious. Then he remembered the old prophet who had anointed him to be king. He found Samuel in Ramah, at the school of the prophets named Naioth. To be able to confide in such a man proved an enormous relief to the confused young David.

But it wasn't long before word came that a detachment of soldiers had been sighted coming up the hill. Once again, the churning in the pit of the stomach. What hope had an old man and a group of theological students against armed fighters? But by the time the soldiers reached the hilltop, a spontaneous celebration of worship had broken out among the students. Brutality was no match for such joy. The soldiers were caught up in the ecstasy and found themselves flat on the ground. Reinforcements arrived and then yet more troops, and each time they fell to the ground, overcome by the Spirit of God. Finally Saul himself graced the hill with his presence, and before they could sing, "God save the king," he had torn off his royal finery and was prophesying along with the rest of them. This lasted all day and the better part of the night.

Long before Saul regained his wits next morning, David was gone.

———————————————

Jonathan was horrified when David told him what had happened. "There's no way my father wants you dead."

"If you don't believe me, then watch how he reacts when you make excuses for my absence at the banquet tomorrow night."

"David had family business to attend to," Jonathan explained when his father asked where he was.

"You stupid good-for-nothing!" Saul roared, jumping to his feet and spilling his drink. There was shocked silence round the table. "You are a disgrace to your family. Don't you realise that so long as that man lives, your succession to the throne is in jeopardy? Now bring him to me, for he must die."

Jonathan made the mistake of arguing the point. In a fury, Saul hurled his spear across the table, narrowly missing his son. White with anger, Jonathan got to his feet and walked from the room, slamming the door behind him.

He met David outside town: "You were right. I can see clearly now that as the Lord was with my father, so he will be with you." There was a pause before he continued quietly, "I fear that God's purposes for you can only be fulfilled if I am out of the way, dead. I want you to make me a solemn promise, choked Jonathan. "When I and my father are both dead, be kind to my family." They both wept, but David was broken, beyond consolation.

The two entered into a formal agreement that day, a covenant of kindness, for they loved each other dearly. Then they called upon God to ratify the covenant. "The Lord is witness between you and me, and between your descendants and my descendants forever." Then they parted company, heartbroken.

14

The Outlaw

Now where to? Having made his escape from home down a rope, David had nothing but the clothes he stood up in – no weapons, no food – nothing. So he headed to Nob, a couple of miles south of Gibeah, the home of the priest Ahimelech. David was well known as a leader of Saul's troops, so Ahimelech was amazed to see him all alone. "I am on a secret mission for the king," David lied. "My men are waiting for me outside of town. But we are in urgent need of provisions. Do you have any food or weapons?"

Ahimelech gave him the consecrated bread that represented the presence of God. "And the only sword I have is the one you yourself took from Goliath." David accepted both with gratitude, even though the sword was still a little big for him.

Just as he was leaving, he caught sight of someone he recognised: Saul's head shepherd, Doeg, an immigrant from Edom. What was he doing in Nob, David wondered? He left with an uneasy feeling.

Where would be the last place on earth that Saul would think of looking for David? It was the sword that gave him the inspiration: Gath, the hometown of Goliath! David kept a low profile, and for the first few days nobody recognised him. But inevitably his presence was reported to the king, who had him arrested. Out of the fat into the proverbial fire. David desperately racked his brain for a way to escape. But no flash of brilliance came to him. So on the spur of the moment, he resorted to acting the fool. As a child, he used to pretend to be mad, just to irritate his brothers, so the act all came back to him. He dribbled and rolled his eyes, then clawed at the door, making incoherent noises.

"The man's insane!" King Achish said in disgust. "Quite mad. Get him out of here!" So they threw him out of town.

David made a temporary home in a cave near the community of Adullam, halfway between Gath and his hometown of Bethlehem. He got word to his family to join him there, since they too were in danger. Saul would be bound to harass them as a way to get back at David. So they joined him in the cave.

Over the weeks that followed, other refugees wandered into the cave: outlaws, fugitives, homeless men and women with no place to call home, no cause to live for. At first it was just a trickle, but soon more and more were arriving every day, till the ranks swelled to around four hundred. There was no way David was going to let them sit around and degenerate into a demoralised group of malcontents, so he began to drill them to become fighters. Soon a sense of purpose and pride transformed them into a disciplined band of warriors.

But Adullam wasn't far enough from Saul to be a safe refuge for David's father and mother. His men might be able to move around to evade capture, but his aging parents could not. So he took them to a high stronghold in the land of Moab, the original home of his great-grandmother Ruth. There in the protection of the king of Moab, he could safely leave them, while he and his outlaws could try to stay one step ahead of King Saul.

One more refugee joined them about that time: no run-of-the-mill outlaw, for he was a priest. When they brought him to David, he told a sorry tale. "I am Abiathar, son of Ahimelech of Nob." David remembered how his father had fed and armed him just a few months previously. Abiathar told how Saul's men had slaughtered his father and his entire family, sacking Nob and killing men, women, and children. "The raid was led by Doeg, the Edomite."

"I knew it! I was sure he'd tell Saul the moment I saw him there,"

David said, recalling his unease at seeing him. *"That man is a disgrace in the eyes of God. But his day will come. God will bring him down."* David recorded his resentment by writing it as a sonnet.

Then to Abiathar: "I feel responsible for your loss. Stay with me. You'll be safe here."

Saul's obsession with catching David distracted him from his responsibility to care for his own people who were vulnerable to the Philistine raiding parties. David felt a degree of responsibility for the nearby town of Keilah, so he asked the Lord if he should lead his men in their defence.

"Go," was the clear answer.

But his men were less certain: "We already have Saul on our tails, and now you want to antagonise the Philistines as well?"

So David took the question back to the Lord.

Before fleeing Doeg's slaughter, Abiathar had had the presence of mind to snatch up some of the precious tools of the priests' trade. He had grabbed the cape from a peg on the door, in a pocket of which were kept the Urim and Thummim, a couple of holy dice by which he could discern God's will in any given matter. And it was by this means that God clearly affirmed: "Go to Keilah, and I will give the Philistines into your hand." And just so it happened. This was the beginning of many occasions when the anointed but yet uncrowned king would spring to the defence of his people.

When word reached Saul that David was in Keilah, he was overjoyed. "He's trapped! Keilah will be his prison."

On the advice of the trusty Urim and Thummim, David made a swift exit and was long gone by the time Saul arrived. From there, they were constantly on the move. To the south they went, hiding amongst the rocks and ravines in the desert region of Ziph. The locals sent word to Saul that David was amongst them, so further south they went to Maon, deeper and deeper into the hills.

The life of a fugitive, responsible for the well-being of a company of men now numbering over six hundred, was no walk in the park. Sometimes, it all got on top of him. *"I am in distress. O God; my eyes are red with tears, my soul and my body wracked with grief,"* he wrote in his journal. *"My strength is draining away. It seems I am the utter contempt of those around me. And even my friends have forgotten me as though I were dead, like a fragment of broken pottery thrown aside."*

One day, just as David was feeling really sorry for himself, into the camp walked Jonathan. How he had found him no one knew, but there he was, large as life and smiling encouragement. Exactly what they said to each other stayed between them, but suffice it to say that David's strength and confidence in God was completely renewed.

"There's no doubt in my mind that one day you will be king in my father's place," Jonathan concluded. "And when that day comes, I want to be your right-hand man, under your command. Swear to me that that is how it will be." Before Jonathan left, they renewed their covenant.

As it turned out, Jonathan didn't have far to go to rejoin his father. He was right there in the desert with three thousand men, hot on David's trail. The chase was relentless. David's six hundred moved around silently, daring not to light a fire or make a sound. And day after day, Saul closed in. David led his men to En Gedi, an oasis on the shore of the Dead Sea. There was a deep cave in which they could find cool shelter from the relentless desert sun. And that's where Saul caught up with them. All six hundred of David's men were crowded into the back of the cave. They had taken care to brush over their tracks to hide the evidence of their presence. If Saul realised they were there then they would be finished, caught like rats in a trap. Each man held his breath, straining his ears. Then their worst nightmare happened: the sound of army boots crunching gravel just outside the cave. But worse was to come. Into the cave walked no less a person than the king himself. Not a man breathed, let alone coughed.

Now if Saul had been expecting privacy as he answered the call of nature, then he would have been disappointed. Six hundred pairs of eyes watched him remove his cloak, throw it over a rock, and then get down to business.

"This is your big chance, the one the Lord promised you," breathed someone. "You have him with his pants down."

David crept forward with his knife between his teeth. Then, when he was very close, he paused – paused for a long time. Then taking the knife in his right hand, he silently cut off a corner of Saul's royal cloak, then crept back to join his outraged men. He held up a hand to stifle their protests.

"God wouldn't let me touch him. He is the Lord's anointed king. It's bad enough that I ruined his robe."

With business completed, Saul vacated the cave and went on his merry way, unaware of his narrow escape. David gave him a head start, and then, when he judged him to be at a safe distance, he ran out of the cave. "My lord the king!"

Saul froze, recognising the voice. He turned, and there was his enemy, face down on the ground, and behind him hundreds of men crowding out of the cave. "Why do you listen to those who tell you that I am determined to harm you? Untrue! Today the Lord put you at my mercy back there in the cave. Yes, there were those who urged me to kill you, but I refused. 'I will not lift a finger to harm my master, the Lord's chosen one.' I admit that I did cut off the corner of your robe, but I did not kill you. I have no desire to harm you in any way. So why do you hunt me? I am a nobody, a dead dog, a flea in comparison to who you are. May the Lord be judge between you and me."

It was a huge risk, and for a moment the silence was tense. Then the king began to sob. "Is that really you, David, my son? You have returned me good for all the evil I have tried to do to you. May the Lord reward you for this." There was a long pause. Then he continued with a note of resignation: "Now I know for sure that one day you will be king in my place. But I want you to swear to me, by the Lord, that when that day comes, you will be kind to my family. Don't kill them or wipe out the memory of my name." David gave his oath – from a distance, for Saul was not to be trusted. But Saul did go home that day, and David maintained his distance, establishing his base in a natural mountain fortress, almost impregnable from every side.

About that time, some bad news reached the fortress: Samuel was dead, the last of the dynasty of the judges. To attend the funeral would be to give himself up to Saul. So they grieved from a distance.

More bad news was that Saul had further insulted David in absentia by giving Michal, David's wife, to another in marriage. Loneliness there in the desert must have threatened melancholy. So, to cheer himself up, and to send the message that the insult had been as water to a duck's back, he married Ahinoam, a local girl who, by happy coincidence, shared the same name as Michal's mother, Saul's wife.

Provisioning his army must have been a constant headache for David. How do you feed six hundred men in the desert? There was wild life to be hunted, but you can only stand so many barbecued rabbits. There were remnants of the peoples who had been missed in Joshua's day, to be mopped up and plundered. Living there were also local Israelis who were vulnerable to the attack of these same hostile foreigners and needed protection. And for that service, David won the gratitude and generosity of many of his countrymen. But not all were grateful.

Nabal was a prosperous sheep farmer on a spread called "Carmel." David's men knew Nabal's herdsmen and had often protected them from rustlers and thieves, but never had Nabal sent so much as a thank-you card.

It was shearing time, with the accompanying celebrations. David sent ten men to convey his greetings and good wishes to Nabal and to drop the hint that a slice of the pie would not go amiss.

"Just who exactly is this 'David' of whom you speak? Is he one of those runaway servants who have betrayed their masters? There's a plague of them these days. But in any case, why would I even consider taking some of the meat I have slaughtered for my men and give it to who knows who, coming from who knows where?"

When they told David, he was furious. "Grab your swords," he growled. In hot-headed anger, he led four hundred of his men to slaughter Nabal and his servants. He was just descending a ravine from the mountains into the flat grassy valley where Carmel was located, muttering curses and promises of vengeance as he went, when he found his way blocked by a small procession of donkeys and mules, laden with provisions. At the rear of the cavalcade was a beautiful woman, who immediately dismounted and, to David's amazement, prostrated herself before him.

"I am Abigail, wife of Nabal. May I speak with you for a moment?" David motioned for her to continue. "I fear my husband is a fool, but I have come to ask for your forgiveness. Let the blame be all mine. I should have stopped him, but I wasn't aware that your men had visited him till it was too late. Please forgive me. And be good enough to accept these offerings as a gift for you and your men." All the wind was spilled from David's sails.

But Abigail wasn't done yet. "I know that one day you will be king, but I would hate to think that when that day comes you might have on your conscience the crushing burden of needless bloodshed. Leave time for God to do the punishing. It is his business to avenge."

The lecture over, Abigail fell silent. Had she overstepped the mark? "Oh, one more thing," she added (might as well be hung for a sheep as for a lamb). "When the Lord does act on your behalf, don't forget me." How could David forget a pretty face?

"Praise God for sending you to stop me. And bless you for your good judgment and wise advice." David wheeled round and headed for home. And that night, they feasted at Nabal's unwitting expense.

It wasn't till next morning that Abigail told Nabal what she had done. Was it shock at how close he had come to death, or was it anger? Hard to say, but Nabal had a heart attack, right there at the breakfast table, and died ten days later.

When David heard the news, he was overjoyed: "It really is God's business to avenge, just as Abigail said." He recalled her parting words: "When the Lord does act on your behalf, don't forget me."

Forget her? Never! He married her.

True to form, Saul tired of repentance and set out on yet another hunting expedition with three thousand of his finest, and in company with his trusted general, Abner. Since the incident in the cave, David had been careful to post lookouts. So he was aware of Saul's approach long before he got anywhere close. David and his men watched as Saul's men pitched camp by the road that wound up and over a hillside. He saw them settling down for the night, Saul and Abner safely surrounded by their troops, snug in their sleeping bags, oblivious to watching eyes.

"Let's go and have a chat with Saul. Who's coming?" His nephew Abishai volunteered. Good lads, those sons of his sister, Zeruiah. There were three of them: Abishai, Joab, and Asahel, all fearless warriors. So David and Abishai crept into the camp, expecting to be stopped at any moment. But no challenge came – just the sound of men snoring. They got right to the centre of the camp, and there was General Abner, sleeping like a baby, and next to him, the king with his spear stuck in the ground by his head, and his flask ready for his morning swill. That spear! Twice it had narrowly missed taking his life. What an opportunity for David to take his revenge.

Remembering David's reticence in the cave when faced with a similar opportunity, Abishai whispered, "Let me do it. One swift thrust with that spear, and he'd be nailed to the ground for good."

"Don't touch him! I don't want any guilt to be attached to you. Remember, it was God himself who anointed him to be king. If the Lord wants to change that appointment, then it's up to him to do so whenever and however he pleases. Just grab the spear and that water bottle, and let's get out of here." So they withdrew, and still no one stirred.

They climbed to the top of the hill. When they had caught their breath, David shouted back at the camp, "Hey Abner! Are you awake yet?"

Struggling into consciousness, Abner replied, "Who's that?"

"Are you a man or a mouse, you who are famed to be Israel's bravest? What kind of a bodyguard are you to the king, sleeping at your post? If an enemy came into the camp, the king would be a dead man, thanks to your negligence. Frankly, Abner, you ought to die for such a failure to protect the Lord's anointed."

"But they didn't come into the camp, did they? The king is unharmed."

"So where's his spear and flask then, if no one came into the camp?"

Awkward silence while he looked.

"Is that you, David, my son?" It was the king.

"Yes, it is I, my lord. Why are you hunting me? Is it the Lord who has put this plan in your heart, or is this someone else's idea?"

"I have sinned, David. Come on home. I promise I will never try to harm you again. I have been foolish. I'm sorry."

Once bitten, twice shy. David had no confidence in Saul's promises. "I will leave the spear and the water bottle here, so one of your men can retrieve them."

"Blessings on you, David. You will do great things and triumph in the end."

David and his men melted away into the night, and in the morning, Saul went home.

"This truce won't last," David realised. "I have to find a safe place for my men and their families to settle. Gath!" Surely they would be safe amongst the Philistines. Saul would never dare follow them there. The last time David had been in Gath, he had been alone, but now he was in the company of a couple of thousand people: six hundred fighting men and their families.

Surprisingly, King Achish welcomed him like an old friend. "You can live in Ziklag," he told him generously, after the crowded conditions in Gath were beginning to get on everyone's nerves. Ziklag was a town some forty miles to the south. A place to call home at last!

Killing two birds with one stone – the need for provisions, and the necessity to cement his relationship with Achish – David conducted raids on some of Israel's traditional enemies far off to the south: Geshurites, Girzites, and Amalekites. He took care to leave no survivors, so no one would ever know exactly where he had been plundering. When asked by Achish, he would let on that he had been raiding the communities of his own people in Israel.

"He can never go home now," Achish concluded. "They will hate him. He's my man for life."

Things came to an unexpected head when the lords of the Philistines set their sights on northern Israel. They established their camp at Shunem, in territory belonging to the Israeli tribe of Issachar, on the northern slopes of the plain of Jezreel.

Saul rose to the challenge and made his camp on the hill of Gilboa, on the south side of the valley, presumably with the thought that the plain of Jezreel between them would offer a level playing field, a fine site for a battle.

Naturally, Achish was included in the Philistine invasion force. "It's understood," Achish announced to David, "that you and your men will accompany me."

"But of course," David replied. "Now you will see for yourself what we can do."

"Then you will act as my personal bodyguards."

So now what? Saul, his true king, Jonathan, his best friend, and many soldiers that he himself had led in the early days were facing them in the Israeli camp over the valley. Here was the ultimate conflict of interests.

But for the time being, they played along. The next day, Achish summoned him: "We have a problem, and I'm not sure quite how to put this. Let me start by saying that from the very first you have been nothing but loyal. But …"

"But what?" David said, feigning shock.

"But my fellow Philistine lords don't know you like I do. They fear that once the battle is joined, you may turn on us."

"Outrageous!" spluttered David. "Have I ever let you down?" He protested long enough, but not too long. Then with apparent reluctance, but heart-felt relief, he led his men on a three-day march back to Ziklag.

How sweet to be going home! But the sweetness turned bitter, for as they drew closer, they saw smoke rising in the southern sky. They covered the last few miles at the double, and there were the ashes of what had been their homes, the city burned to the ground. Everyone was gone: wives, sweethearts, children. The jubilation of the homecoming turned to despair and then to anger.

Someone had to be blamed. The boss! "Let's stone him!" someone shouted, but what good would that have done? David was as devastated as was everyone else, for his two wives, Abigail and Ahinoam, were also gone. What to do?

First, he took time to talk it over with the Lord. That helped. Then he asked him specific questions and, with the aid of the Urim and Thummim, got some straight answers. "Yes, pursue them. Yes, you will succeed in the rescue."

"Let's go!" David shouted at the angry mob. Off they set at a run, keeping up a furious pace for some twenty miles.

On reaching a steep ravine, some of the older or out-of-shape men were unable to go further. "Hopeless!" they reasoned. A couple of hundred stayed by the stream, and the other four hundred left their backpacks in their care and continued with a lighter load.

A couple of miles further down the road, they found an Egyptian man, dying by the roadside. They took time to revive him with water and some food. He told them he had been slave to an Amalekite who had abandoned him three days previously when he fell sick. His master was part of a raiding party who had burned Ziklag, amongst other places. "What of the women and children?" they asked him anxiously. He assured them they were unharmed and that the Amalekites were moving slowly, since they were driving a large number of stolen livestock ahead of them.

As it turned out, it didn't take long to catch up with them. There they were, spread out haphazardly. No discipline. No thought of vigilance. All the pent-up anger and frustration that had been misdirected at David was now unleashed on the Amalekites. If the slaughter was intense, then the joy of reunion was overwhelming; families reunited, David a hero.

When they got back to the two hundred by the ravine, some grumbled that they deserved no share in the plunder, but David insisted: "Not so. It was God who gave us all this stuff and our families back unharmed. Therefore, we owe it to him to be generous, as he is generous to us. The share of those who guarded the kit is the same as for those who fought." And that became a rule from that day on.

When they got home and sorted out the plunder, they found that there was way more than had been taken just from Ziklag. So David continued his policy of generosity and sent shares to the Israeli towns all over the region of Judah, with his best wishes. David's stock rose, and a good thing too, for things were not going well for Saul, still facing off with the Philistine army over the plain of Jezreel.

Saul's confidence was at a low ebb: advancing years and declining health; he was not the man he used to be. He went personally to reconnoitre the enemy camp, but that only made things worse. He was terrified at what he saw. He prayed, seeking God's wisdom, but the heavens were shut up tight. No one home. Samuel was dead and buried, so now he had no one to turn to.

"Find me a medium!" Saul demanded. One was found close by in Endor. Disguising himself as a peasant, he and a couple of his men paid a visit on this lady. It was night, and they were dangerously close to the Philistine camp. The three of them were jumpy as crickets. Was it spooks or Philistines that most rattled them? They huddled close together as they crept through the shadows.

The door creaked open when they knocked, and there was the witch.

"We want you to consult a spirit for us."

"Are you trying to get me killed? King Saul has made the craft illegal, you know."

"Listen. I swear by the Lord himself that you will not get trouble for this." No problem giving that assurance.

"Well, who is it you want to consult?"

"The prophet Samuel."

"Very well."

They all sat there in silence, just the sounds of night birds calling outside and the occasional rat scurrying across the floor. They could see in the faint light of the candle that the lady was slowly rocking back and forward. Then her eyes rolled back, and she started to moan. They leant forward expectantly. Suddenly she screamed. They jumped and the hair rose on their scalps.

"Why have you tried to deceive me? You *are* Saul!" she yelled, pointing.

"Don't be afraid," snapped Saul. "What do you see?"

"I see a spirit rising from the ground."

"What does it look like?"

"He's an old, old man, wearing a cloak."

"Samuel!" Saul remembered that cloak. He had torn the corner off it that day long ago, when Samuel had accused him of failure to obey the Lord's command. In an instant, he was prostrate on the ground.

Then the woman spoke with a man's voice: "Why have you disturbed me?"

"I am in terrible trouble. The Philistines are attacking me, and I can't seem to get any answer when I pray. So I have no one else to turn to. What shall I do?"

"Why should I help you, since the Lord has become your enemy? This is exactly what I told you would happen that day when you tore my cloak. The Lord has torn the kingdom from you and is giving it to another: to David. Tomorrow, the Lord will give over the Israeli army to the Philistines." Then in a chilling finale: "You and your sons will be here with me by tomorrow evening."

Saul was finished, out cold on the ground. It was the woman who eventually roused him. "You need something to eat," she said kindly, and his men, who hadn't eaten all day, agreed with her. She fussed around, and when they had eaten a good meal, they all felt better. They headed back to Gilboa before it got light.

And sure as the witch had foretold, the battle began that morning.

From the start, it was a disaster. Almost immediately, the Israeli line broke, and in panic, they started a disorderly retreat. Back up the slope towards the camp on Mount Gilboa they fled. The Philistines were intent on taking out Saul himself, for the fighting intensified all around him. To Saul's horror, he saw Jonathan fighting for his life and then hacked down in a flurry of bloody mayhem. His best men formed a protective wall around Saul, keeping the murderous spears and swords back. It was the archers who eventually got him, an arrow finding a gap in his armour.

"If those fellows reach me, they will abuse me," Saul gasped, leaning on his spear for support. He knew that once he was down, they would be on him like a pack of wolves. "Finish me off quick before they can have their sport," he croaked to his bodyguard. But the bodyguard was unwilling to take the life of the Lord's anointed king. So Saul threw his full weight on his own sword tip and died in a gurgle of blood. The bodyguard then followed suit and died right there, next to his king.

Seeing their king was dead, the remaining troops simply turned and ran. In each town they passed through, they spread the word that Saul was dead and that Israel was defeated. The panic was contagious, and soon the inhabitants of all the towns in northern Israel had abandoned their homes and stampeded to the comparative safety of the east bank of the Jordan River.

The town of Jabesh Gilead now became a refugee camp. That was the town from which wives had been taken to repopulate the depleted tribe of Benjamin, back in the days of the judges. The good citizens of Jabesh Gilead regarded the Benjamites as family and Saul as one of their own. So when word came that the Philistines had hung the corpses of Saul and Jonathan on the wall of Beth Shan just over the river, some of the men of Jabesh made a night sortie and retrieved the royal bodies, bringing them home. There they cremated the mutilated remains and gave the bones a royal burial under a tamarisk tree. Then they fasted and mourned for a week.

An Amalekite arrived in Ziklag with urgent news for David. "Three days back I happened to be on Mount Gilboa," he panted. "And there I saw King Saul, critically wounded with the enemy closing in on him. He called out to me. 'What can I do to help?' I asked him. 'Finish me off before those Philistines get me.' There was no way he was going to recover, and the enemy was very close, so I killed him, as he asked," he lied. Then more truthfully: "I rescued the crown from his head and this band from his arm, and I have brought them straight to you." Doubtless the fellow was a scavenger, seeking to profit from the fallen. The discovery of the dead king with the crown still on his head must have seemed like the mother lode. Who would be the highest bidder for such a trophy? Likely the one Saul had been known to hunt these past years. Greed is a powerful motivator.

The response was not at all as he had expected. David was grief stricken, as were those around him. Clothes were torn and tears were shed. Then turning back to the messenger, David asked, "Why were you not afraid to kill the Lord's anointed?" The wretched man had no idea how highly Saul was honoured by these, his supposed enemies. "You have just testified against yourself. Your blood be upon your own head." Then turning to one of his men: "Kill him!"

15

The King

With the death of Saul, there was no further reason to be a fugitive in a foreign country. And to continue to live in Philistine territory might have been misunderstood by his own countrymen. In any case, Ziklag was a burned-out wreck of a place. So, taking direction from the Lord, he moved his family and all his men to Hebron where he had many friends left over from his outlaw days. Conveniently, it was not far from the family home in Bethlehem, to which his parents were thrilled to return after their exile in Moab.

But this was also a historically significant city, where was the family tomb still containing the dust of Abraham and Sarah, as well as that of Isaac and Jacob.

And it was in Hebron, nearly a quarter century after Samuel had anointed him, that the men of Judah, David's own tribe, anointed him their king.

But Israel was divided. Only Judah followed David. Ish-bosheth, Saul's surviving son, was recognised by the rest of Israel as successor to the throne. Abner, Saul's general, had lived through the battle with the Philistines, and it was he who set Ish-bosheth on the throne. Abner was a hard-bitten fighting machine who had accompanied Saul on his many hunting parties to track down the renegade David. Now here was that same outlaw, continuing his rebellion against the house of Saul.

Ish-bosheth was a weakling, a puppet king, content to permit the real power to be exercised by the military leader, Abner. Ish-bosheth made his headquarters in Mahanaim, on the east side of the Jordan River, not far from Jabesh Gilead, where his father had recently been buried. This was a secure location, safe from Philistines in the west and David in the south.

When Ish-bosheth was securely established on the throne, Abner led the somewhat depleted Israeli army down south to Gibeon. Hearing of their advance, David sent Joab and his men to head them off. They met just outside Gibeon. There was a pool, and the opposing forces faced each other over the water. It was hard to tell at first if this was a reunion or a face-off. Many of the men knew each other. Taunts and good-natured insults were shouted across the water. Eventually, they all sat down and ate their lunch.

Abner and Joab had a parlay. "Let's have a bit of fun," Abner suggested. "A dozen of your youngsters against a dozen of ours." It was agreed.

The combatants paired off, each armed with a short sword. When the whistle was blown, they all used the identical tactics they had learned at the same military academy. They grabbed the opponent by the hair and stabbed a lethal blow upwards into the other's stomach. Every one of them died there, slowly writhing in their own blood. If ever there was a demonstration of the senseless futility of a war organised by generals, sitting in safety away from the danger zone, then surely this was it.

Both sides watched in fascinated horror. Then they jumped to their feet to a man and ran at each other, screaming vengeance. How quickly wars escalate! The fight was intense but brief. There were casualties on both sides, but many more of Abner's men fell. Realising they were beaten, the demoralised men simply turned and ran back toward Mahanaim, with Joab leading David's troops in pursuit. Joab was running with his brother Abishai, but their younger brother Asahel, the fastest runner in the family, was way out in front. He had picked out the unmistakable figure of Abner, presumably thinking that if he could get him, then the war would be over.

"Is that you, Asahel?" panted Abner.

"It is indeed."

"Then pick on someone your own size, why don't you? How can I ever face your brother if I have to kill you?"

But Asahel was determined. With every step he closed the gap, and when he was just a few paces behind him, Abner abruptly stopped dead in his tracks and rammed the butt of his spear into Asahel's stomach and clear out his back. When his two older brothers came to the spot, there was Asahel, dead on a skewer. And now they had compelling cause to redouble their chase. It was personal.

As the sun was setting, Abner made a stand on a small hillock, rallying his men into a tight square, bristling with spears. "How long are you going to keep this up, Joab?" he yelled. "This is going to end in terrible bitterness, you know."

"We are ready to chase you all night if need be. But what's the point?" Joab sounded the cease-fire and the battle was over. Abner limped back to Mahanaim, while Joab and Abishai carried their brother back to Bethlehem, where they buried him in the family cemetery.

The war between Israel's divided tribes dragged on for years. David became stronger, while Ish-bosheth became weaker. David also increased his strength on the home front by siring several sons. To help this project along, he married a couple of extra wives besides the two he already had, and half a dozen sons were added to the family home there in Hebron.

Not content with four, David also wanted his original wife back (as though he didn't have enough without her). So he sent a message to Ish-bosheth, demanding the return of Michal, for whom he had paid Saul the princely sum of two hundred Philistine foreskins. That was fine with everyone except Paltiel, Michal's new husband, who was heartbroken. No one bothered to ask Michal what she thought.

Meanwhile in Mahanaim, a squabble had developed between Ish-bosheth and Abner. Abner was accused of having sexual relations with one of Saul's concubines, who now all belonged to the new king. Abner played the outraged innocent and devastated Ish-bosheth by announcing his intention to turn the whole kingdom over to David. Abner made good his threat and sent a letter to David, offering to help to unite the kingdom as one under David's rule. David was delighted.

Abner wielded considerable influence and in short order had convinced the elders of Israel that since the Lord had promised David the kingdom, it was about time they all fell in line and recognised him as their true king. When consensus was pretty well achieved, Abner went to Hebron with a delegation of twenty men. This was the first time in many years he had actually seen David, face to face. David entertained him royally, laying on a special banquet in his honour. When the toasts were all done, Abner told David, "So I will go and call an immediate assembly of all Israel, and they will make you their king." David sent him off in peace.

No sooner was Abner out of the door than Joab arrived back from a raid that had taken him out of town for a few days. Joab was furious to hear that Abner had been in Hebron. He knew nothing of his deal with David but suspected Abner's visit as being but an excuse for espionage.

Joab sent messengers after Abner, asking him to come back for further talks. When he arrived, Joab took him aside and then stabbed him in the stomach, just as Abner had stabbed Joab's brother, Asahel. Vengeance!

When later he heard what had happened, David was horrified. This surely was the end of his hopes for a unified kingdom. He called down curses on Joab and went to elaborate lengths to distance himself from the murder. He gave Abner an elaborate funeral with full state honours and even composed a special song to mark his passing. What else could he have done?

A day or so later, two of Ish-bosheth's men arrived, demanding an audience with David. Opening their backpack, they pulled out a severed head.

"Who was that?" David demanded.

"Your rival, Ish-bosheth, son of Saul, who tried to take your life. Now you are avenged!" they announced triumphantly.

"You murdered an innocent man in cold blood," David said, staring them down icily. "Why should I not demand your blood in return?" And he did, hanging their dismembered bodies out to dry on the wall as an example to all who might ever mistakenly think they were doing the king's service by murdering innocent people. But Ish-bosheth's head was given a decent burial next to Abner.

Next day, the elders of Israel arrived. They made a fine speech to David, recognising his service to the nation and the obvious call of God on his life. Then they anointed him king of all Israel.

David wrote in his journal that evening: *"How wonderful it is when brothers live in unity! It is like precious oil on the head. It's as though the dew of Hermon were falling on Mount Zion. Unity! That's where the Lord sends his blessing – Life!"*

Hebron, currently the capital of Judah, would not do for the new national headquarters for all Israel. Gibeah had been Saul's capital, so it might be difficult for David to rule from there, surrounded as he would be by the old king's family.

He recalled that as a teenager, when he had commuted from his home in Bethlehem to Saul's court in Gibeah, he had frequently looked up to the Jebusite fortress of Jerusalem. *That would make a fine capital city,* he had always thought.

"But it's impregnable!" Joab reminded him. "No one has ever managed to dislodge its Jebusite inhabitants, not even in the victorious days of Joshua. It's not for nothing that those Jebusites have a saying: 'Even blind and lame soldiers could defend Jerusalem.'"

"I think I know a way in that the lame and blind haven't thought of." David said. "Through the water system."

Joab led the way in, wiggling out of the water duct in the middle of the city, drenched to the skin but triumphant. He opened the gates and let David's army march in. For that, David forgave his former indiscretions and made Joab his general.

Jerusalem was indeed a magnificent site for a capital. It was renamed "City of David," and immediately they went to work to develop its potential. Carpenters and stonemasons, along with building materials, were lent by Hiram, king of Tyre, up on the Mediterranean coast. Cedar was the most available lumber, so they built a magnificent palace for David and his ever-expanding family. In an attempt to fill the space, he married yet more wives and added a handful of concubines for good measure. The inevitable result was still more kids.

Understandably, the Philistines were not pleased that David was now king of all Israel. Poor Achish must have heard a few "I told you so's" from his fellow Philistine colleagues. "This upstart has got to be stopped," they reasoned and marched their troops to within a couple of miles of Jerusalem.

"Shall I go out and attack them?" David asked the Lord.

"Go!" was the clear reply. So he went and thrashed them. But they rallied and came back the next day for a rematch.

"This time go round behind them," responded the Lord to David's request for marching orders. "Wait there till you hear the sound of marching feet coming from the tree tops." Not sure what that meant, David took up the specified position and waited. Then they heard it, marching boots over their heads. "Up and at them!" shouted David. "The armies of heaven have gone ahead of us." That day it was a rout, and the Philistines were chased right out of the hill country.

To consolidate his position, it next seemed expedient to David to make Jerusalem the religious capital of Israel. He pitched a fine new tent in a prominent position and then marched thirty thousand men the ten miles west to Kiriath Jearim to fetch the ark of God, where it had been stored in the house of Abinadab ever since it had been returned by the Philistines in the days of Eli the priest. The ark had originally arrived there on a cart miraculously pulled by two cows, and it was a state-of-the-art new cart that Abinadab made for its transportation in the grand procession to Jerusalem. How proud he was of his two sons. Ahio was guiding the oxen who, it appeared on this journey, needed some human intervention to guide them in the way they should take. Uzzah was sitting on the cart, right next to the ark. There was music and dancing and a marching band for the soldiers. What a spectacle! They had gone but a mile of so, when one of the oxen missed its step, giving the cart a shake. Uzzah reached out a hand to steady the ark and died right there on the spot.

The whole procession came to a staggering halt. The band quit like a dying gaggle of geese. David demanded to know what was the matter. And there was Uzzah, stone cold dead beside the ark.

Anger was David's first reaction, but then the hair rose on his scalp, and he was terrified. Why had God done this? He heard that Uzzah had touched the ark. But who was he, David, to imagine that he could have such a terrible object close to him? He made arrangements for it to be stored in the nearby barn of Obed-edom and then went home, still shaking.

When he had recovered from the shock, he consulted with Abiathar, his priest, and Nathan, a prophet who was becoming a valued advisor. They told him that the cart was the problem. There was a clearly defined way that the ark was to be transported. Only the priests were ever to touch the ark, and then only remotely as they inserted carrying poles into the rings designed for the purpose.

Three months went by, and word was that Obed-edom was doing well, clearly blessed by the presence of the ark. "Then I must have it here with me in Jerusalem," said David.

So a second time they set out to fetch the ark, but this time there was no cart, just humble priests who carried the ark on their shoulders, supported by long poles. When they had walked a few steps, they paused while a bull and a calf were sacrificed. Then they moved on towards Jerusalem. They may have started out nervously, but by the time they reached Jerusalem, there was a party happening: shouting and singing and dancing, waving banners and flags. Even David himself stripped off his royal robes and danced with all his might in just his boxers. They took the ark and placed it in the new tent. Then the food was brought on, a feast for the thousands of soldiers and civilians who had participated in the parade. Finally, David stood up and made a speech of gratitude. He pronounced a blessing on the whole crowd and then sent them home to bed. He arrived back in the palace, exhausted, but deeply satisfied.

He was met in the hall by his first wife, Michal. "Well, well!" she exclaimed with heavy sarcasm. "Didn't the king of Israel distinguish himself today, dancing almost naked in full sight of even the servant girls?"

"Michal, it was before the Lord that I was dancing," David returned, shocked. "It was he who made me king in place of your father. I don't care how undignified I may appear to others when I am worshipping like that."

The years that followed were the glory years for Israel. Everywhere they went, there was victory. Everything they touched turned to gold. All the surrounding nations were conquered and became subservient to Israel: the Philistines, the Moabites, the Arameans, the Ammonites, the Amalekites, the Edomites – north, south, east, and west – all were subject to David's rule. And David reigned fairly, doing what was just and right for all his people.

He was well served with good men taking responsibility: Joab, his nephew, continued to be military commander. Serving the spiritual needs of the people were Zadok and Ahimelech. Ahimelech was the son of Abiathar, who had joined David's outlaws back in the desert days. Touchingly, he had named his son after his father, who had been slaughtered by the wretched Doeg. Seraiah was secretary of state. And surrounding David were his sons, royal advisors every one.

Just one thing rippled the calm surface of David's peace. It didn't seem right that he should live in a cedar palace while all the ark of God had for protection from the elements was a tent. In any case, a grand and imposing temple might impress on visitors the virtue of worshipping the God of Israel, David's God. He discussed the matter with Nathan the prophet.

"Go right ahead. Whatever you have in mind sounds good to me." But even prophets don't always get it right.

Next morning, Nathan was back with an extraordinary message from God. "This is what God says to you: 'Have I ever asked anyone to build me a home? What possible use would I have for a wooden house, anyway? And, even were I to need one, what makes you think you would be the right man to do the building?

"'In case you think you are something, let me remind you that it has been I who have been doing all the building so far. I took you from being a simple shepherd to become ruler of Israel. It was I who put down those who opposed you. And it will be I who will make you great, I who will give Israel a safe home, I who will give them peace.

"'No, it's not you who will build a house for me, but rather I who will build a house for you. And it is not you who will raise many sons to secure your dynasty, but it is I who will raise up one unique son after you. I will be his father and he will be my son. I will discipline him, yes, but I will never stop loving him, no matter what happens. He is the one who will build a house for my name. Your house and your kingdom will endure forever before me; your throne will be established without end.'"

David was speechless at first, but when what God had promised began to sink in, he responded, "Who am I that you have blessed me this far and have promised so much more for the future? Is this how you normally deal with people? No, but for some reason you have picked Israel from all the nations on earth to be a demonstration of your greatness. Indeed how great you are, oh Sovereign Lord! There is no one like you.

"So, yes! Please do exactly as you have promised. Your words are always to be trusted. It is you who have promised these good things, you who have spoken, and you who will bless the house of your servant forever."

What an amazing paradox. David the servant had wanted do some great thing for his Master. But instead, the Master had promised to do great things for his servant. Like so many others who since then have found such an incongruity too amazing to swallow, David was overcome, his world turned upside down, inside out.

What could he do in response to such undeserved kindness?

"Kindness." Yes. That triggered a memory. His best friend Jonathan had made him swear: "When I and my father are dead, be *kind* to my family." Even Saul had extracted a promise from David: "Swear to me, by the Lord, that when that day comes you will be *kind* to my family." Kindness. But to whom could he show it?

He asked his personal assistant: "Find out if there is anyone left from the household of Saul." They came up with a name: Ziba – one of Saul's servants. He was summoned to the royal presence.

"Is there anyone still alive from Saul's family? I want to demonstrate God's kindness."

"Yes, there is still a son of Jonathan. He is severely disabled."

"Bring him to me!" David ordered.

There were, in fact, several survivors from Saul's family, but Ziba was only aware of the one. On the day he had received the news of the death of both his father and grandfather, Mephibosheth, then just a child of five years, had suffered a crippling fall. Since then he had lived up north, close to his father's grave.

The summons to appear before King David must have been terrifying. He had heard conflicting reports about this man, good reports originating from his father Jonathan, and bad ones probably coming from his grandfather Saul, or his uncle Ish-bosheth. But common sense told him that his last day on earth had probably now come.

Ziba wheeled him into the throne room. He sat there, trembling like a leaf.

"Mephibosheth," the king said warmly, "don't be frightened. I am going to show you kindness for the sake of your father, Jonathan. That was my promise to him years ago when we were both young. And what is more, I will restore to you the family farm in Gibeah, where your grandfather and your father lived. But I want you always to eat here at my table."

Mephibosheth did his best to bow. "Who am I that you should even notice a dead dog like me?"

Then David charged Ziba with the responsibility of acting as the estate manager of the farm in Gibeah, answerable to Mephibosheth, who would in future be found in the royal palace in Jerusalem.

16

The Fall

Life was good. David had a wonderful home and a loving family in a magnificent city where he successfully held down the best job in the world. He was pleased with himself. To cap it all, Joab was away with the army, laying siege to Rabbah, a troublesome Ammonite city east of the Jordan, so life in Jerusalem was peaceful.

David woke from his nap one beautiful spring afternoon with nothing more important on his mind than what was for supper. He went up onto the flat roof of his palace to stretch his legs. As far as the eye could see in any direction was his kingdom. What more could a man want? But then he knew …

On the flat roof of his neighbour's house was a woman, sunbathing by her pool, buck-naked. Spectacular! No harm in looking.

"Who is that beautiful woman?" David asked of his butler.

"Her name is Bathsheba, sir, and she is the wife of your neighbour Uriah, who I believe is currently away with the army at Rabbah."

"She must be lonely," mused David. So he invited her over for a neighbourly cup of tea. But it turned out to be more than tea that they enjoyed together that afternoon. That perfectly ordinary day became the turning point in David's life and that of the whole nation. Small things can have such devastating repercussions.

That might have been that, were it not for one little sperm that entered a tiny egg, and Bathsheba was pregnant. The time in the month was long passed, and there was no sign of menstruation, so she sent David a discreet note simply stating the problem: "Dear David. I am pregnant. Love, Bathsheba" – or something along those lines.

How to solve this problem ... If Uriah might be called home on some pretext, then he would be bound to sleep with his wife and no one would know who was the father of the premature child seven months later.

What had started out as an apparently harmless contravention of the tenth commandment – *Don't covet your neighbour's wife* – had quickly led to the flouting of the seventh: *Don't commit adultery.* Now number nine was in danger of toppling, the prohibition of false witness. Where would it end?

Uriah arrived at the palace and reported to the king. "So how is General Joab?" David enquired. "And are the troops in good spirit? The siege is dragging on a bit, don't you think? Do you anticipate a positive outcome soon?"

"Indeed I do, sir," the soldier reported in clipped military fashion.

"Well done indeed, Uriah. You deserve a break. So go on home now and enjoy a night with your wife. Dip your feet in that roof top pool I know you enjoy so much. Let your hair down."

Next morning, the butler whispered in David's ear, "You might like to know, sir, that Uriah did not go home last night. He slept on the palace steps."

David called him in. "So, Uriah, I hear you slept at my front door last night. Why would you do a thing like that when your home is just next door?"

"Didn't seem appropriate to enjoy the comforts of home, sir, what with the ark of God and the rest of the army sleeping rough on the battle front."

"Very commendable, I'm sure, but quite unnecessary. Stay another night, in fact, stay the weekend."

Uriah stayed but stubbornly slept on the palace steps. In desperation, David invited him in for supper. They ate a gourmet meal together and drank the health of the army, General Joab, Abishai, and all the other officers, until they had drank to almost the entire army, man by man. Uriah was thoroughly smashed. "Now go on home, and dip your little feet," slurred David. But Uriah was too far gone to walk down the palace steps.

Next morning, David fought his hangover to write a note to Joab: "Dear Joab. Put Uriah in the front line so that he will be killed. Yours sincerely ..." He carefully sealed it up and wrote "Private and confidential" on the envelope. "Give this to General Joab with my greetings," he ordered the washed-out-looking Uriah. "Be sure to put it into his hands only!"

And off Uriah set, with his fate sealed and in his pocket.

A few days later, a messenger arrived from Rabbah: "Bad news, I'm afraid, sir. Some of their men came out of the city and attacked us, but we drove them back to the city gate, but in the process got too close to the wall and within range of the archers. Some of our men were killed, including, I fear, your neighbour, Uriah."

David was not nearly as upset as the messenger had anticipated. "Tell Joab not to let this setback get to him. These things happen. The sword kills indiscriminately, and no one can be blamed. Press on and take that city!"

Naturally, Bathsheba was sad to get the news, but David did his best to cheer her up by marrying her. The whole city rejoiced when yet another royal son was born in the palace, and only six months after the wedding! That's royal blood for you!

So there they were. The whole affair neatly covered up, the broken commands now were crowned by number six: murder. But it wasn't really murder, was it? "The sword kills indiscriminately, and no one can be blamed." Adultery? Well, not really. He had married the woman, after all.

But God was not pleased. He sent Nathan to David with a heart-wrenching story of a poor man who had a little lamb, a family pet that he had personally bottle fed and now behaved as one of his own children. The shepherd in David identified with the tale. "Then one day a visitor came to the home of one of his rich neighbours. Unwilling to kill so much as one animal from his own flock, the rich man tore the little lamb from the arms of the heartbroken family and slaughtered it, setting it before his guest."

David was outraged. "Anyone who would do a callous thing like that should be made to pay big time. Who is guilty of this crime?"

There was a long, pregnant silence. Eventually: "You are that man!

"This is what the Lord has to say to you: 'I delivered you from Saul and anointed you king. I united the kingdom under your rule. I gave you a palace to live in and wives to love. And if all that had not been enough, you had but to ask for more. Why did you despise my word, doing such evil? You murdered Uriah through the Ammonites as surely as if you had wielded the sword personally. And you took your neighbour's wife as though she were your own. And in so doing, you have utterly despised me.

"Know therefore that the sword will never again leave you in peace. And know that in the days to come, calamity will originate from your own home. You may have tried to cover it all up, but the consequences will be public. It may have been in secret that you did this thing with Bathsheba, but it will be in broad daylight that another will violate your wives for all the world to witness.'"

David didn't argue. There was nothing to be said. "I have sinned against the Lord," he whispered. So wretched was he that he must have anticipated death right there and then.

"You won't die," Nathan reassured him. "Your sin has been taken away. The Lord has laid on him, the child, your iniquity. He will die."

Sure enough, the baby became unwell, getting progressively worse as the days went by. For a whole week, David fasted and prayed, prostrating himself on the ground before the Lord. "*I know my transgressions and am only too conscious of my sins. Against you have I sinned and done what is evil in your sight. There is no question but that you are right when you judge me. But please ...*"

Then the baby died. The servants were hesitant to let David have the bad news, but when he heard them whispering together, he guessed. He got up and, for the first time in a week, took a shower and ate some food.

"While the child was still living, I fasted and wept because there was still hope that the Lord might change his mind," he explained to his baffled servants. "But now that he is dead, what's the point?"

He later wrote down his continuing prayer: "*God, have mercy on me according to your unfailing love. Don't send me away from you or take your Holy Spirit away from me. Wash away all my iniquity. Make me whiter than snow. Create in me a pure heart and a loyal spirit. Give me back the joy that I have lost.*" But joy was elusive, for shame clung to his shoulders like a shroud.

David did his best to console Bathsheba, and she became pregnant once again. When the baby was born a full nine months later, it was a boy.

They called him "Solomon." Halfway through the birthday celebration, there arrived an uninvited guest: Nathan, the prophet. David went white, and Bathsheba nearly fainted. No! What horror stories might he have to tell this time?

"I have for you a message from God," the prophet announced in the shocked silence. "You are to give the child an extra name: 'Jedidiah.'"

"What does that mean?" quavered Bathsheba.

"It means 'Loved by the Lord.'"

"But why?"

"My dear, simply because the Lord deeply loves him."

Rabbah eventually was taken, with David himself leading the final assault. The crown was removed from the lifeless head of the defeated Ammonite king and victoriously placed on David's. But was the glorious moment marred by the memory of Uriah? Even his victories were tainted by shame. *I know my transgressions and am only too conscious of my sins.*

David's family was "blended," with multiple wives and numerous half-brothers and -sisters. David himself was handsome, and all his wives were beautiful, for David was not attracted to the plain. Consequently, a better-looking group of people than David's family would have been hard to find. It was not surprising, therefore, that sooner or later mutual attraction would confuse the normal flow of sibling harmony.

Amnon, David's firstborn through Ahinoam, fell passionately for his half-sister Tamar. He looked and looked, but he dared not touch. Desire hidden in his heart was building a dangerous head of steam.

Amnon had a cousin, a shrewd man named Jonadab. He was quick to notice that Amnon was off colour. When he discovered the reason, he advised, "Simple solution, cousin. Feign sickness, then ask your father to send Tamar to your house to cook some of the family favourites."

So that's what he did. Tamar arrived, and Amnon watched her lustfully as she went about the baking in the kitchen next to his bedroom. "Come and eat, brother," she invited.

But he refused. "I can't move from my bed. I'm too sick," he moaned. "Get rid of all those people. I can't stand the noise. Then come and feed me in my bedroom."

When she came in with a delicious tray of baked goods, he knocked it from her hand and grabbed her. "Come to bed with me, my sweet!"

She struggled, appalled. "No, brother! Neither of us could live with the shame. Don't force me to do this wicked thing. Why not ask the king? He won't stop you marrying me." Even their ancestor Abraham had set the precedent by marrying Sarai, his half sister. But Amnon was aroused, and there was no stopping him. He pulled her into his bed and raped her.

When the deed was done, he lay panting on the bed. Something profound changed in his heart. The love he had thought would turn to a butterfly, turned instead to a grub – revulsion. "Get out of here, you slut!" he yelled.

"Oh, don't make matters even worse," she pleaded.

"Throw this woman out of here!" he ordered his servant. "And lock the door behind her."

Tamar staggered away, desolate. She tore her dress and threw dust on her head, weeping aloud. It was her full brother Absalom who met her wandering down the street. He took her to his own home and did his best to comfort her. "You can live here with me for as long as you like," he assured her.

When David heard what had happened, he was furious. But he did nothing about it. After all, who was he to judge another? *I know my transgressions and am only too conscious of my sins.* Nathan had predicted that his sin would be the cause of calamity, originating from his own family. His confidence as a father was gone and with it his ability to rule his own household as he should.

Absalom hated Amnon, the perverted little creep. But he didn't say a word to him, just bided his time. And that time came a couple of years later.

The occasion was the celebration of the shearing of Absalom's sheep. There was all the usual roast lamb and good wine, as well as the inevitable shearing competitions. All the brothers were there, even Amnon who joined the party, drinking like there was no tomorrow. And, as it turned out, he was right. At a signal from Absalom, his servants stepped in and murdered the inebriated half-brother. Of course, that was the end of the party. All the boys jumped on their mules and galloped home.

News reached the palace that Absalom had murdered all the king's sons, so when all but Amnon clattered into Jerusalem on their exhausted beasts, David was almost relieved.

Absalom fled to the protection of his grandfather on his mother's side, the king of Geshur.

David felt as though he had been bereaved of two sons: Amnon, obviously, but in a way Absalom also. He longed to have him back home. But there was no way he could take the initiative to invite him.

Years went by, and Joab hated to see the king unhappy. How could he find a way to get Absalom home? He hatched a plan ...

He paid an old woman to make out she was in deep mourning and then come to the king and tell him a tale of woe, for which Joab gave her the script.

"Sir, I need help. I am a widow left all on my own with but two sons. Well, the boys were out in the field, where they got into a fight, and one killed the other. So now everyone wants me to hand over my only surviving son so they can put him to death for justice's sake. But then I would be completely alone and there would be no one to carry on the family name."

"I will write an order protecting him," said the king.

"But I don't want that any criticism should attach itself to the king for such an order."

"Don't worry about me," David assured her.

"Would the king go so far as to invoke the Lord's name to protect my son from anyone who might seek vengeance?"

"As sure as the Lord lives, not a hair of your son's head will be damaged."

There was a pause, then she continued: "May I say one more thing to the king?"

"Speak your mind, woman!"

"If you say you are willing to do all this for me, don't you convict yourself, since you also have a banished son?" A dawning comprehension spread over David's face. But the woman wasn't finished: "Water spilled on the ground cannot be recovered, neither can a life be restored once taken. But God is not in the business of distancing people; rather, he devises ways to bring home the estranged."

The king was silent for a moment, and then he leant forward and said very deliberately, "I want you to tell me just one thing. Is all this Joab's idea?"

"Who can keep a secret from one so wise as you, oh king? Yes, it was your servant Joab who put these words in my mouth."

Then David turned to Joab. "Very well. Go bring back the young man. But he may not see my face."

Well, it was a step in the right direction, and Joab was thrilled. After all, it is the greatest joy of the servant to see his master's wishes fulfilled, even if he is a stubborn old goat sometimes.

Absalom's homecoming was not the success he had anticipated. He was not permitted to enter the king's presence but was confined to his own home. After two years, he grew impatient and sent repeated messages to Joab, asking him to intercede on his behalf. Joab made no reply. Finally, in desperation, Absalom had his servants set fire to Joab's field, and that brought him running.

"Look, I have been trying to get your attention for weeks. I simply want you to tell the king I want to come home. Frankly, there's no point in my being here in Jerusalem if I am excluded from the family. Tell my father that if I am guilty of anything, then he should go ahead and put me to death. If not, why am I a prisoner in my own home?"

"Guilty of anything"? Sure, Absalom was guilty. He had murdered his brother. But had not Amnon deserved punishment for how he had mistreated Tamar? And who was David to judge, anyway? How could he condemn one son for murder and another for sexual promiscuity when he himself was guilty of both?

I know my transgressions and am only too conscious of my sins.

The invitation to the royal presence finally arrived. Absalom bowed to the king, and his father kissed him. Thereafter, Absalom had the run of the city. All the girls agreed that he was the perfection of manhood. Indeed, it seems everyone noticed his fine looks, including himself. He could not pass a mirror without a second look. He was particularly proud of his hair, a fine flowing mane that grew thick and long. He bought himself a state-of-the-art chariot drawn by a team of horses and employed fifty men to run ahead of him so no one could be in any doubt that a royal prince was approaching. He even erected a statue in honour of no less deserving a person than himself.

His practice was to go to the city gate and intercept those bound for the palace, promising them that he would give them justice, if only he were in a position to give it. When any made to bow down before him, he would raise him up and embrace him like an old friend. And by this means, he quickly won the hearts of many people from all over the country.

After four years of campaigning, Absalom considered the time had come to make his move. With the king's permission, he went to Hebron, the town of his birth, ostensibly to offer a sacrifice. Ignorant of the true purpose of the journey, some two hundred men from Jerusalem went along with him, including David's chief advisor, Ahithophel. As soon as he arrived, he sent messengers all over Israel, summoning his supporters: "Absalom is king in Hebron." A few hundred malcontents flocked to join the rebels in Hebron, nothing that David's well-trained army could not have quashed in an afternoon. But David's confidence was gone. Guilt rode him, whipping him with shame down the road to self-destruction. *I know my transgressions and am only too conscious of my sins.*

"Come on!" he urged his courtiers. "We must evacuate the city before they kill us all." And so the most powerful army in the whole country, together with courtiers, religious leaders, and officials, simply abandoned the impregnable fortress city and headed out to the wilderness. But who was David to take a stand? Was not this exactly what God had warned him would happen? *Against you have I sinned and done what is evil in your sight. There is no question but that that you are right when you judge me.*

David left ten of his concubines to take care of the palace and the priests; Zadok and Abiathar to care for the ark of God. "Keep your ears to the ground," he instructed them, "and send me word of what you hear via your sons, Ahimaaz and Jonathan."

David's friend and counsellor Hushai would have accompanied him, but David made him return since one more pair of ears in Jerusalem would be invaluable. "Whatever you hear, tell the priests, and they will get word to me. Oh, and do what you can to confuse Ahithophel's treacherous advice to Absalom. May God turn his wisdom to stupidity."

A sad procession wound its way down the steep hill from Jerusalem to the shadows of the Kidron Valley and so on up to the Mount of Olives. Looking back at Jerusalem, David and his disciples wept for the city, clothes torn in anguish. So many memories. Now all their hopes were dashed.

Their spirits were temporarily raised by the arrival of Ziba, Mephibosheth's steward. He had with him a string of donkeys laden with provisions.

"Where is Mephibosheth?" David asked.

"Oh, he has stayed in Jerusalem, hoping that this will prove his opportunity to get his grandfather Saul's kingdom back," lied Ziba.

Just then, a shower of stones rattled on the ground near David. A figure ran along a ridge above the path they were following. Someone recognised him as Shimei, a relative of the dead King Saul. He was shouting and throwing handfuls of dirt down onto them: "Go on! Get out of here, you bloody man, you scoundrel! At last you are getting what you deserve. The Lord is repaying you for all the blood you shed in the household of Saul. You have come to ruin because you are a man of blood!"

I know my transgressions and am only too conscious of my sins.

Abishai, David's nephew, was furious. "I'll have his head! Why should that dead dog be permitted to curse the king?"

"Have you considered that perhaps the Lord told him to curse me? Since my own son is trying to kill me and no one stops him, why should not a Benjamite be permitted to curse all he likes? And who knows? Perhaps if I accept this indignity without protest, the Lord will vindicate me some day."

And so the dispirited procession, splattered with dirt and bloodied by stones, wound its painful way on down the hill towards the lowest place on earth, the Jordan Valley. They were exhausted.

Meanwhile, back in Jerusalem, all was anarchic celebration. Absalom took up residence in the royal palace. Just to make sure that no one was in any doubt that all links with David were forever severed, a tent was pitched on the flat roof of the palace, the same vantage point from which David had first cast eyes on the naked Bathsheba. There before the cheering crowds below, Absalom took his father's concubines and publicly violated them. Just as Nathan had predicted to David: *It may have been in secret that you did this thing with Bathsheba, but it will be in broad daylight that another will violate your wives for all the world to witness.*

Later, Absalom called for his advisor, Ahithophel, now joined by Hushai, who had unexpectedly materialised just as Absalom was arriving in Jerusalem, swearing to him his allegiance. "So what is the next step? How do we secure the advantage we have gained?" Absalom asked them.

"We should strike immediately. Leave tonight and attack while they are tired and confused. Just take the king, then all the rest of the army will give you their support." Ahithophel's advice was at first well received.

But then Hushai spoke up: "I know how wise the advice of Ahithophel has been in the past, but this time he is wrong. We all know that the army with your father is comprised of seasoned warriors, well disciplined and experienced in all kinds of conflict. For sure they will hide your father in a hole some place we will never find him. So my advice is to raise a huge army from all over the country and then mount a well-organised attack, which will completely obliterate them all."

Hushai's plan won the vote. Ahithophel accepted the decision with bad grace: he went home and hanged himself.

Hushai communicated the plan to Zadok and Abiathar, who dispatched a servant girl to pass on the information to their sons, Ahimaaz and Jonathan: "Tell David that I think I have won him some time. He should cross over the Jordan immediately. Don't delay for a moment!"

Recognising the strategic importance of the intelligence they had received, the two set out to convey it to David. But they were followed by Absalom's men. The two spies hid down a well till the hue and cry died down and then fled fleet foot to tell David what was going down. They found him in Mahanaim, some distance east of the Jordan. There some of David's old friends had brought provisions for the humiliated army.

Absalom quickly raised his own army and set off in pursuit. He appointed Amasa as his general, crossed the Jordan, and advanced to what he assumed would be the decisive victory that Hushai had promised him.

David sent his men out with strict instructions that Absalom was to be taken alive.

The battle was fought in the forest, and right from the get-go, the result was never in doubt. Absalom's troops caved and fled for their lives into the trees. So desperate was their flight that many simply impaled themselves on the tree branches. Among the victims was Absalom himself. He made the mistake of trying to escape on a mule – not a smart plan in a dense forest. His magnificent hair got caught in the branches of an oak tree, but the mule kept going, leaving Absalom a victim of his own vanity. And that was how he was found, hanging in midair, alive but helpless. Ignoring David's final instructions, Joab wasted no time but ran him through with his javelin; "Frustrating young upstart!" Then he cut him down and dumped his corpse in a hole. Others joined in heaping stones over his grave.

The joyful news of the victory was for David eclipsed by the grief of Absalom's death, so the victory parade was turned into a funeral march as the army slunk back into the camp, shamefaced.

"O my son Absalom! If only I had died instead of you!" wailed David.

Joab was sickened by David's whinging: "You are humiliating your men by behaving like this. They have just risked their lives to save you and your family, and here you are snivelling as though they had done you wrong. Seems you love those who hate you and hate those who love you. I suppose you would be glad if we were all dead, if only Absalom were alive in our place? Now get up and go out to publicly congratulate the men, or I promise you they will all desert you, and you will be in a worse mess than before."

So a second disaster was averted, but David resented Joab for his rebuke.

Word quickly spread that King David was on his way back to Jerusalem. Crowds came out to welcome him. Mephibosheth, Saul's grandson, was there. "So why didn't you come with me, Mephibosheth?" David demanded when he spotted him.

"I tried to, but as you know I am lame. I got as far as saddling my donkey, but Ziba wouldn't let me come. And now I understand that he has said terrible things to you about me." Who was telling the truth, Ziba or Mephibosheth?

"Divide the estate equally between Mephibosheth and Ziba," David ordered. You can't get fairer than that.

Also in the crowd was Shimei, the one who had hurled dirt and insults at David during the retreat. He prostrated himself before David in abject apology.

"Let me kill the little rat!" growled Abishai, Joab's brother.

"Shimei shall live!" snapped David.

To everyone's surprise, Amasa, Absalom's general, had escaped the slaughter and somehow made it back to Jerusalem. And what was even more surprising was that in a snap decision, David appointed him general of his army in place of Joab. Perhaps this was designed to be an insult to Joab for his rebuke, or possibly it was a political manoeuvre to win support from the defeated members of Absalom's army. Either way, David justified his decision by pointing out that Amasa was his nephew, but since Joab was also his nephew, the rationale was questionable.

But the troops found themselves in terrible confusion, and a group of rebels broke off and headed north. David, recognising the danger of this breakaway faction, ordered Amasa to give chase. But Amasa was slow off the mark, and his appointment as general quickly proved a disappointment, so David dispatched Abishai to take over. Joab went along, ostensibly to support his brother, but the family pecking order quickly reasserted itself and scarcely had they left the city when Joab was once again taking the lead. Any question over who was in charge of the army was finally settled when Joab put a knife in Amasa's stomach: "Waste of space, that fellow!"

Nearly one hundred miles of hard marching, and they had the rebels holed up in a northern town named Abel Beth Maacah. They quickly surrounded the city, threatening to pull it down brick by brick if necessary.

A woman's voice cut through the clamour of destruction: "General Joab!"

"What do you want?" he replied.

"Why are you trying to destroy a peaceful city? We here are faithful citizens."

"You are giving shelter to a gang of no-accounts who have rebelled against the king. Hand over their leader, and we will leave you in peace."

A few minutes later, a bloody head came flying over the wall and landed at their feet. Thank goodness for wise women.

So order was restored in Jerusalem. Joab was once more officially recognised as general, and others whose loyalty had weathered the storms of rebellion were confirmed as members of the king's cabinet.

---- **17** ----

The Intercessor

Ever since the days of Abraham, his descendants had been promised to be innumerable, uncountable as the grains of sand on the seashore or the stars of heaven. But David made the mistake of trying to count those God had designated uncountable.

He commissioned Joab to go through his kingdom and conduct a census to number all the fighting men. "I want to know how many men there are at my disposal," David insisted. "How else can I estimate what kind of opposition I dare confront?"

"But sir, don't forget that the Lord could multiply the number of your men a hundred times over if necessary? Why would you want to know the number, since God's economy is limitless?"

But the king was the king, and Joab knew better than to rebuke him a second time.

Just over nine months later, the numbers were added up, revealing a total of 1,300,000 fighting men at David's disposal.

No sooner was the census complete than David's conscience smote him. "I have sinned! I have done a very stupid thing!"

Next morning, the prophet Gad arrived with a message from God: "I am giving you three options. You may choose which one I am to carry out against you."

"What are the choices?" stammered David.

"Three years of famine. Three months of defeat by your enemies. Or three days of plague. Now which do you choose?"

Three years of famine was a long time. Enemies were anything but merciful, by very definition. That left plague, presumably one that would be under God's direct control, and David knew God to be the epitome of mercy. "Let me fall into the hands of the Lord, for his mercy is very great."

That very morning, the plague broke out, and thousands died from the north to the south of the land. The census was nonsense, out of date before the ink was dry. Lack of faith masquerading as wise precaution often tilts the odds against those who should be trusting God.

To the victims, the plague was but a faceless menace that killed indiscriminately. Indeed, it wasn't till the plague reached the outskirts of Jerusalem that David was himself able to put a face to it. It was on the hilltop in the heart of Jerusalem that David saw him. That particular hill belonged to one of the original inhabitants of the city, a Jebusite named Araunah. But a thousand years previously, it had been there on that same hill that Abraham had nearly sacrificed his son Isaac. Abraham had been willing to sacrifice his one and only child, through whom God had promised innumerable offspring. Now David had sought to count the innumerable offspring, and thousands had died. Abraham might have believed God, but David had doubted.

It was right there in that significant location that, to his unspeakable horror, David saw the angel of God's wrath. He was hovering between earth and sky with his blood-dripping sword stretched out over Jerusalem. The Plague!

David cried out, "Oh Lord, I am to blame. I am the guilty one who has sinned and done this wrong. But these people in my city, these sheep, what have they done? Nothing! Let your hand fall upon me and my family, but spare my people."

That was perhaps the bravest of all the actions of David's life. To stand there with the very sharp end of God's wrath at his own throat and intercede for his own people! That was courage. To trust God's love in the face of his fury! That was faith. To cast himself on God's mercy when he was unquestionably guilty! That was repentance.

"Enough! Withdraw your hand!" The same voice from heaven that had stayed the hand of Abraham now stayed that of the angel of death.

David was still standing there, trembling, when the prophet Gad came up to him. "You are to build an altar to the Lord on this flat rock," he panted.

Next up came the owner of the land, Araunah. "Why has my lord the king come to his servant?"

"I would like to purchase this hilltop with its flat rock, that I believe you use to thresh grain. I want to build here an altar to the Lord so that this plague can be stopped."

"Take it, please do. It's yours. No charge."

"No, but I insist on paying. I can't call it a sacrifice if it costs me nothing, now can I?"

So that day, David bought the land for fifty shekels of silver, and Araunah threw in some oxen for good measure. Surely that was the real estate deal of all time, since all the money in the world could never repurchase that flat rock from that day to this.

The altar was built on the very place where Isaac had been laid a millennium earlier, and the sacrifice was offered. And there and then, the destroying angel sheathed his sword, and the plague was ended.

"This will be the site for the house of the Lord!" declared David. A place of intercession.

David would have loved to build the temple, but the Lord had made it clear that since David had been a man of war, responsible for much bloodshed, he would not be the right man for the task: "But your son Solomon will be a man of peace, and I will give him rest from his enemies. He will build the temple for my name."

From then on, David started to amass building materials. A stockyard stacked high with best-quality stone blocks, flats of imported cedar beams, and bars of smelted bronze were the basic building materials, with iron nails by the bucket full. And in the royal vaults there were precious metals aplenty: four thousand tons of gold and forty thousand tons of silver. David also started to recruit skilled workers from home and abroad, people who could not only do the work, but could train apprentices in their various trades. David's enthusiasm and personal generosity towards the project were contagious, and soon others chipped in.

David would dream of the magnificent building that would one day rise on that mountaintop, to the admiration of people from all over the world. The Lord inspired in his mind detailed plans for the temple and its furnishings, which David faithfully committed to paper. He foresaw how the temple servants would be ordered, the kinds of worship that would be offered, the appropriate songs for different festivals and seasons throughout the year, even the musical instruments to be used in the orchestra.

The young Solomon was fascinated by all these preparations and took a keen interest in all that was going on. "One day when you are king in my place, you will build a magnificent temple to honour the name of the Lord," David would tell him.

This work became something of an obsession for David in his latter years and kept him happily occupied till he became too old to do anything much, and he was virtually confined to bed. Even there he just couldn't get warm, so they found him a beautiful young lady to cuddle in bed. Abishag was her name, and she cared for all the king's needs. But David had no sexual relations with her.

———————————————

Now that David's days were clearly numbered, the question of his successor became the buzz. Adonijah, who had been born back in the days when David was newly made king in Hebron, fancied his chances of the throne. Absalom, his late older brother, had always been something of a role model to Adonijah. Adonijah shared Absalom's fine looks and consequent vanity. Like his brother, he bought himself an impressive chariot drawn by magnificent horses, and also hired the fifty men to run ahead of him.

Old General Joab threw his hat in to support Adonijah's bid for the throne, as did one of the priests, Abiathar. But Zadok, the other priest, Nathan the prophet, and Benaiah, David's bodyguard, declined to join his supporters.

Adonijah went ahead anyway and invited many of the leading men of Judah to a special sacrifice just south of town. His siblings were also invited – all except Solomon, that is.

Ever since Nathan had announced to David and Bathsheba that their son Solomon was specially loved by the Lord, Bathsheba had held a special place in her heart for the old prophet. So not surprisingly, it was Nathan who alerted her to what Adonijah was up to: "Here's what you must do. Go quickly and tell King David what is happening, and I will come in and confirm what you are saying."

So Bathsheba went to see the aged King, lovingly cared for by the beautiful young Abishag.

"What can I do for you?" David asked of Bathsheba, as she bowed low before him.

"My lord, did you not swear by the Lord that Solomon our son would be king after you?"

"Indeed I did."

"Well now, Adonijah has made himself king without your being aware of it. He has the support of Abiathar the priest and of General Joab. All Israel is looking to you for your decision in this matter. You must realise that as soon as you are dead, my life and that of Solomon will be in jeopardy."

At that moment, right on cue, in came Nathan and confirmed the disturbing report.

Then David spoke clearly enough, though his voice was cracked and shaky with age: "As surely as the Lord lives, Solomon will be king after me. Now call in Zadok the priest and Benaiah, my warrior."

When they arrived, the king gave his final orders: "You are to anoint my son Solomon as king. Then with a fanfare of trumpets announce to the world, 'Long live King Solomon!' Finally take him up to the palace and seat him on my throne."

And that is what happened. The sounds of cheering and music were so great that the ground shook with the celebration. The clamour even reached the ears of Adonijah and his guests. They were terrified when they learned the cause of the commotion. Most of the guests fled, but Adonijah ran to the altar for sanctuary. But Solomon sent him back to his own home.

A few days later, it became clear that David's end was very close. Solomon was brought to his bedside. "I am about to die," the old man wheezed. "So here is my charge to you. Be strong and do what the Lord requires of you. Walk in his ways, keep his decrees, obey his commands. Then you will do well, and the Lord will be able to keep the promise he has made to me: 'If your descendants walk faithfully before me with all their heart and soul, you will always have one of your family on the throne of Israel.'

"Now my son, as you know I had it in my heart to build a house for the Lord, but he would not permit me. But may the Lord be with you, my son, as you now do the building. Devote your heart and soul to seeking the Lord your God. Start building. Be strong and get on with it. It will be a wonder for all the world to see."

Then David breathed his last, after forty years' reign over Israel.

18

The Wise

Solomon was just a youngster, barely twenty years old, when the crushing responsibility of kingship was placed upon his shoulders. He was the youngest of his siblings, just as David had been when he had been anointed to be king. To further challenge his confidence, there had been that fiasco with his much older brother, Adonijah, making a last-minute bid for the throne. On that day, Solomon had been wise to send Adonijah back to his home in peace, but to leave that state of affairs unaddressed would be bound to cause trouble, sooner or later.

Things were brought to a head sooner than expected. Adonijah sought Solomon's permission to marry Abishag, the young lady who had kept David warm during his final days. But it was the sole right of the king to inherit his predecessor's harem. Was this a threat to his throne? Solomon smelled trouble. He immediately dispatched his faithful general, Benaiah, to execute Adonijah before he could do more damage. No way was Solomon going to make the same mistake his father had made when he had permitted Absalom to ferment rebellion unchecked.

Now what was he to do with Abiathar, the priest, and old General Joab, who both had supported Adonijah in his ambition? Abiathar was easily dealt with by being given early retirement and put out to pasture. But Joab was a ruthless man of war. Benaiah was dispatched to perform the execution, but finding him clinging for sanctuary to the altar in the tabernacle, Benaiah hesitated.

"No question, but that he deserves to die," insisted Solomon. "In cold blood he murdered two innocent men in my father's day, both better men than himself." So Joab died right where he was, in the tabernacle.

Then there was Shimei, who had cursed David during that terrible retreat from Jerusalem, but who David, on his return, had promised not to kill. His father may have promised the wretch his life, but that didn't tie Solomon's hands. Yet he couldn't very well just kill him in cold blood for no apparent reason, so he placed him under house arrest, telling him that he was free to go where he would in the city of Jerusalem, but he would forfeit his life should he ever set foot outside the city. Shimei agreed and promised to abide by the restriction.

All was fine for the first three years, but then a couple of his slaves went AWOL, and Shimei made the fatal mistake of pursuing them outside Jerusalem. Before Benaiah dispatched him, Solomon reminded Shimei of his crime against the Lord's anointed, so he went to his grave knowing that the line he had crossed was far more serious than just the city limits of Jerusalem.

Around that time, Solomon took a wife. It was largely for political reasons that he chose a daughter of the Egyptian pharaoh, but he loved her and promised to build her a palace in Jerusalem.

Solomon's coronation had been perforce a hasty affair with none of the usual pomp and ceremony. So Solomon called all the army officers, judiciary, leaders, and family heads to a religious assembly in Gibeon, some seven miles north of Jerusalem. The natural geological features of this locale had long given it significance: a great rock standing beside a pool of water. But the feature that leant it the greatest significance was that in recent years, it had been the home of the original bronze altar built by Bezalel, nearly five hundred years previously, when Israel had just come out from Egypt. And there still stood the tattered remains of the old tabernacle that had somehow survived since those long-ago days of Moses. It seemed significant to Solomon that a link should be established between this ancient tent of meeting and the glorious temple he was soon to build.

The occasion was impressive, with all those dignitaries in attendance. A thousand animals were sacrificed and long prayers offered. That night, the young Solomon fell into an exhausted sleep. He dreamed that God appeared to him and said, "You may ask me for anything you desire."

"What more could I ask than you have already given?" Solomon replied. "You showed such extraordinary kindness to my father, and now, just as you promised him, you have made me king in his place. I rule over a people as numerous as the dust of the earth, again as you promised to my forefather Abraham. So here I am, but a child, with the responsibility to govern this great people. What I need is the ability to choose right, to discern the good from the bad. I ask for wisdom."

God was pleased with Solomon's reply: "You might have requested wealth, honour, power, or long life, but instead you have asked for wisdom and knowledge. So wisdom and knowledge you shall have, but I will also give you what you did not ask for: wealth and honour, and if you walk in my ways, I will give you a long life to enjoy it all."

When he awoke, it was only a dream. Or was it?

One of the many responsibilities of the king was to act as a final court of appeal, a kind of supreme court to which disputes could be brought for a royal decision. The dream was still fresh in Solomon's memory when two women with a baby came before him, both spitting mad. Clearly the baby was the cause of the argument. It came out that these women who shared a house had both given birth around the same time.

"She," said the first woman, pointing disparagingly at the other, "rolled her considerable bulk over in the night and crushed her baby to death. But then she had the gall to swap her dead child for mine. So when I woke in the morning, there was her dead baby in bed with me, while she was nursing this child, my child."

"No, that's my baby!" said the other.

"Liar! He's mine."

"My baby!"

"Mine!"

Seemed they would tear the child apart between them.

"Bring me a sword," said Solomon. So a sword was put into the king's hand. He held it for a moment and then handed it to one of his bodyguards. "Cut the baby in half and give an equal share to each of these ladies. That should settle the matter."

There was a horrified gasp from around the court. How could the young king be so cruel?

One of the women said, "Good plan. Cut him in half, and we'll each have our share."

But the other woman was appalled: "Oh no, my lord. Don't hurt the child. Let her have him, if only he can live."

"So it's clear that you really are the mother," the king replied kindly. "He is yours."

Word of this ruling got around, and it quickly became known that the new king was possessed of a godly wisdom, way beyond his years.

Probably the most significant expression of his wisdom was Solomon's ability to discern people. He had the uncanny knack of appointing the right man to the right job. He soon had his kingdom organised with good people, each with his specific job description, taking care of his part of the responsibility. Provisions arrived at the palace on time from all over the country and abroad. The borders of the kingdom extended north, south, and east, limited only by the sea to the west. Trade agreements were signed with foreign powers, and prosperity abounded.

One of his most honoured trading partners was King Hiram of Tyre. In exchange for wheat and olive oil, Hiram organised an army of loggers to strip the mountainsides of Lebanon of the mighty cedars that abounded on those slopes. He would haul them to the waterfront and form them into great booms that he would sail down the coast to a log sort near Joppa. There they would be cut into planks and beams, then hauled up to Jerusalem or wherever the latest construction project required lumber.

Luxury in the court reached unprecedented heights. But it wasn't just the king who benefited. The whole nation enjoyed a higher standard of living than they had ever known. They had ample food and drink, owned their own homes, and were happy.

Solomon had an insatiable appetite for learning. He studied plant life, from the tiny hyssop that grew from the cracks in the walls of Jerusalem to the towering cedars in the western hills. He observed the minute insects that scurried across the floor and studied the huge lumbering beasts in the forests. He was an ornithologist, fascinated by the colours and flight patterns of the myriad birds that inhabited his kingdom. He even observed the flashing fish in the rivers, lakes, and ocean to the west. He sketched what he saw and wrote down his observations, accumulating a veritable encyclopaedia of knowledge so others could benefit.

But people were the object of his most intriguing observations. *"Better to be a nobody with a servant than to pretend to be a somebody but have nothing to eat,"* he noted. He was enthralled by the way people interacted. He observed patterns of behaviour that time and again would result in predictable consequences. *"The man who works hard on his land will have plenty of food, but a dreamer lacks sense."* His observations encouraged people towards goodness. *"The righteousness of a good man keeps him on the right track, but the wickedness of a sinful man is his downfall."*

He would reduce his observations to simple statements that he would write down for the benefit of everyone. He called them "Proverbs." In all, he recorded some three thousand such sayings.

He anthropomorphised wisdom, giving her personality: *"Don't forsake wisdom, and she will keep you safe; love her, and she will watch your back. Honour her, and she will promote you; embrace her, and she will honour you. She will crown you with grace and splendour."* Like his father before him, Solomon loved music and wrote over a thousand songs.

As his fame spread, people from all over the world would come to Jerusalem just to listen to his lectures. And admission to these lectures was not free. "Gifts" enriched his palace with exotic objects and works of art from a thousand cultures.

Four years into his reign, Solomon began to build the temple. He had the blueprints that David had drawn but added many of his own ideas. The building was a three-story, rectangular structure, ninety feet long, thirty wide, and forty-five feet high, with an entrance foyer at one end. Narrow recessed windows high up on the walls let in the light of day. On both sides and at the back of the building were ancillary rooms on three floors, accessed by circular staircases. Construction was basically of huge stone blocks, some as large as fifteen feet long, but all of which were cut to exact size at the stone quarry, so that no sounds of hammer or saw were ever heard on the holy construction site. The wood ceiling was supported by cedar beams; in fact, the whole building was panelled with cedar, finely decorated with carvings of cherubim, palm trees, and flowers. When that was finished, then the wood was overlaid with pure gold: floors, walls, and ceiling.

At the far end, opposite the entrance foyer, was a thirty-foot-square room: the Most Holy Place. This was accessed from the main temple area by ornate double doors. Against its inner wall stood two magnificent gold cherubim, fifteen feet tall and each having a wingspan of fifteen feet. So, as they stood side by side, they together spanned the full width of the room.

One of the chief craftsmen was a man named Huram. His mother was an Israeli and his father had been a foundry worker from Tyre. His skill was in casting bronze, which he did chiefly down in the Jordan Valley. The furnishings of the temple were his responsibility. He cast two magnificently decorated pillars to stand at the entrance of the temple that became affectionately known as "Jakin and Boaz."

Then there was a huge round tank that held eleven thousand gallons of water, shaped like an open lily, fifteen feet across and seven feet deep. It was supported on a stand resembling twelve oxen. This also merited a nickname, one inspired by its size: "the Sea." To fill it Huram cast ten bronze water carts that would convey over two hundred gallons each from the source to "the Sea."

In addition to Huram's work, there were the gold furnishings: the altar for the sacrifices; the table on which the loaves representing God's welcoming presence would be displayed; and the gold lamp stands. There were floral decorations, cups, basins, dishes, tongs, lamps, snuffers, and fire pans – all of them gold.

It took a combined labour force of around a hundred thousand men to complete the construction of the temple, and they did it in seven years.

So there it stood, crowning Mount Moriah, sparkling in the sunshine. Old King David would have been thrilled. The dedication ceremony was planned months in advance to coincide with the annual Festival of Booths. Special invitations were sent to all the tribal leaders and heads of families.

The festivities started early in the morning, at the site of the tent that King David had erected to house the ark of the covenant. The ark was transported by the priests using the designated carrying poles, and the crowds followed excitedly. Arriving at the huge square in front of the temple, the priests paused to set down the ark while innumerable sheep and cattle were sacrificed. The blood, the smoke, and the smell of roasting meat permeated the area all morning. While the sacrifices were finishing, the priests once again hoisted the ark onto their shoulders and proceeded on into the temple. They passed through the foyer and into the main room of the temple. Without pausing, they proceeded on through the ornate doors and up into the Most Holy Place. Though the crowds didn't see what happened, the ark was reverently placed on the platform designed as its resting place, and there beneath the outstretched wings of the gold cherubim, the ark found a home. Someone took note of the fact that the ark contained nothing except the stone tablets on which was inscribed the covenant between God and Israel. Moses had put them there when Israel was at Mount Sinai, some 480 years previously.

As the priests came back out of the temple to join the crowds, suddenly a bright cloud like a mist enveloped the whole temple area, and a holy awe came over all the people. So intense was the sense of the presence of God that the ceremony had to stop for a while. Someone whispered, "This is how it must have been in the old days when Moses used to meet God in the tabernacle."

As the afternoon wore on, King Solomon stood up to address the multitude. A respectful silence descended on the people. "Ladies and gentlemen, blessing and thanksgiving are due this day to the Lord, the God of Israel, the faithful promise keeper. He has kept the promises he made to my father, David. He wanted to build this temple, but the Lord would not permit him. 'Your son will build it instead of you,' the Lord promised him. And here before you today is the fulfilment of that promise."

Then Solomon fell to his knees, lifted up his arms towards the heavens, and prayed, "O Lord God of heaven and earth, there is none like you. Will you really make your home down here with us on earth? Even the infinity of heaven is too small for you, so how much less this temple.

"Now here is the prayer we offer this day. Would you please watch over this temple day and night. May it be a perpetual house of prayer. Please always be attentive to the humble, earnest prayers offered towards this place by your people, no matter where they may be. Hear us from your home in heaven.

"When your people cry to you for mercy because their sins cause them to be defeated by their enemies, hear from heaven and forgive.

"When your people pray and call on your name because their sins have shut up the skies and there is no rain, hear from heaven and forgive.

"When your people pray because of famine, plague, crop failure, infestation of locust or caterpillar, or even enemy invasions, hear from heaven and forgive.

"And not only your own people Israel, for people from all over the world will hear the fame of your miraculous power and be drawn to pray toward this temple. Hear them from heaven and grant their requests also.

"If ever your people should so sin against you that you permit them to be taken into exile in a foreign land, and if the people there repent and admit, 'We have sinned and done evil,' and if they turn back to you wholeheartedly and pray toward this temple, then hear from heaven and forgive."

Then Solomon stood, and at the top of his voice, he shouted:

"Praise the Lord! May the Lord always be with us as he was with our ancestors before us! May he never forsake us! May he give us the will to obey him in all things! May all these requests that I have just made be answered in full! May people the world over know for sure that the Lord alone is God! And may you people present here today always be faithful to the Lord, obeying his laws and commands!"

And after the crowd roared their unanimous approval in a great "Amen," then the sacrifices got going again. Hundreds of thousands of sheep and oxen were offered.

The celebration continued for two whole weeks, and then Solomon dismissed the people, and they went home rejoicing because of the goodness of God.

The night after they had all gone, Solomon had another dream. Again God spoke to him: "I have heard your prayer and I have set apart this temple as a place where my name will be honoured. And yes, I will watch over it, just as you requested.

"As for you personally, if you will continue to follow me with integrity and godliness, then I will establish your dynasty forever, just as I promised David, your father.

"But if you, or one of your descendants, should turn away from me and worship other gods, then know this: I will uproot Israel from this land and make them the object of ridicule. I will also reject this temple and make its destruction so appalling that all who see it will scoff and ask, 'Why did the Lord do such a terrible thing to this place?' And the answer will be plain: 'Because this people forgot the Lord their God and worshiped other gods.'"

The temple was not the only impressive building in Jerusalem constructed at that time. There was a huge hall dubbed "the Forest of Lebanon," inspired by the forty-five gigantic cedar pillars that supported the roof. There was a second hall, half the size, "the Hall of Pillars." Then there was "the Judgment Hall," where Solomon heard legal questions.

Solomon's private living quarters were at the back of these municipal buildings and were constructed round a courtyard. All these buildings took a further thirteen years to complete.

But still bitten by the building bug, Solomon next turned his creativity to the construction of other cities as supply centres and as stabling for his many horses. He conscripted into his labour force many of the non-Israeli peoples who still inhabited the land, appointing Israeli citizens as supervisors. He built a fleet of trading ships that he stationed on the Gulf of Aqaba, from whence they would travel the world, returning with cargos of gold, silver, ivory, and exotic livestock such as apes and baboons.

Perhaps it was these trading ships that carried the news of Solomon's greatness to far-off kingdoms such as Sheba in Africa, that dark and mysterious continent. The queen of Sheba was drawn by the stories of a kingdom crowned with great buildings, presided over by a king of unfathomable wisdom, who worshiped an invisible god who ruled by love.

News reached Jerusalem that a camel train nearly a mile long was approaching from the south. So when the important guest arrived, the red carpet was cleaned and rolled out. The "Forest of Lebanon" was the venue for the meeting, festooned with banners and with five hundred gold shields lining the walls. And there, at the far end, was the throne. To approach it, one had to mount six steps, each with a gold lion standing on either side. The throne with its rounded back and armrests was covered in glittering gold, with fancy inlaid ivory. It was unlike anything that the queen had ever seen.

For Solomon's part, his breath was taken by the stately woman who approached. She was jet black, tall and regal in her bearing and dazzlingly beautiful. When the formal introductions were satisfied, Solomon asked to what he owed the honour of this visit.

"I have many issues to discuss with the one whose wisdom is famed far and wide. And I am fascinated by the relationship you enjoy with he whom you call 'the Lord.'"

And so the talk began. Discussion it was not, since Solomon had an answer for everything and was so clearly right that counter-suggestions would have been pointless. They walked around the impressive new buildings and along the flower-festooned terraces. Everywhere they went, there were footmen, valets, and servants to meet their every need, all dressed in the royal livery. All the cups and plates were gold. The meals that came from the royal kitchens were haut cuisine par excellence.

But then they came to the temple. The beauty of the building, the robes of the priests, the spectacle of the sacrifices, the inspiring music: all simply overwhelming.

The queen's breath was quite taken away. "I didn't think for a moment that the report that reached me back in Sheba was true. Stories always get exaggerated the further they travel. But now I see that the half was not told me. I can quite see why your citizens are so happy and contented. Who wouldn't be if they were within earshot of your wise words and had you to oversee the affairs of the country? But I think that credit is due to the Lord your God, who placed you on the throne of Israel. It must be because he loves this people so deeply that he has made you king to maintain justice and righteousness."

If the queen was impressed, then so was Solomon. He had written many love songs, but his Song of Songs seemed fitting in the presence of this amazing woman who graced his court those memorable days.

"How beautiful you are, my dear! Your beauty is flawless. Your eyes sparkle

like doves. Your hair is a fine tapestry. Your teeth are like a flock of freshly shorn sheep. Your lips are a scarlet ribbon. Your cheeks are beautifully adorned with earrings and your neck with strings of jewels. Your breasts are like clusters of fruit. Your waist is a mound of wheat. Your navel is a rounded chalice. Your graceful legs are a work of art. How beautiful your sandaled feet! You carry the fragrance of a spring garden. You have completely stolen my heart. You are so beautiful, my dear."

Then the queen presented the gifts she had brought, dozens of camel loads of gold, spices, and precious stones. Neither did she go home empty handed, for Solomon gave her all she asked and then heaped upon her treasures from his royal bounty. Doubtless she would have liked to stay, but duty called. She too had a kingdom to administer.

19

The Fool

Once a man has seen the greener grass on the other side of the fence, it can be difficult for him to settle back to his own pasture. The queen of Sheba had certainly been a glimpse of verdant grazing land hitherto unimagined. It was not that he no longer loved Pharaoh's daughter, but he realised that there were just so many beautiful women in the world and so little time to love them all. And just as the works of art that daily arrived in his palace were from all over the world, so perhaps the horizons of his amorous possibilities need not be limited by his national boundaries. So Solomon began to make a collection of beautiful women from all over the world. Those from royal extraction he married, and the others he simply treated as concubines. There were a thousand women in his collection: seven hundred wives and three hundred concubines.

Housing must have been a challenge, but even that posed no real problem to so prolific a builder. But Solomon was often heard to mutter, *"Better to live on a roof top than to share a house with a nagging wife. She is like a constant dripping on a rainy day."*

The more serious problem was the baggage these women brought with them. Coming from many different cultures and traditions, they had diverse views on religion. Solomon might have kidded himself that so impressive was the Lord, represented by his magnificent temple, that it would not be long before his wives would convert. However, such proved not to be the case, and soon Solomon found himself forced to make certain concessions to domestic multiculturalism. All manner of shrines, minarets, sanctuaries, and holy places sprang up all over town.

And time was stretched thin. At night, he had to satisfy a thousand women, and during the day, he had to attend a plethora of religious services. Some of these religions appeared relatively harmless, but others were the more sinister brands, some even involving child sacrifice. But while that may have been inconvenient to Solomon, it was abhorrent to the Lord who had made him king.

For all his own wisdom, Solomon had neglected to heed many of the warnings from the book of Wisdom, written by Moses centuries earlier:

"A king must be careful not to build up a large stable of horses for himself, and in no circumstances must he send buyers to Egypt." Solomon had twelve thousand horses scattered in stable cities around his kingdom, and many of these animals had indeed been purchased in Egypt.

"A king must not accumulate for himself vast wealth in silver or gold." The streets of Jerusalem were virtually paved with the stuff.

"A king must not marry many wives for they will be sure to lead him astray from the Lord." Solomon had a thousand of them and, exactly as predicted, he was fast losing his first love for the Lord his God. He knew it was happening, but his love for women was so strong that nothing would turn him from his addiction.

So the Lord told Solomon, "Since this is the way you are behaving, I will take the kingdom away from you and give it to one of your servants. But for David's sake, this will not happen in your lifetime, but during the next generation. And even then, I will still preserve one of the twelve tribes for your son to rule."

So the inevitable trouble happened. Solomon's reign, which up to that time had been so peaceful, was suddenly plagued by enemies. Hadad, an Edomite, returned from Egypt, where he had been in exile for years, and started to conduct raids from the south. Then there was another malcontent, Rezon, who set up headquarters in Damascus and caused trouble for Solomon in the north.

But the most troubling of all was one of his own officials: Jeroboam, son of Nebat. Jeroboam was a smart young man who had caught Solomon's eye early on as a good candidate for promotion. He had been set over a large section of the labour force.

Trouble started one day as Jeroboam was heading home for the weekend. He fell into step with Ahijah, a prophet. They chatted about this and that, and then suddenly the prophet removed his brand new cloak and started to rip it into twelve squares.

"This is what the Lord says. I am about to rip the kingdom from the hands of Solomon because he no longer follows my ways. Ten tribes I will entrust to you to rule but one tribe I will preserve for Solomon's son to rule, for the sake of David. If you follow my decrees and walk in my ways, I will establish your dynasty for years to come, and you will rule over all that your heart desires."

There were only the two of them present when this happened, but as is the way of things, word got back to King Solomon, who was not at all pleased. In fact, he sent to have Jeroboam killed. But somehow the young man slipped away unharmed and went to live as an exile in Egypt.

Solomon's unparalleled success and near genius had its down side. In his latter years, he suffered from depression. He saw things with jaundiced eyes and wrote gloomy verse to express his disappointment with life: *"Meaningless. Everything is pointless. I can't help but think that the dead are happier than the living, but happier still the man who has never been born in the first place. In the end the same fate overtakes the wise man and the fool alike. And I suppose the fate of the fool will soon overtake me also. So what do I gain by being wise? All the things I have worked for I must leave to the one who comes after me. And who knows whether he will be a wise man or a fool? So I despair!"*

For all his morose moods and negative thoughts, Solomon was still the possessor of the wisdom God had given him on that long-ago night on a hilltop near Gibeon. His concluding thought that he passed on to another generation before he died was wise indeed: *"Remember your Creator in the days of your youth, before trouble comes and pleasure flees. This is the conclusion of the matter: Fear God and keep his commands, for this is what life is about."*

Forty years on the throne finally came to an end, and all that he had accumulated passed to his son, Rehoboam.

--- **20** ---

The Rift

To say that Rehoboam had it made is perhaps an understatement. He inherited a fortune, lived in a gold palace, enjoyed the good will of everyone, and was king of all he could see. And all this without lifting a finger.

Now that King Solomon was dead, the fugitive Jeroboam returned from Egypt, where he had been in exile ever since Ahijah had prophesied that one day he would be king. He had left as a hated taskmaster, but absence having worked its proverbial magic, he now returned to a hero's welcome. Riding a wave of popularity and leading a delegation of representatives from the northern tribes of Israel, he approached the young King Rehoboam.

"Your father laid on us all a heavy burden of taxation and conscription. Give us a break, and we will be your devoted subjects."

Rehoboam sought the guidance of his father's advisors. They stroked their long white beards and recommended leniency: "A tax break will always win supporters."

Next he consulted some of his buddies, young men he had grown up with: "Don't even think of going soft on this rabble. Be the king!"

So when Jeroboam returned to hear the verdict: "Give you a break? Is that what you are expecting? You haven't seen anything yet. I'll chase you with scorpions, not just whips! My little finger is thicker than my father's waist. Now back to work!" Nobody moved.

He turned to the foreman of his labour force: "Adoniram, get these slackers moving, why don't you?" Whips cracked, and still no action.

"We owe no allegiance to the family of David. Let's get out of here," said Jeroboam to his delegation. Then turning back to Rehoboam: "You guys are on your own from now on."

One last fateful time, Adoniram cracked the whip before the first rock hit him. Rehoboam jumped into his chariot and fled for his life.

Scarcely had the dust of his departure disappeared over the hill, before they had crowned Jeroboam king of Israel.

That was the end of the united kingdom of the twelve tribes.

Initially, Jeroboam established his headquarters in Shechem. But his makeshift palace was no match for the gleaming towers of Jerusalem. He surmised that the people would be bound to follow their accustomed religious pattern of annual pilgrimages to the temple in Jerusalem, and it would not be long before they would be drawn back to serve King Rehoboam. Something had to be done.

Once again on the advice of his young advisors, Jeroboam resolved to dream up his own religion. "No need to trouble yourselves any longer with expensive trips to Jerusalem," he assured the people, unveiling two golden calves he had commissioned. "Behold your gods!"

He set them up in two convenient locations, one in Dan in the north and the other in the south, at Bethel. He established a new priesthood, comprised of volunteers drawn from all the tribes, not just Levi, and he reorganised the calendar with a new set of religious festivals to replace those established by Moses.

Convenient for the people it may have been, but God was not well pleased. This false worship became a trap that ensnared the people of Israel. Worship divorced from truth is a slippery slope that ends in destruction.

A prophet arrived from Judah, just as Jeroboam was offering a sacrifice on his new altar in Bethel. "This is what God has to say to this altar," cried the man of God. "The day will come when a descendant of David named

Josiah will burn the bones of your self-appointed priests on this altar. And in token of that event, this altar shall now split asunder."

"Seize him!" Jeroboam roared imperiously, pointing at the prophet. As the words were still on his lips, his arm shrivelled to a stump, and the altar burst open with a crack like thunder.

"Pray for me," whimpered Jeroboam. The arm was restored, but not Jeroboam's heart. He remained unrepentant.

With stubborn determination, he taught Israel to follow his false teaching. He insisted that his people should worship his gods in his way, establishing a tradition that was to endure for generations to come. In fact, he would become labelled by future historians: "Jeroboam, son of Nebat, who caused Israel to sin."

Rehoboam, now king of only Judah, made little attempt to worship the God of his fathers. Instead, he fostered the multicultural chaos his father Solomon had imported along with his wives.

"Because you have abandoned me, I will abandon you," God told him, and next year the Egyptians looted Jerusalem, carrying off a fortune in gold from the temple and the palace. Rehoboam reigned seventeen insignificant years and then died, passing the kingdom to his son, Abijah.

Abijah was a busy lad, for during his brief three-year reign, he married fourteen wives and sired twenty-two sons and sixteen daughters. In his spare time, he did his best to carry out reprisals against the rebel Jeroboam, who had stolen most of his father's kingdom.

Abijah's son Asa was next on the throne. Initially he did his best to get Judah back on the straight and narrow, but later forgot to fully trust the Lord. So his latter years were a disappointment. "The eyes of the Lord range the world over, looking to strengthen those who are fully committed to him." But apparently Asa was not one of them.

He died a bitter old man and was succeeded by his son Jehoshaphat.

Jehoshaphat picked up the baton and set out on the road towards reformation with determination. He made a purge of pagan symbols and practices. He diligently sought to know the Lord and to teach his people to obey his commands. He appointed judges to preside over each city in

Judah. "See to it that you judge justly. Serve wholeheartedly in the fear of the Lord," he warned them.

The fear of the Lord was indeed felt throughout the land and even beyond its borders. Tribute poured in to enrich the royal coffers. Jehoshaphat used it wisely to fortify and garrison the cities of Judah. Perhaps less wisely, he built a fleet of ships in the Gulf of Aqaba with the intent of importing gold from Ophir to replace that which the Egyptians had stolen. But the whole fleet was wrecked in a storm before it even left port.

Jeroboam, the usurper of Israel, didn't live long. But then neither did any of the following five kings of Israel. Most of them died at the hands of assassins. Omri, king number six and himself an assassin, survived long enough to purchase a hill where he established a city he called Samaria which became the capital of Israel. Omri's other significant achievement was to sire a wretched little boy called Ahab, who eventually succeeded him on the throne.

Ahab made the terrible mistake of marrying a Sidonian princess named Jezebel, a dedicated disciple of the pagan god, Baal. Doubtless at her insistence, Ahab built a temple to Baal right near his palace in Samaria. Jeroboam may have made Israel to sin, but Ahab and Jezebel between them made them do it with style.

Such rebellion had to be confronted.

21

The Contender

Elijah was a rugged outdoorsman. Ahab knew he was in trouble the moment he saw the wild man dressed in animal skins. "There will not be a drop of rain for the next few years till I say so." Not waiting for a reply, Elijah turned on his heel and walked out into the desert.

He made camp east of the Jordan in a deep ravine by a stream. The weather was perfect for the outdoor life, since not a cloud darkened the sky. He had no need of supplies, for every morning and every evening, a flock of ravens would settle near his shelter and leave scraps of bread and fresh meat. All was well till the stream dried up.

The Lord sent him north to a coastal village in Lebanon, to the home of a widow. He met her gathering sticks to make a fire. "Might I trouble you for a drink of water?" he asked politely. "And a slice of bread while you are at it."

"Bread?" she asked. "As sure as your God lives, I have no bread. I am down to my last handful of flour and am just about to bake one final meal for my son and myself so we can eat it and then die."

"No worries," said Elijah. "Go make your meal, but give me the first share. Then you and your son can eat all you want, for here is God's promise to you. You will have all the flour and oil you need till the famine is over." And so it happened, just as Elijah promised.

All might have been well, had not the child fallen sick and died. The woman was understandably upset. "What have I done wrong that you come here to remind me of my sins and kill my child?"

"Let me have him," Elijah said, and taking the lad in his arms, he carried him up to his room. Having closed the door, he laid him on his bed and knelt to pray. "Why have you let this happen?" he asked the Lord. "Please let him live again."

The kid stirred. Elijah picked him up and gave him back to his mother, alive.

Meanwhile, the famine in Samaria was grim. Ahab was desperate to save his horses from the knacker, so sent his servant on a nationwide search for pasture. In the process of his fruitless search, the servant bumped into Elijah. "Go get your master," Elijah told him.

"Is that really you, you troublemaker?" greeted the king when later they met.

"It is hardly I who am the troublemaker, but rather you and your father's family in your refusal to obey God's commands, and your worship of Baal. But now, call an assembly of all Israel on that mountaintop over there," he said, indicating Mount Carmel. "And be sure that your prophets of Baal attend."

It took some time to call the assembly, but eventually streams of weary people started arriving from all over the land. They were sullen and weak from malnutrition as they dragged themselves up to the mountaintop. And there were the ghoulish prophets of Baal, looking stronger than the general populace, since they had enjoyed the generous hospitality of their benefactor, Queen Jezebel. They gathered under the relentless sun. To their west sparkled the blue waters of the Mediterranean, but to the east, the land was a dustbowl.

Early next morning, when most everyone was there, and before the sun was too hot, Elijah called the meeting to order: "Hear me and hear me well. I want to know how much longer you will live your lives in limbo, wavering between two conflicting opinions. It's time to make up your minds once for all. If the Lord is God, then follow him. But alternately, if Baal is God, then follow him."

The crowd was silent, sullen, ambivalent.

"Very well, here is what we will do. We will build two altars, one to Baal, and one to the Lord. We will each sacrifice a bull, but put no fire to the wood. The one who sends fire, he is God. Agreed?"

The people had often witnessed such miracles in the temple of Baal. A child would be placed on the altar, and as the priests prayed, the fire would spring up from nowhere to consume the infant. So the people readily agreed to so unbalanced a contest. Baal was good at that kind of thing.

The prophets of Baal were not so happy, since unlike back home in their temple at Samaria, the secret underground tunnels beneath the altar, from which the wood could be ignited, were embarrassingly absent on that barren mountaintop.

"You may go first since there are more of you," Elijah offered graciously. A bull was slaughtered, butchered into convenient portions, and then arranged on a stack of bone-dry faggots of wood. No flame was permitted near the altar. "Now go ahead and ask Baal to light it!"

"O Baal, answer us!" they mumbled.

"You can do better than that," taunted Elijah. "Shout a bit louder!" So they did. No answer.

"Come on! He's a god, isn't he? So perhaps he's meditating, or tied up for the time being, or even out of town. It's exhausting work being a god, so perhaps he's taking a nap. Wake him up!" The noise crescendoed into wails and screams.

Then they started to dance round the dead animal, and the flies buzzed and bit. The dance turned to a frenzy, and the blood began to flow as the priests slashed themselves with knives in their vain attempt to attract the attention of an entity that had no ears to hear (except in the distorted imaginations of its followers).

The sickening ritual went on all morning and into the afternoon. Eventually, Elijah brought the fiasco to an end: "Enough already! Now come over here."

The crowd watched as Elijah arranged exactly twelve stones in a ring, one for each of the twelve tribes. This was not a contest between the ten tribes of the north and Judah in the south. This was the Lord of all twelve tribes against ignorance and superstition. Then Elijah dug a trench around the ring of stones and neatly stacked the wood in the centre. Finally he butchered a second bull and arranged the meat on top of the wood.

When all was finished to his satisfaction, he told the people, "Now dowse it with water." The people watched the water soaking into the wood and turning the dust to mud. "Do it again!" and they did. "Now a third time." By now everything was soaked, and even the trench was filled.

Then Elijah lifted his hands, and a great silence fell on the people. "O Lord, God of our fathers, Abraham, Isaac, and Israel, please make it clear today that you alone are God. Answer me, oh Lord, so that these people will no longer be in any doubt who you really are. Draw their hearts back to yourself."

Scarce were the words out of his mouth when a ball of fire fell from the heavens, and instantly the wood was ablaze. The crowd fell to the ground, prostrate, and someone shouted, "The Lord, he is God!"

"Then do away with these false prophets who have been leading you in this terrible deception. Round them up and kill them!" And it was done.

Ahab was still standing there with his mouth hanging open, shocked rigid. "You'd better have your supper quick, because it's going to start raining soon," Elijah told him.

As the crowd dispersed, Elijah and his servant climbed back to the top of the mountain. There, Elijah knelt with his face on the ground and prayed for rain. After a while: "Go look to the west over the sea."

"Not a cloud in the sky," said the disappointed servant.

After a few more minutes: "Go have another look."

"Nothing."

This went on six times, but on the seventh: "There's a tiny cloud, big as your hand, just rising over the horizon."

"Go tell Ahab to jump in his chariot and head for home before the rain slows him down." The sky grew black as night.

Jezebel was not happy when her soaking-wet husband told her what had happened to her precious priests. "Tell Elijah that by this time tomorrow, he will be as dead as they," she announced imperiously.

When the message was delivered, something snapped inside the courageous prophet. Elijah's confidence melted, and he fled for his life. He ran south, way south, out into the wild wilderness of the Negev, where David had hidden from Saul.

He eventually collapsed in the shade of a tree and prayed for death. "I have had enough, oh Lord," he moaned. He fell asleep of sheer exhaustion. When he awoke, there was an angel offering him a fresh baked loaf and a jug of cold water. He ate and drank, then drifted off to sleep again.

What seemed like no time later, there was the angel once again with more refreshments: "Get up and eat. This has all been too much for you."

Fortified by the food, Elijah continued south and kept going for six weeks. He wandered way down into the desert, till eventually he came to Sinai, the mountain where God had met with Moses. He climbed high up the mountain till he came to a cave. For all he knew, it may have been the place where God had revealed his glory to Moses. "Let me see you," Moses had prayed, and that same desire must now have been heavy on the heart of this distressed prophet.

"What are you doing here, Elijah?" asked a voice from the swirling mists outside the cave.

"I am very upset," he replied lamely. "Your people have broken the covenant you made with us on this mountain. They have killed your prophets; in fact, I am the only one left, and now they are trying to ill me too."

"Come out here," said the voice, "for the Lord is about to pass by."

Elijah stumbled outside the cave and stood on a ledge. At once, what felt like a tornado screamed across the face of the mountain. Elijah retreated into the cave for shelter. Then the ground began to shake in a violent earthquake, and as the rocks began to fall from the roof of his cave, Elijah fled for the safety of the open air. Scarcely had the ground ceased to rumble when a fire swept across the mountainside, and it was back into the cave for protection.

Elijah waited with his heart pounding for whatever would happen next.

Then he heard a quiet voice, little more than a whisper: "What are you doing here, Elijah?" Elijah went and stood outside the cave on the ledge. Stubbornly, he repeated the same answer as before.

"Well, go back the way you came," said the quiet voice, "to the place where you lost your way. I still have work for you to do there. First you are to anoint Hazael to be the next king of Aram in place of Ben-hadad. Then find Jehu and anoint him to succeed Ahab in Israel. Finally, your successor is to be Elisha. Anoint him also. And just so you know, I still have seven thousand prophets faithful to me in Israel, who have not worshipped Baal. You are by no means alone."

And so Elijah retraced his steps north. When he eventually arrived back in the region near Carmel, where the contest had been held, he found Elisha working on the family farm. Without a word of explanation, he walked up to the young man, threw his cloak over his shoulders, and then walked on. Elisha was stunned. Of course he recognised the hero of Mount Carmel, but why the cloak thing? So he ran after Elijah. "Hey, yes. I'll follow you, but let me nip home and say good-bye to the folks." Elisha went home, smashed his plough to firewood, sacrificed his yoke of oxen, kissed Mom and Dad good-bye, and left home on a whole new adventure.

To King Ahab, the grass always appeared greener on the other side of the fence, and that was most certainly true of the vineyard pertaining to Naboth that bordered Ahab's winter palace in Jezreel. "That south sloping land would make the perfect vegetable garden," he insisted. "I'll give you a fair price, or if you prefer, I'll trade you an even better parcel of land." But Naboth valued his family inheritance more than just any old field, so he refused.

Ahab was not used to being snubbed, so he went and lay down on his bed in a sulk. That was where his wife found him.

"What's up with you?" Jezebel enquired. Ahab explained. "Are you not the king around here? Cheer up. I'll get your precious veggie patch for you."

And so she did, but not at the fair price Ahab had offered. She arranged for Naboth to be publicly accused of treason and then stoned to death. When the news of the tragic demise of their neighbour reached the palace, Jezebel sent word to Ahab: "Naboth is dead, and the vineyard is now yours. Enjoy!"

And that was where Elijah met him, the first reunion since the Mount Carmel affair. "So we meet again, my enemy," greeted Ahab.

"This is what the Lord has to say to you: 'You have murdered an innocent man and stolen his property. So in the very place where the dogs licked up Naboth's blood, there shall they lick yours. And not just your blood, for I will make an end of your whole family, every last one of them. But the dogs will actually eat Jezebel by the wall of her palace.'"

In recent years, relations between Israel and Judah had warmed somewhat. Matters had been helped along by a marriage between Jehoshaphat's oldest son, Jehoram, and Ahab's daughter, Athaliah. Athaliah was a true chip off the old block – the old block being her mother Jezebel, and she made it her business to influence her new Judean husband in the worship of Baal, her family religion.

So now Jehoshaphat and Ahab were all one happy family. Jehoshaphat went to visit his fellow in-laws in Samaria. An impressive feast was held to celebrate the happy alliance.

Eventually, they got down to talking business. Apparently Ben-hadad of Damascus had reneged on a previous agreement to cede certain cities to Israel. "I have in mind to go and take back Ramoth Gilead," said Ahab. "Would you come along with me?"

Jehoshaphat readily agreed but felt that it might be smart to seek the guidance of the Lord before doing anything precipitous.

"Okay with me," agreed Ahab, and he sent for four hundred prophets, not those of Baal, since Elijah had caused them to be in short supply, but rather his national prophets who served Jeroboam's two golden calves.

The two kings sat on their royal thrones in the city square, near the main gate of Samaria. In the prophets all came, a strange group by all accounts. One had made a metal helmet with horns, much like those of the sacred cows he served: "With these you will gore the enemy," and all the prophets agreed that victory was assured.

But Jehoshaphat was not convinced. "Don't you have any prophets of the Lord in Samaria?"

"Well, yes. There is one. But I can't stand him. He is so negative. Never has a good word to say for me."

They sent for Micaiah. "Make sure you prophesy victory like all the others have done," hissed the messenger, who escorted him to the royal presence.

"I'll tell him what the Lord tells me," snapped Micaiah. Then before the two kings: "Oh yes. Go right ahead. Victory is assured. This many prophets couldn't possibly be wrong."

"How many times must I warn you to tell me only the truth," grumbled the phony Ahab.

"Oh, it's the truth you want, is it? Very well then. I foresee all Israel scattered over the hills like terrified sheep."

"I told you so," Ahab muttered to Jehoshaphat. "Never has a positive thing to say. Throw him into prison, and give him nothing but bread and water till we return victorious."

"If you return at all, then the Lord has not spoken through me."

So off they went to Ramoth Gilead. Lest he should be picked out as a prime target, Ahab went in disguise as a regular soldier. Nevertheless, in the course of the battle, a chance arrow found its deadly way through a chink in his armour. They propped him up as best they could in his chariot so as not to discourage the troops, but he was dead by evening, and the retreat was sounded. They conveyed his body in his own chariot back to Samaria, where they buried him, and then drove the chariot to the pool where the local prostitutes normally did their ablutions. But before they got to washing the chariot, the dogs had first dibs on the dried blood. Those dogs had been developing a taste for human blood ever since Naboth, the vineyard owner, had been stoned to death on that exact spot. Elijah was proved right.

Jehoshaphat, however, made it back to Jerusalem in safety.

Ahaziah, Ahab's son, suffered an unfortunate setback not long after assuming his father's throne. He fell from an upstairs window and was seriously injured. In deep distress, he turned to the religion of his parents, consulting a prophet of Baal – "Baal-zebub," or "Lord of the flies," as they called him. Exactly what he expected in response is not clear, but what he got was most certainly not what he wanted.

A message came from Elijah the prophet, the nemesis of his father Ahab. "Is the Lord so unavailable that you are forced to seek the help of Baal-zebub? Be aware, therefore, that you will certainly not recover from your injury."

The enraged king sent fifty men to arrest Elijah. "Come with us at once!" ordered the haughty captain. Fire fell from heaven and consumed him and his soldiers. The same fate was suffered by the next detachment.

The third captain was more tactful, adding "please" to his summons. This time, Elijah obliged, but when he came to the bedside of the injured king, he simply repeated his original message. So Ahaziah died of his injuries. He was childless, so his brother Joram took his throne.

By then, Elijah was an old man and glad of the support of his understudy. Elisha had faithfully followed him ever since he had thrown his cloak over his shoulders on his return from Sinai. Being prophets, both men were aware that Elijah's last day had come. Elisha followed his master, first to Bethel and then to Jericho. In each town, local prophets warned Elisha of what he was already well aware.

"As certainly as God lives, I will not leave your side," Elisha insisted when Elijah bade him go.

The two of them came to the bank of the Jordan, close to the place where Israel had crossed under Joshua's leadership. Elijah took off his cloak, rolled it up, and struck the water. As it had for Joshua, the water divided right and left, and the two walked through on dry ground.

As they walked together up the far bank, Elijah asked, "Have you one last request before I leave you?"

With no hesitation, Elisha responded, "I would like a double share of your spirit."

"Difficult one. I tell you what: if you see me as I am taken from you, a double share will be yours."

They walked on, chatting about this and that, when suddenly a fiery tornado came galloping across the sand like a coach and four. Elijah went with it.

Elisha, shocked to the core, shouted, "Father! My father. The chariots and horsemen of Israel!"

Gradually his wits returned to him. Stooping down, he picked up Elijah's cloak, which had fallen from his shoulders, the same cloak that had been thrown over his own shoulders that day when Elijah had found him ploughing on the family farm.

He strode back towards the river. On the far bank stood a group of spectators, prophets who had been unable to follow since the parted waters had returned, denying them passage. Elisha rolled up the cloak, just as he had seen Elijah do but an hour earlier. "Where is the God of Elijah?" he shouted and struck the water. Same thing. Elisha walked confidently through the dry river bed.

A murmur ran through the crowd: "Now the spirit of Elijah is on Elisha!" They all bowed in respect. Even so, those prophets wasted several days searching in vain for any trace of Elijah.

"I told you not to bother," Elisha said when they eventually gave up. While he was there, he threw salt into their polluted well and cured the water that had been undrinkable as long as any of them could remember.

Elisha did not cut as striking a figure as had Elijah. Short, fat, and bald has never been in fashion. As he began the ascent to Bethel, a gang of hoodlums followed him, shouting insults: "Get out of here, Baldy!" Elisha turned to face them, and out of the trees came a couple of vicious bears that attacked the kids and sent them running for home, mauled and bleeding.

From then on, Elisha made his home in Samaria, where Joram had recently inherited his brother's throne. So when King Joram, in company with King Jehoshaphat of Jerusalem, set out to teach the Moabites a lesson, Elisha tagged along with them. The Moabites who lived to the east had reneged on their agreement to supply Israel with wool, and Joram felt compelled to press his claim with military might. The two kings set off side-by-side, allies, family. They took a roundabout route, necessitating a seven-day march through the desert. They don't call it desert for nothing, so they shouldn't have been surprised when the water supply gave out.

"I should never have trusted the Lord," moaned Joram. "This must be his trick to hand us over to the king of Moab."

"So perhaps we should consult one of his prophets," suggested Jehoshaphat.

Elisha was summoned. He considered the problem and then, inspired by the music of a harpist, gave orders that the whole army was to set about digging drainage ditches in the parched ground. No one was particularly thrilled about such a thirsty and pointless exercise, especially when the problem they faced was the lack of water, rather than its surfeit. Drainage ditches indeed!

"This is what the Lord says," Elisha assured them: "'This valley will be filled with enough water for you and your livestock to drink. And these ditches will also prove the downfall of Moab.'"

Sure enough, next morning the ditches were full of water. The Moabites, seeing in the distance the rising sun's blood-red reflection on the surface of the water, took it as a good omen. "That's blood! They must have slaughtered each other! Let's grab the plunder!" They charged headlong in pursuit of the booty, only to find a well-prepared army of very much alive soldiers waiting for them. The wool supply was restored, and everyone kept warm that winter.

Once home in Jerusalem, Jehoshaphat received news that a vast enemy army was approaching from the south. Word was that it was a coalition of peoples from east of the Dead Sea. His scouts informed him that they had advanced as far of En Gedi. Having learned his lesson from the fiasco with King Ahab, Jehoshaphat was determined to seek the Lord's leading before doing anything. He sent messengers to every city in Judah, telling all his subjects to assemble in Jerusalem, praying and fasting as they came.

Thousands gathered in the great court in front of the temple, and when they were all there, King Jehoshaphat himself led the people in prayer. The occasion was reminiscent of when King Solomon had prayed at the dedication of the temple on those same steps.

"O Lord, God of our fathers, it was you who gave this land to our forefathers, who built this sanctuary in your name so that whenever trouble threatens your people, they may come and stand here before you and cry to you for protection. So here we are, faced with this vast army that is intent on driving us from our inheritance. We are powerless before them and have no idea what to do. But we are looking to you for help."

The people stood there in silence, just standing there, hand in hand, husbands and wives, little children and babies in arms, terrified of losing each other, dreading what the future might bring.

Then the voice of a Levite broke the silence: "King Jehoshaphat and all present, this is what the Lord has to say to you today: There's no need to be afraid or discouraged. This fight is not yours, but God's. Tomorrow you are to march out to face them. There will be no need to do anything, just take your stand and see what God will do."

There was dead silence. Then the king got down on his knees. Were those tears running down his cheeks? Soon everyone was kneeling, tears of relief and hope flowing free. A faint whisper of singing began somewhere among the Levite choir and then spread through the people till soon the whole crowd rose to their feet and joined the worship, a great crescendo of praise, echoing through the streets of Jerusalem.

Early next morning, they marched out towards the south. As they left, the king stood at the gate of the city, encouraging the troops: "Have faith in God and his promises. You will most certainly be victorious."

The Levite choir preceded the soldiers and led the people in praising: "Give thanks to God, for his love lasts forever!" They were still singing when they reached the ridge that overlooked the desert. And there was that vast army, all dead, every man jack of them. Seems they had fallen out with each other and fought to the last man standing, then even he had fallen. It took three days to gather up the plunder. On the fourth day, they all massed on the two sides of a nearby valley and sang and worshipped till their throats were sore. Thereafter that place was known as the "Valley of Worship." When they could sing no more, they processed back to Jerusalem, where the worship broke out all over again in the temple.

After that, no one dared threaten Jerusalem. Everyone was terrified of the Lord their God. So Jehoshaphat enjoyed peace till the day of his death, when he was buried in the family tomb after twenty-five successful years on the throne. He left several sons, but it was his oldest, Jehoram, who inherited the throne. Jehoram, married as he was to Athaliah, the daughter of the late King Ahab and his widow, Jezebel, followed the religious perversions of his in-laws. To secure his throne, he wasted no time before killing off all his brothers along with other men of influence in the land. He re-established all manner of pagan practices and suffered the unpopularity of his own people and neighbours alike.

One day, a letter was delivered to the palace, purporting to be from the late prophet Elijah himself. Now it was well known that Elijah was no more, caught up in a chariot of fire, so the story had it. It was therefore with a sense of foreboding that Jehoram slit open the envelope: "The Lord, the God of your father David, says to you: 'You have led the people of Jerusalem to prostitute themselves in much the same manner as did King

Ahab. Furthermore, you have murdered your brothers, who were all better men than you. So prepare yourself for the worst.'"

Whoever the author of the letter may actually have been, trouble did indeed follow – in spades. Marauding bands from the surrounding nations broke into Jerusalem and plundered Jehoram's palace, killing most of his family. Ill health knotted his intestines till they oozed out of him, and he died in terrible agony. No one was sorry to see him gone.

Ahaziah, his son, succeeded him. Names must have been scarce in those days, since he took the same name as his uncle, the unfortunate king of Israel who had fallen from that upstairs window.

Ahaziah was just twenty-two when he came to the throne. His mother, Athaliah, daughter of the malevolent King Ahab, was a powerful force in his life and gathered round her son an evil council made up of members of her evil family. They made it their business to mould him in the ways of Ahab and caused him to forge a close alliance with his uncle, King Joram of Samaria.

22

The Thaumaturgist

Unlike his reclusive predecessor Elijah, Elisha enjoyed company. He made his base in Samaria but spent much time on the road, mentoring the younger prophets. Near Gilgal down in the Jordan Valley, not far from Jericho, was a seminary where a hundred student prophets lived. Some had been around long enough to have known Elijah and had even witnessed his departure in the chariot of fire. So it is not surprising that in the course of his peripatetic ministry, Elisha often stayed there and shared meals in the refectory. Doubtless he was a welcome guest, particularly since he was the one famed for having restored their water supply.

On one visit, they had just sat down to eat, and the chef was ladling stew out of an immense cauldron, when one of the prophets started to choke. "There's poison in the pot!" he spluttered.

Turned out that one of their number had found a wild vine out in the fields and had added it to the mix, thinking to bring a little spice to the brew. Since they were in the throes of a famine and the seminary was experiencing a severe food shortage, no one wanted to throw the stew away.

"Add a little flour to the mix," Elisha told the chef. No one suffered so much as a stomach ache after that.

Next morning, there was no bread for breakfast. Now it happened that exactly at the time when they all sat down to eat, a man arrived at the door with a gift for the visiting prophet. It was a small basket of buns.

"How kind," Elisha said to his servant. "Now we can all have breakfast."

"Just how far do you think these few buns will go among a hundred hungry prophets?" asked the cynical servant.

"They will all have enough and there will be leftovers," Elisha assured him. And so there were.

After breakfast, they invited Elisha to go out with them. "Where are you going?" he asked.

"Logging, down by the river. We are building an extension on the dormitory, since accommodation is a little tight these days."

Elisha watched the enthusiastic young students at work. Suddenly, a cry of dismay attracted his attention. "What's the matter?" he enquired.

"The head came off my axe, sir, and it fell into the river. That always seems to happen when you borrow something."

"Where did it fall?" Elisha asked. "Show me."

Elisha cut a stick and threw it into the water near where the axe had last been seen. To everyone's amazement, the metal floated to the surface.

"Grab it!" Elisha shouted. Everyone was astonished.

It wasn't just the prophets themselves who shared that community. There were wives and children as well, even a few widows. One of these ladies came to Elisha and asked if she might have a word.

"As you know, my husband is dead. Since he died, we have been terribly short of cash. Prophet he may have been, but he was not wise with money, and he died with outstanding debts. Now his creditor is threatening to take my two sons as slaves in payment of the debt. Can you help us?"

"What assets do you still have at home?" Elisha asked kindly.

"Well, nothing really, except perhaps a few drops of oil left in the bottom of a jar."

"Right, well, send your lads out to all your neighbours and borrow every container you can lay your hands on. Be sure to get as many as possible. Then go home, lock the door, and start pouring your oil into those containers."

And so she did. The joy and laughter that filled that sad house went on for hours as mom poured, and the boys brought the containers. "Quick, bring me another!" she said eventually.

"There are no more, Mom. That's the last." Then the oil stopped pouring.

She ran off joyfully to tell Elisha what had happened. "Great!" he said. "Now go and sell the oil. Pay your debts, and I think you will find that there will be enough money left over for you and your boys to live on."

Gilgal wasn't the only place where Elisha was welcome. Up north in Shunem, there was a grand home where he loved to stay. The house owner was rich and farmed a big spread. His wife was young, but sadly they had no children.

"Let's build the man of God an upstairs room of his own," the woman suggested, and they both agreed that this would be a great idea. That room became something of a home away from home for Elisha.

"What can I do for you in return?" he asked gratefully.

"We really don't need a thing," she answered. "We have a home among our own people. What more could we want?"

Elisha discussed the question with Gehazi, his servant. "They have no children," Gehazi pointed out, "and the old man's no spring chicken."

"Now that's a plan," agreed Elisha.

"Lady," Elisha said as she was standing in the door. "About this time next year you will be nursing a son."

"Get away with you," she objected. "Don't joke about something like that." But it was no joke, and soon a healthy boy brought joy to the household.

At least he did for a few years. Then he got sunstroke out in his dad's harvest fields and died in his mother's arms.

Elisha was not there at the time, but even so the grief-stricken mother carried him upstairs and laid him on Elisha's bed. Quickly, she saddled a donkey and set off at a gallop to find the prophet. Eventually, she caught up to him some thirty miles away on Mount Carmel.

"Here comes the lady from Shunem," Elisha said to Gehazi. "Run out to meet her and see what she wants."

"Everything is fine," she said, brushing past him. When she got to Elisha, she fell and grabbed his feet. Gehazi made to push her away.

"Leave her be," Elisha said. "Something is seriously wrong, and the Lord has not told me what it is."

Eventually, out it all came in a tumble of grief and anger. "Did I ask you for a child? And when you told me I would have a son, didn't I tell you not to raise my hopes for nothing?"

"Gehazi, take my staff and run back to the house as fast as you can. Don't stop for anyone. When you get there, lay the staff on the boy's face." Elisha followed with the lady on the donkey.

"How is he?" Elisha asked Gehazi when they arrived.

"He hasn't stirred, sir."

There the boy was, lying on Elisha's bed, stone cold dead. Elisha shut the door, knelt down beside the bed, and prayed. Then he got up and stretched out on top of the child, full length. Gradually, the child's body grew warm. Elisha got up, paced around the room, then stretched out on the boy once again. Suddenly, the boy sneezed and opened his eyes. "Gehazi! Call the lady!"

When the celebrating was all done, Elisha had a quiet word with the couple: "The Lord has told me that there is to be a severe famine in this part of the world. You should travel for a while till it's over." So they left for what turned out to be a seven-year sojourn in Philistine territory.

But they did not escape trouble during those years. For one thing, the husband died, and the lady was left alone with her son. And for another, when eventually they got back home, they found that the family farm had been seized, presumably to cover property taxes. She was destitute, with no recourse but to go and plead her case before King Joram in Samaria.

Now it just so happened that she arrived at the palace while the king was having a friendly chat with Gehazi, Elisha's servant. By then, Elisha was something of a legend in Samaria, and the king wanted to hear first-hand some of the amazing stories that seemed to follow Elisha around. Gehazi had just told him the best story of all, the amazing account of the Shunammite woman whose son had been raised to life. Suddenly Gehazi broke off his narrative. "Well, I'll be ... There she is, sir, the woman I was just telling you about! And if I'm not mistaken, that tall young man must be her son." The lady confirmed all Gehazi had been saying.

The king was so amazed that he gave orders that all the land she had lost should be returned to her, together with interest for lost revenue.

Ever since the battle at Ramoth-Gilead, when Ahab had been killed, Israel and Aram had been picking at each other. It was not outright war so much as scuffles and skirmishes. A raiding party from Aram had taken captive a young Israeli girl and sold her as a slave back in Damascus. She was bought by no less a person than Naaman, field marshal of the Aramean army. Naaman was something of a hero because of his daring exploits and many victories. But no amount of adulation could counterbalance his secret shame. It had started as a sore, which he could keep hidden under his shirt, but eventually the terrible truth came out. He was a leper.

One day, the Israeli slave took it upon herself to speak to her mistress: "My lady, if only there was some way that my master could visit the prophet who lives in Samaria. I know he would cure his leprosy."

When you are desperate and there is no cure offered by conventional medicine, you will try almost anything. So, with the blessing of King Ben-hadad, Naaman set off for Samaria with a covering letter from his king. Quite the entourage went with him: a camel train carrying silver and gold and the latest fashions from Damascus.

A company of Arameans would have felt as welcome in Samaria as a swarm of wasps at a swimming hole, so Naaman went straight to the palace and handed in Ben-hadad's letter. Joram slit it open and turned white as he read the contents: "I am sending you my servant Naaman so that you may cure him of his leprosy."

"Who does he think I am?" spluttered Joram. "God? Is this some kind of a joke or possibly a pretext to start another fight?"

"Send him to me," Elisha told the king when word of this reached him.

Naaman halted his grand procession outside the back-street dwelling that Elisha called home. In answer to his knock, a mere servant came to the door: "My master says you are to go and dip yourself seven times in the river Jordan and you will be healed."

Naaman was outraged. "He could at least have come out to speak to me and called on the name of the Lord and waved his hand over the spot – something dramatic! But just a message through a servant? And another thing … The Jordan – that muddy little stream? We have much better rivers in Damascus if it's just a wash I need. Why not one of them?" And he stamped off in a dudgeon.

"My lord, a word in your ear, if I might," said a tactful servant. "If the prophet had told you to do some grand thing, would you not have done it? So when he tells you to do so simple a thing – 'Wash and be healed' – why not?" Ah, the voice of reason.

So the procession made its way down to the Jordan Valley. It was indeed a muddy little stream at that time of year, but at least it was cool. Surely one dip would suffice, but when he looked, there was no change. … five, six, and finally seven dips. Yes! His skin was clean, with the complexion of a child!

Back up the long hill they went, back to the home of the prophet, who came out to greet him this time. "So it's true. There really is a God in Israel, and he is doubtless the only God in all the world. So yes. I have gifts for you."

"As sure as God is God, I will accept no gift." Elisha refused all offers. "Go in peace." He sent him on his way.

Gehazi could not stand there and watch all that wealth just walk off over the horizon. So when Naaman had got out of town, he ran after him.

"What's up?" asked Naaman. "Is everything okay?"

"Yes, everything's fine. It's just that a couple of young prophets happened by," he lied. "My master thought it would be nice to give them a suit of clothes each and perhaps a talent of silver to help them on their way."

"By all means," agreed Naaman, delighted. "We'll give them a talent each." He even sent a couple of servants to help Gehazi carry the stuff home.

Gehazi hid the booty in his own home and then went back to serve Elisha his supper.

"Where have you been, Gehazi?" his master asked when he got in.

"Nowhere special."

"My spirit was there with you, watching when the man alighted from his chariot to greet you. Do you really think it is appropriate to accept money and possessions? So now Naaman's leprosy will cling to you forever." Gehazi went out from his master's house, a leper from head to foot.

One might imagine that a cure for leprosy for his field marshal would have warmed the heart of Ben-hadad towards Joram. However, such was not the case. He continued with his raids, yet for some reason that he found difficult to understand, the Israelis were inevitably ready for him. No matter where he planned to strike, his enemy was there first.

"We have a spy in our ranks," growled the Aramean king.

Elisha's name was well known in Damascus, since the healing of Naaman must have caused no small stir. Someone suggested, "Has it occurred to you, oh King, that since that prophet who Naaman brags about is so clever, perhaps he knows all your secrets, even the very words you say in the private of your bedroom?"

Ben-hadad blushed red at the thought. "Go and bring him to me," spat the embarrassed king.

They received intelligence that Elisha was visiting Dothan, a city just a few miles north of Samaria. During the night, Ben-hadad's soldiers quietly surrounded the city so there could be no escape.

Early in the morning, Elisha's new servant got up and went for a stretch. There, before his horrified eyes, was an army of soldiers and horsemen hemming them in. He went running in to wake Elijah: "What are we going to do?"

"No worries," said Elijah. "We have them outnumbered. Take another look!" Gradually the young man discerned through the morning mists that the hills all around them were alive with horses and chariots, like flames in the brush.

Elisha strode out to meet the Arameans, with his servant reluctantly tagging along behind. "Lord, please strike these soldiers blind," Elisha prayed as they walked. As they approached, it became plain that there was confusion in the camp: men stumbling about, bumping into each other.

"Are you fellows having difficulty finding your way?" called Elisha. "Hey, I know the man you are looking for, and I'll lead you to him, if you like."

Like sheep to the slaughter, they followed as Elisha led them right into the city square of Samaria, where they were instantly surrounded by Israeli soldiers. "Now open their eyes, Lord." Panic!

"Should I kill them?" asked King Joram.

"No! That's no way to treat prisoners of war. Give them a good meal and send them home." And so they did.

"A gentle answer turns away wrath," Solomon had included amongst his proverbs, but on this occasion, Solomon was proved wrong. Joram's gentle answer did nothing to quell Ben-hadad's wrath. He marched his entire army to lay siege to Samaria. Surrounding the city so no one could come or go, he ensured no provisions could enter the city to feed the starving citizens. Prices rose as stocks dwindled, till you would be lucky to buy a donkey's head for an entrée and a slice of pigeon dung pie for dessert.

King Joram was taking a walk round the city wall to assess the situation. An emaciated young woman called out to him for help.

"Help? Where are you expecting to get help? Oh, from our overflowing storerooms and wine cellars, perhaps? Get real! Only God can help us now. Why don't you ask him?" Then realising that his sarcasm had perhaps been over the top, he went on, "But tell me, what's the matter?"

The woman's reply made his stomach churn: "This woman here suggested that we should eat my son and promised that when he was all finished, we would eat her son. So we cooked my son and ate him, but when I came to ask her to produce her son, she had hidden him. It's not fair!"

Fair? What had fairness got to do with anything? In rage and frustration, Joram tore his royal robe, and the people could see that underneath, he was wearing the sackcloth of a penitent. "God help me if I don't take Elisha's head for this!" Well, someone had to be blamed.

The king dispatched an executioner but then, thinking better of it, ran after him to Elisha's house. He stormed in to find the house already crowded with city elders holding some kind of council meeting.

"This mess is all God's fault!" raged the king. "So there's no sense in waiting around for him to help us, is there?" Just what suggestions he had in mind for more immediate implementation than intervention by the Almighty, he never explained.

"One more day," soothed Elisha. "By this time tomorrow, the Lord assures you that there will be flour and grain aplenty in the market."

Standing next to the king was an effeminate young officer. "Oh come on! Even if the Lord should open wide the floodgates of heaven, I doubt you could be right."

"Oh, you doubt it, do you? Well, I assure you that you will see it with your own eyes, but you will never taste it."

Outside the city gates lived the poorest of the poor, a demoralised group of lepers. In better days, they may have lived off the garbage that was dumped over the city wall, but when donkey's heads and pigeon dung are sought-after commodities in the market, then you don't even throw away the potato peelings. They were starving.

There was no place for them to go, since as lepers they were not permitted to enter the city. And they couldn't escape to the country, since they were surrounded by hostile Arameans.

"There's nothing we can do."

"If we sit here we are dead men."

"Even if we could go into the city, there's no food there, so we'd die of starvation there, same as here."

"If we go to the Arameans, they'll kill us for sure."

"Well, we can't just sit here and do nothing," insisted the optimist in the group. "Let's go and make a grand surrender to the Arameans. Perhaps they'll give us a last meal or something, before killing us. We'd be no more dead there than we will soon be sitting here."

It was unanimous, so off they shambled. As they neared the camp, they expected to be challenged at any moment, or worse – a swift blade to the neck. But nothing. They came to the first tent. The campfire was smouldering and the supper was cooked, but no one was home. Starving men don't wait for an invitation, so they quickly ate what was before them and then cautiously reconnoitred the next tent. Same story. Not only was there food and drink in abundance, but valuables there for the taking: silver and gold and fine clothes to replace their beggars' rags.

As the evening turned to night and their appetites were more than satisfied: "Hey, you guys. This isn't right, you know. We can't stay here stuffing ourselves. This is a day of good news, and good news is meant to be shared. If we sit around here all night, bad things may happen to us. Let's go and tell this in the city."

The city gates were locked up tight, so they shouted their news up to the sentries who were guarding the walls. The sentries passed the report to the palace. The palace servants woke the king.

"It's a trick!" he growled, struggling into consciousness. "They will ambush us as soon as we set foot outside the city. I'm going back to bed."

"But sir, shouldn't we at least check?"

"And who would risk their necks by venturing into the Aramean camp? They'd be killed."

"But no more dead than they will soon be by staying here."

"Very well," the king relented.

A couple of nervous horsemen clattered out of the city gates and galloped towards the enemy camp. No challenge. No arrows. Nothing. They galloped right round the camp. Not a soul there. Then they began to follow the trail of discarded clothes and equipment that gave evidence of the panicked flight of a terrified army. They followed the trail of detritus for miles, most of the way to the Jordan. Same story all the way.

In the morning, when the news spread through the whole city, there was joyful looting, and the market was abuzz for the first time in weeks.

"Let there be order here!" yelled the king, dispatching the effeminate young officer to oversee the chaos. But the people were not going to put up with regulations on such a day as this. The young man was knocked over in the scrum and trampled to death. Yes, he caught a glimpse of the grain and flour in the market stalls, but he never even got a taste, just as Elisha had predicted.

Some time later, it was revealed that the Arameans had fled because they had heard the sound of what they took to be a great army. "Run for your lives!" Of course, there was no one there. Or perhaps there was an army: the fiery horses and chariots of the host of heaven. Who knows?

This on-going dispute with the Arameans reminded Elisha that there was an item lurking deep in a pending file, unfinished business, that he had to take care of. Years earlier, up Mount Sinai, God had instructed Elisha's predecessor, Elijah, to anoint Hazael to succeed Ben-hadad as king of Aram. So far as Elisha knew, Elijah had never carried out that commission. So when news reached Elisha that Ben-hadad had fallen sick, he realised that something had to be done quickly. Elisha travelled to Damascus, ostensibly to pay the king a hospital call. When Ben-hadad heard that Elisha was on his way, he sent Hazael to greet him. "Ask him if I will get better," he told him, sending along a generous gift in hopes of a positive reply. Perhaps he might even be healed, like Naaman?

"Your servant Ben-hadad has sent me to ask if this sickness will prove fatal. Will he die or will he recover?" Hazael asked when the pleasantries had been exchanged.

"You can tell him, 'The sickness will not kill him.'" Elisha fixed Hazael with an icy stare and held it till Hazael dropped his eyes in shame. How had Elisha discerned that he was secretly planning to assassinate his master while he was incapacitated?

Then Elisha's chin began to quiver, and in the next moment, he was overcome with grief.

"Why is my lord so sad?" Hazael asked, embarrassed.

"Because I know what's in your heart and in your future. I see all the pain you will inflict on Israel, the burning, the destruction, the violence, rape, and murder."

"But how could I, a mere nobody, achieve such a thing?" asked the cold-hearted Hazael.

"The Lord says that you will be the next king of Aram." There! He had said it. It didn't rate highly as an anointing, but Hazael believed it, and next morning, he smothered Ben-hadad with a wet towel and stole his crown.

23

The North

Ramoth Gilead, situated as it was on the border between Israel and Aram, was something of a bone of contention between the two nations. Like two terriers with a stick, they pulled it this way and that. When Hazael took up the reins of power in Damascus, he made it a priority to settle the dispute once and for all. He attacked the city, and true to form, King Joram of Israel responded. At some point during the battle, King Joram was wounded. Déjà vu! His father had been fatally wounded during a previous battle over Ramoth. Now it was his turn. He took off for home, leaving the ongoing battle in the capable hands of his commander-in-chief, Jehu.

Jehu was holding a council of war with his fellow officers when a wild-looking young man walked in on their meeting. "I have a message for you, from God," he announced.

"A message for who, exactly?" demanded Jehu.

"For you, commander, in private, if you don't mind."

Jehu excused himself and went with the young man, who appeared nervous and agitated. They found a place where they could be alone. Immediately, the young man pulled from his pocket a flask, and before Jehu could stop him, he had poured oil over his head. "I hereby anoint you king of Israel. You are to annihilate the whole family of Ahab, avenging the blood of the Lord's prophets that Jezebel shed. She will be eaten by dogs by the wall of her palace, just as Elijah prophesied."

Not waiting for a moment, the young man fled from the room.

Jehu must have looked shaken. "Is everything okay?" his colleagues asked him when he got back to the meeting. "What did that nutcase want?"

"Oh, nothing special. You know the kind of madness these fellows come out with."

"No. Tell us what he said," they insisted.

"Well, if you must know, he anointed me the next king of Israel."

As quick as rain turns to sunshine at the end of a summer storm, their scorn turned to adulation. They threw down their cloaks at his feet and shouted: "Long live King Jehu!"

For one who had appeared bashful at first, Jehu was remarkably quick off the mark to get started on his divinely ordained mandate. Off he went to Jezreel at a furious pace, with his troops doing their best to keep up.

Back in Jezreel, King Joram was convalescing from his wounds. His mother Jezebel was in residence, there at their winter palace. When you are hurting, there is nothing like a mother's touch to speed you on the road to recovery, even if your mother is cold hearted as a witch.

Hearing the news of his uncle's troubles, Azariah had travelled all the way up from Jerusalem to encourage him and to visit his great-aunt Jezebel in her old age.

"Troops approaching!" shouted the lookout on the wall of Jezreel.

"Who is it?" Joram asked from his bed.

"Whoever it is, he's driving like a lunatic. Looks like Jehu, if you ask me."

Joram couldn't wait to get news of the battle in Ramoth Gilead, so he insisted on being helped into his chariot to drive out to meet him. Anxious not to miss out on whatever was happening, Azariah tagged along in his own chariot.

It so happened that the place where they all met up was the entrance to the vineyard that Jezebel had taken from Naboth by having him stoned to death.

Joram was halted in his tracks by the hostile expression on Jehu's face, so the positive greeting died on his lips: "Have you come in peace, Jehu?"

"Peace? What chance has peace while your mother continues her idolatry and witchcraft?"

Recognising that trouble was staring him in the face, Joram had his driver wheel the chariot around and fled, shouting a warning to Azariah as he went: "Treason, Azariah! Treason!"

Jehu grabbed up his bow and shot the retreating Joram in the back. "Kick his body out of the chariot right there, where you are," Jehu yelled to the terrified driver. "Dump him in Naboth's vineyard so Elijah's words can be fulfilled. Ahab will finally pay a fair price for that piece of land: the blood of his son."

The arrow that hit the fleeing king of Judah was not quite so deadly. Azariah got away, but only got as far as Megiddo before he succumbed to his wound.

That day, both Israel and Judah lost their kings.

But the day was not over. Jehu had only just started on his deadly agenda. He rode into Jezreel. Jezebel was sitting like a gargoyle in her upstairs window, face painted, hair braided. "So, you traitor, is this a peaceful visit?" she called down to Jehu in the street below.

"Push her out of the window!" Jehu shouted to her attendants. Her screaming body hit the ground, and her blood spattered up the wall. Just to make sure of the business, Jehu rode his horse right over her. Leaving her mangled body where it fell, he went into the royal banqueting room and slaked his thirst. When they went back an hour later to bury Jezebel, all they found were her skull, feet, and hands. Dogs had eaten the rest. Jehu thought it appropriate that Jezebel's final resting place would be in a pile of dog excrement.

There was still some mopping up to be done, so Jehu wrote to the elders in Samaria, demanding the heads of any of Ahab's sons who remained. By return he received seventy heads. Anyone in Israel who was in any way related to Ahab, or even had liked him, followed a similar fate. Some visiting relatives of the late King Ahaziah made the mistake of admitting they had come to visit the families of Joram and Jezebel. "Off with their heads!"

Samaria was the centre for Baal worship. Jezebel had built her famous temple there, so stone and wooden idols proliferated.

"So this is where Ahab revered Baal, is it?" Jehu asked in a loud voice. "Well, you haven't seen anything yet. Watch how I will honour him! I intend to hold a great sacrifice to Baal, and I want all the prophets and priests of Baal from all over the country to participate. None of them will want to miss what I have in mind!"

Into town they all came, eagerly anticipating the promised festival. Thousands of them crowded into the temple, packed in like sardines. At Jehu's command, they were all wearing their official priestly robes.

Jehu stood up and addressed the throng: "We don't want any of those wicked servants of the Lord in on this. Look around and make sure this gathering is not polluted." Any servants of the Lord who had accidentally strayed in were identified and turfed out. Once outside, they were amazed to see the whole building surrounded by soldiers, who motioned to them to be silent, not to betray their presence.

"Now let the sacrifice begin!" shouted Jehu. In rushed the troops, who hacked down the Baal worshippers. None escaped. Then they smashed the idols, demolished the building, and torched the ruins. That site was thereafter used as a public latrine so all comers might personally insult its former purpose.

So Jehu had done what the Lord had asked of him. However, he stopped short of destroying the golden calves that Jeroboam had set up years earlier, a failure that dogged his family footsteps for the following several generations.

Hazael lived up to the predictions Elisha had made for him, harassing Israel mercilessly, but Elisha lived just long enough to predict that Jehoash, Jehu's grandson, would one day return the complement by inflicting significant pain on the Arameans.

Elisha died soon after and was buried in a cemetery outside town. Perhaps it was a less dramatic send-off than that of Elijah, but it had its moments. Some men were in the process of burying a friend, but before the body was in the ground, they were interrupted by the unexpected arrival of a raiding party of Moabites. Before they fled for cover, they just had time to hide their friend's corpse, tossing it into Elisha's vault. Imagine their surprise when they later returned to find their friend alive and well, sitting on Elisha's tombstone. Seemed there was yet power in those old bones!

The Lord sent to King Jeroboam II a word of encouragement in the next generation. It was delivered by another most unusual prophet. Jonah had a fascinating story. Seemed that God had sent him to deliver a warning of God's coming wrath to the Assyrian city of Nineveh, but Jonah had been unwilling (or perhaps too fearful) to go. Instead, he had taken a ship bound for Spain at the far end of the Mediterranean. Not long out of port, a violent storm had threatened to sink the ship. In desperation, the sailors had thrown Jonah overboard in an attempt to placate the gods. From there, Jonah's testimony got really strange. Story was that a huge fish had swallowed him, and there in the guts of the monster Jonah had prayed. God must have heard, for Jonah survived the ordeal, and three days later found himself on the beach in a pile of fish vomit. Naturally, when Jonah finally arrived in Nineveh, bleached white by the bile in the fish's belly and telling the most amazing big fish story that anyone had ever heard, it was difficult to ignore his message. The whole city repented.

But Jonah's reaction to their contrition had been a bizarre one from any self-respecting preacher. Instead of being pleased at their change of heart, he had been disappointed that God had forgiven them. Perhaps he could foresee the horrors the Assyrians would soon bring upon Israel.

But whatever the reason, when Jonah arrived in the court of King Jeroboam II with all that in his portfolio, it was not surprising that the king also took him seriously. His words sparked hope in the demoralised king, who proceeded to recapture from the Arameans huge areas of land, restoring much that had been lost over the previous lean years.

It was but a temporary reprieve, and soon things were back on their accustomed downhill track. Unfaithfulness saddened the Lord, and he grieved for their lost love. To address this, he sent another unorthodox prophet, Hosea.

Hosea married Gomer, a woman of questionable morals. Three children were born to the couple, though doubts were expressed over who really had been the father. Each child was given a name guaranteed to bring a blush to his face when called out in class. Names like "Not Loved" or "Not My

People" were unlikely to rival Tom, Dick, or Harry in popularity. But this strange nomenclature was just God's way of communicating to Israel his displeasure with their idolatry.

Inevitably, the marriage came to a sad end, and after a few wild affairs, Gomer was forced to support herself through prostitution. Yet even this was no accident, but God used Gomer's profession as a deliberate rebuke to Israel for her spiritual prostitution and idolatry.

But Hosea's message had a positive ending. Years later, he found Gomer for sale in a slave market, all her beauty gone, a haggard wreck of a woman. He purchased her, brought her home, and lavished his love upon her.

"And so will it be for Israel. You who were once called Not My People will be called My People. And you will not call me Master, as might a slave, but Husband. For I will betroth you to myself in righteousness, love, and compassion. I will betroth you in faithfulness, and you will acknowledge me and no other."

Much as Gomer had been reduced to the slave market, so the grim days of slavery and exile to come were beginning to cast their ominous shadows over Israel. Some sought solace in their religion, a mixed hodgepodge of truths and superstition that offered no more than wishful thinking. Their prophets and priests fanned the flames of the deception, promising peace to the people as they continued their march to perdition.

One prophet stood out in contrast: Amos, a shepherd, and an arborist. He vehemently challenged these deceivers, attacking their arrogant lies and laying bare their falsehood.

"Woe to you who are complacent, secure in your religion. 'I despise your feasts and your burnt offerings,' says the Lord. 'I can't stand your singing and your endless strumming of harps! Instead let justice roll on like a river, righteousness like a never-failing stream!'

"Woe to you who look forward to the day of the Lord as though that would bring you relief from your troubles. Out of the fat, into the fire; flee from the lion, into the bear; safe in the house, bit by a snake."

"Long live the king" was not a chant that carried much credibility for most of the last nine kings of Israel. They were probably no worse than their predecessors, but sadly they were no better. Jeroboam, son of Nebat, may have been credited with being the first to cause Israel to sin two hundred years earlier, but his successors had done their best to perfect those sins ever since. Only because of the Lord's great mercy had he given them slack till this point, but now the rope was all paid out, and the frayed end had come.

During those turbulent years, Israel had made the mistake of antagonizing the Assyrians way up north by attacking one of their cities. The Assyrians demanded compensation.

So the spark that eventually precipitated the end was as simple as Israel's failure to pay their taxes. Like every revenue-collecting agency, the Assyrians took a dim view of this, and before anyone could blink, their army was banging on the door demanding payment.

They started by simply rounding up the unprotected inhabitants of the northern part of Israel and marching them away into exile.

That left the survivors holed up in Samaria, their fortress now their prison. In the confusion, the penultimate King Pekah was assassinated by Hoshea who appropriated what was left of the throne. The siege lasted for three more weary years before the inevitable happened. The remaining Israelis were chained up and marched away to join their fellow countrymen in exile, five hundred miles northeast of home, deportees from the land of promise.

Politics is one way to understand this momentous change of the map, but the underlying reasons were spiritual. The Israelis had sinned against the Lord. Seven hundred and twenty years ago, the Lord had delivered them from slavery in Egypt. He had driven out the previous inhabitants and given the land to Israel as their own home. But it was the pagan gods and customs of that land that had fascinated the Israelis so that they secretly did things against the Lord. They set up sacred stones and Asherah poles, and then burned incense to strange gods. By their wickedness, they provoked the Lord's anger against them. Again and again, he sent prophets to warn of the consequences of such actions, but they would not listen. In following worthless idols, they made themselves worthless. They broke every one of the Lord's commands. They cast gold idols shaped like cows, worshipped the stars, and bowed down to Baal. They sacrificed their own children in the flames of their shameful passions. In fact, they sold themselves to do evil. So the Lord was very angry with them and finally banished them from the land he had promised to give them.

When the last Israeli had vacated the land, the king of Assyria, realising that the land could not be left unpopulated, brought in other peoples from other lands that he had conquered to take their place. This mixed race hodgepodge of newcomers made themselves at home in Samaria and the surrounding towns of what had previously been Israel. They brought with them their own religions and traditions, none of which included the worship of the Lord.

The land was depopulated for some time while this changeover was taking place, giving the wild life the opportunity to multiply. The result was that when the new immigrants arrived, there was a rash of lion attacks. The king of Assyria took this to be the Lord's judgment on them for not respecting the appropriate form of religion for that land. He addressed the problem by sending back one of the Israeli priests he had just deported so he could act as guru to the newcomers, teaching them how to worship the Lord properly. This priest made his base in Bethel.

The immigrants cottoned on slowly to this new Israeli religion, but the problem was that they refused to abandon their old ways. So what emerged was a mosaic of religions. They worshipped the Lord, yes, but they also served their own gods, following the traditions of the nations from which they had been brought. They took over the shrines the Israelis had left behind them, installed their own priests, and practiced their own brand of worship. So the land mourned.

24

The South

The sad saga of the demise of the northern kingdom of Israel, from the rebellion of Jeroboam to the deportation, spanned some two hundred years in all, and half of those years had elapsed since the zealous reign of Jehu, when he had killed both Ahab king of Israel and Ahaziah king of Judah in one terrible day. So to pick up the thread of what was happening in Jerusalem, the story rewinds one hundred years to the day when Judah found themselves with no king.

With Ahaziah dead, the obvious choice for a successor would have been one of the royal princes, sons of the late lamented Ahaziah. But Athaliah, the dowager queen mother, widow of the late and unlamented King Jehoram, had other plans.

Just because there had never previously been a queen on the throne in Jerusalem did not preclude her from setting a new precedent. And what did it matter that she was no descendant of David? She was royalty, a daughter of King Ahab and Queen Jezebel of Israel! So she murdered her grandsons, the royal princes, and usurped the throne as her own. The royal line of David was finally extinct, the promises of God broken; at least that was what she thought.

Unknown to her, a slender thread of David's line remained: a tiny baby boy named Joash. Horrified at the wicked intentions of her aunt Athaliah, Jehosheba, wife of the high priest, had snatched up her infant nephew Joash just moments before the assassins had burst into the room where the royal princes were being kept. She had hidden him in a spare room, then spirited him away to the temple, where his crying was less likely to be detected.

Athaliah had little interest in the temple of the Lord during her reign. She was building a proper temple in honour of Baal, just as her mother Jezebel had done in Samaria. She was confident that the outmoded traditions that perpetuated the worship of the Lord would soon fade out in favour of the much more exciting worship of Baal.

But there in the temple of the Lord, under the watchful eye of Jehoiada the high priest and his wife Jehosheba, baby Joash was growing. His existence was a closely guarded secret. Nobody knew, except Jehoiada and Jehosheba and the child's nurse.

Then in the seventh year, Jehoiada invited the captains of the guard and the leading priests and Levites to meet with him in the temple. When they were all there, Jehoiada closed the door. He reminded them of the promises of God about the royal line of David, and the traditions that had been maintained since David died 140 years previously. When he was satisfied that they all shared a common grief that the old days were dead and gone, he took the ultimate risk: "What if I told you that there is a son of David who still lives?" There were gasps.

"Where is this man?" someone asked.

"Ah, that's the question, but before I could reveal the answer, you would have to swear fealty to him in absentia." They each swore an oath, still not knowing about whom they were talking, but longing for the truth of what Jehoiada was telling them.

"Wait just a moment," Jehoiada said, and then he called the child. In came a seven-year-old with the ruddy good looks of the house of David. Those hardened soldiers and holy men gasped and then got to their knees, tears on their cheeks.

"Now here's the plan ..." No one was to know about the king before the given date. The coup would take place on the Sabbath at the changing of the guard. Those taking over the guard would take their normal stations so as not to arouse suspicion, while those going off duty would come straight to the temple, instead of going home. They were to become the personal bodyguard of the king. Any suspicious intruder approaching him was to be killed immediately.

"But those going off duty will be required to leave their weapons at the armoury, so they will all be unarmed," someone pointed out.

"You are forgetting the ancient weapons that King David himself left that have been preserved here in the temple to this day. Remember, your priority is the king. Stay close to him wherever he goes."

No one knew of the plan except those who had been in the room when Jehoiada had revealed the lad. So on the agreed day, the off-duty soldiers were directed to go to the temple as soon as their shift had ended. Mystified, they were handed antique weapons and then stationed around the temple. Then a child was brought out and escorted up onto the royal dais. To the amazement of the soldiers, their captains called them to present arms to the boy. The high priest then put a crown on his head, placed a copy of the law into his hand, and anointed him with oil. "Long live the king!" he said. Then gradually, as it dawned on the assembly what was happening, the applause started. "Long live the king! Long live the king!" they roared, and jubilant pandemonium broke out.

Attracted by the commotion, Athaliah went to investigate. As she entered the temple, there was a child, standing on a platform, wearing a crown, and flanked by officers of the guard. All the people were clapping him and cheering. Athaliah tore her robe and shouted, "Treason! Treason! Guards?" The guards came to her side all right, but not to her aid – rather to arrest her. They led her out of the temple and into the horse guards' entrance to the palace, where they executed her swiftly before she could cause any more trouble.

The coronation continued in the temple as people gathered from all over the city. Jehoiada led them in making a solemn covenant to serve the king and to be faithful to the Lord. When the service was finished, the crowd surged to Athaliah's temple of Baal. They stoned the priests, smashed the altars, and demolished the building. While that was happening, Jehoiada and the soldiers escorted the king to the palace, where he took his place on the royal throne. There was rejoicing throughout the land. Finally, they had a true king, albeit a very little one.

Jehoiada stayed at Joash's side during the early days of his reign, advising him in all matters of state and the traditions of the law. Consequently, he did what was right before the Lord. Having spent his first seven years hidden in the temple, he was naturally concerned for its state of repair. The buildings were now well over a hundred years old and needed some TLC. So the first thing on young King Joash's regal agenda was the renovation of the temple.

But after the death of Jehoiada, things went pear-shaped. The people abandoned the Lord in favour of idols, King Joash with them.

Finally, it was Jehoiada's own son, Zechariah, who dared to confront Joash in the main temple court. "Why do you so wilfully disobey the Lord's commands? You have forsaken the Lord, so he now forsakes you."

King Joash was furious, and in his rage he forgot the kindness that Jehoiada had shown him right there in the temple while he was a child. "Stone him!" he yelled, and they did. As Zechariah lay dying in the dust of the temple court, he breathed, "May the Lord call you to account for this."

And sure enough he did, for the very next year, King Hazael of Damascus led the Arameans in a daring raid right into Jerusalem. Joash was severely wounded, surviving only long enough to be assassinated in his bed by some of his officials who could not forgive him for the wrong he had done to Zechariah.

Amaziah, his son, inherited his father's throne with a chip on his shoulder. First, he executed his father's assassins. Then he attacked the Edomites, driving them to a cruel death over a cliff top. Finally, he picked a fight with Israel. It started, as is often the case, with insults.

"A weed once demanded the daughter of a mighty cedar tree in marriage, that is, till a cow came along and stomped the weed into the mud! And just who do you think you are to make demands on us?"

In the battle that followed, the Israeli troops stomped Judah into the mud and then went on a rampage right into Jerusalem, looting the temple and the royal palace.

Amaziah survived the battle and lived for another fifteen years before being assassinated. Assassination, it would appear, was the preferred death of kings in those days.

His son, Uzziah, was just a youth of sixteen years when he came to the throne. He benefited from wise and godly counsel in his early years, a foundation that set his feet on the right paths. So he started out well, and his exploits against the Philistines, Arabs, and Meunites were so successful that they brought in huge revenues. Uzziah loved towers and built a forest of them in Jerusalem and the surrounding country. And if he wasn't putting up towers, he was digging holes: cisterns to provide water for his livestock. He loved the soil and delighted in turning the hills and valleys into lush pasture and vineyards.

He maintained a well-trained and fully equipped army of over three hundred thousand men. His artillery was creative, with trebuchets capable of hurling large boulders.

Yes, he was successful, but when he became powerful, it went to his head. Pride was his downfall. What had started out so well was in danger of being derailed. But God has a way of getting man's attention, and it was around this time something happened, guaranteed to get that of Uzziah. A devastating plague of locusts stripped the land bare, leaving his beloved pastures and vineyards like a desert.

The prophet Joel turned the disaster into words: "Despair, you farmers. Wail, you vine-growers. Grieve for the grain fields, because the harvest is destroyed and the joy of mankind is withered away." Joel warned of a coming day when an enemy army would advance on the land to devastate it, as had the locusts.

"'Return to me wholeheartedly,' says the Lord. Tear your heart and not your clothes. Turn back to the Lord your God, for he is gracious and compassionate, slow get angry and overflowing with love."

Joel went on to promise a day when the Lord would repay them for the years that the locusts had eaten. Even the dried-up formalism of temple worship would spring to fresh life. "I will pour out my Spirit on everyone. Your children will prophesy, your seniors will dream dreams, your young adults will see visions. And everyone who calls on the name of the Lord will be saved."

But despite natural disasters and eloquent speeches, Uzziah's personal vanity still clouded his judgment. Perhaps he felt that kings had a divine right to do anything they pleased, so one day he marched into the temple and approached the altar to burn incense, the exclusive preserve of the priests.

The priests courageously confronted the king: "It is not permitted for you to burn incense, King Uzziah. Leave the sanctuary, or you will be dishonoured by the Lord."

Uzziah was furious, and as he stood there in front of the altar, censor in hand, he raged at the stupid priests who dared to defy him. The look of horror that spread over their faces stopped him dead. Then he felt it himself: leprosy spreading over his face. They hustled him out, finding no resistance now, for he was as eager to be gone as they were to eject him.

From that day on, Uzziah never entered the temple again, or any other public building, come to that, for he was an unclean leper, living out his days in isolation. The affairs of the kingdom were handled by his son Jotham, who acted as the king's surrogate till Uzziah's death.

During the same year that King Uzziah died, a young man named Isaiah had a vision of God, sitting on an exalted throne with a long train that coiled down into the temple. He was attended by winged seraphs, who were singing his praise. At the sound of their worship, the temple was filled with smoke and shaken as by an earthquake.

Isaiah was overcome with a crushing sense of unworthiness. "Woe is me!" he cried out.

One of the seraphs immediately flew to him with a glowing ember he had taken from the altar. With this, he touched Isaiah's lips: "Now your sin is gone and your guilt is taken."

That was the beginning of decades of prophetic ministry. Isaiah would become one of the great writers of his day, in vivid verse penetrating the thoughts and intentions of the hearts of the people, challenging injustice and promising hope during the reigns of four successive generations of kings. He would predict the rise and fall of Judah's enemies as well as the coming horrors that would result from Judah's own unfaithfulness. But he would always temper his more negative predictions with dazzling words of hope and encouragement.

He would write of one who would come as a herald, a voice calling out in the desert, verbally building a super highway through a rugged land for the coming of a great king. This king would be called by many names: Wonderful, Counsellor, Mighty God, Everlasting Father, Prince of Peace, and he would reign on David's throne, establishing and upholding justice and righteousness forever.

In apparent contrast, Isaiah would also foretell of one who would be an outcast from society, a reject, a man of great sorrow who would become hideously disfigured by what others would do to him. Some might see this as divine retribution, God giving him his just desserts. But in truth, Isaiah revealed, he would be like a sacrificial lamb, taking upon himself the guilt of others and giving back to them peace and healing. In some amazing way, God would lay on his shoulders the sin of all mankind. But when all that was accomplished, he would live once more.

Isaiah would foresee a day when the doors of the temple would be thrown wide open, not only to Jews, but to people from all over the world, who would come to worship God and rest in his international house of prayer. And even beyond that, he would see a distant day when God would create a whole new heaven and earth in which all would live in harmony. "The wolf will live alongside the lamb, and the leopard and the goat will share a bed. A little child will walk around with a lion on a leash like a pet dog, and a toddler will crawl around with snakes for playmates. They will neither harm nor destroy, for the whole earth will be full of the knowledge of the Lord as water fills the sea."

Living not far from Isaiah's home was a kindred spirit, a fellow prophet named Micah. His predictions of the future resonated with those of Isaiah. "In the last days, the mountain of the Lord's temple will be raised up to a position of prominence. People will stream to it from all over the world. 'Come on!' they'll say. 'Let's go up to the Lord's mountain so he can teach us his ways.' Jerusalem will become a place where disputes can be settled and peace can be negotiated. As a result, nations will redirect their industries from making implements of war to manufacturing farm machinery. In fact, war will be abolished altogether, and people will live out their days in peace and tranquillity, sitting outside their own homes in the shade of their vines and fig trees."

Micah didn't have a good word to say about most of his fellow prophets. They were a corrupt bunch, motivated by money more than inspired by the word of God, saying only what their hearers wanted to hear. "'I will prophesy for you plenty of wine and beer,'" he mimicked. "Yes, a prophet who prophesies such delights would be certain to draw a crowd. A prophesy of coming peace will be guaranteed by a good honorarium, but watch out if you're stingy! Judges take bribes. Preachers expect honoraria. Prophets charge fees. And then they insist that it was the Lord who had sent them!"

Like Isaiah, Micah foretold the birth of a coming king: "From you, Bethlehem in the land of Judah, will come one who will rule Israel. Then she who is in labour will give birth to he who is from ancient times."

With Uzziah gone, Jotham now became king in his own right. And a fine job he did too, just as his father had done at first, but in Jotham's case, he stayed the course. Like his dad, he loved to build towers and did much to fortify many of the towns in the Judean hills. He subjugated the Ammonites to the east of the Jordan and exacted tribute from them. He was powerful precisely because he continued to walk steadfastly before the Lord his God. But alas, after only sixteen years, he died and was succeeded by his son Ahaz.

Ahaz, however, was not a success. Just twenty when he took over the throne of Judah, he ruled for sixteen miserable years. It was not the godly traditions of his family that he followed, but the pagan ones of the kings of Israel. He cast idols for Baal worship and multiplied pagan practices on hilltops and at street intersections. He even went so far as to offer his own son as a burnt offering. He stripped the temple of many of the valuable furnishings that King Solomon had provided, then shut and locked the doors, directing that in future worship should be carried out wherever.

The Lord was not pleased, and the people longed for the good old days. So, when Ahaz died, no one mourned his passing. They declined to give his corpse a space in the royal tomb. Hezekiah, his son, replaced him as king.

As spring follows winter, so was Hezekiah after Ahaz. Within days of assuming the throne, he went to the temple and flung wide the doors. He called an assembly of the priests and Levites. "You are the Lord's chosen ministers, and there is much work to be done. Now let's get this show back on the road!"

And they did, with a will. They rounded up all their lost brothers and set to work to give the temple a scrub from top to bottom. They dumped all the pagan garbage in the Kidron Valley and burned it. Then they retrieved all the temple utensils that Ahaz had removed and sanitised them. In just over a couple of weeks, they were ready for visitors.

The first to be invited in were the city fathers. They, together with the priests and Levites, were party to a rededication ceremony, during which many animals were sacrificed.

In the big clean-up, they found some ancient musical instruments that had been stored since the days of King David. Joy bubbled over as the long silence was broken and Levites began to make music on these special instruments, with the priests adding some volume with their trumpets. They even got some of the old hymnbooks out so the people could sing the favourites of yesteryear, composed by David and his contemporaries. The days of Ahaz were now behind them, and the future was full of hope.

In the course of their reading of the law, they were reminded of the Passover, the feast that celebrated the deliverance from Egypt of their forefathers, back in the days of Moses. "We should do that now," someone suggested.

"Should have been last month," corrected an orthodox.

"Better late than never," was the conclusion, and since the Passover had not been celebrated since the days of Solomon, what difference would a month make, either way?

Invitations and proclamations were sent out to all Judah, and they even sent some to the people in Israel. At that time, Israel was yet to go into exile. "People of Israel," they wrote, "come back to the Lord, the God of Abraham, Isaac, and Israel, that he may return to you. Come and join us in the temple, which he has consecrated forever. If you return to the Lord, he will be gracious and compassionate to you." If only they had listened!

In many towns in Israel, the invitations were torn up in derision, but some came, particularly from the northern tribes of Asher, Manasseh, and

Zebulun. But in Judah, the people were unanimous in their enthusiasm to be about the Lord's business.

So the Passover festival was an unparalleled success and was held over for a further week. As the worshippers eventually dispersed to their own homes, they carried with them the commitment they had experienced at the festival. Wherever they went, they smashed the pagan altars and symbols and hacked down the Asherah poles.

In the course of his purge, Hezekiah came across the bronze snake that Moses had originally set up in the wilderness so that when people were snake bitten, they had but to look at the snake to be healed. But valuable though this symbol had been at the time, it had now become a distraction, an idol to which the people had burned incense. "Nehushtan" they called it. Precious though this artefact was, Hezekiah had it smashed to pieces. Nothing would be permitted to distract the people from loving the Lord only.

To maintain the temple and all this worship would cost money, and salaries would be the biggest budget item. Moses had legislated that the priests and Levites should be supported by the tithes of the other tribes to enable them to concentrate their full-time efforts on the Lord's business. In recent years, this practice had been neglected, so Hezekiah insisted that this be restored. He set the example himself for others to follow by bringing his own tithe to the temple. Soon everyone was doing it, and the impact on temple life was spectacular. Provisions abounded, and generosity was a thing of beauty. Whole Levite families that had wandered off into a variety of secular pursuits were drawn back into the ministry.

So Hezekiah had made a great beginning to his reign, making God his priority and getting worship back at the heart of the nation. The upshot of this was success in whatever else he undertook.

But all around him, his neighbours were suffering. The Philistines to the west had fallen victim to the Assyrians. Then one terrible day, news reached Jerusalem that Samaria had finally surrendered. Their brother Israelis were being led away for deportation to far-off lands in the north.

And now the Assyrian threat was right on Hezekiah's own doorstep, just thirty-five miles southwest of Jerusalem. Initially, Hezekiah tried money, stripping the gold from the temple in an attempt to buy off the enemy. But this offering only served to whet the Assyrian appetite.

Jerusalem was in a panic, refugees were flooding into the city, and fear was palpable. Hezekiah took immediate and urgent action. Water was their most important resource, so he did what he could to divert the flow so that the attacking force would be deprived, while the citizens of Jerusalem would be adequately supplied. For some time, his engineers had been digging a tunnel deep in the ground so that an abundant source of water could be channelled right into the city. In the present circumstances, he was glad he had had the foresight to commence this project. He reinforced the walls of the city and ensured that all weapons were cleaned and sharpened.

Then he called out all the military officers to parade before him in the city square, where he addressed them: "Set an example by showing no fear. He who is for us is infinitely more powerful than this vast army of Assyrians. They have but human resources on their side, but we have the Lord to fight our battles." Everyone cheered loudly.

A day or so later, the Assyrian army arrived at the very walls of Jerusalem and demanded to speak to the king. King Sennacherib of Assyria declined to come himself but sent a spokesman, so protocol demanded that Hezekiah also be represented. He sent his administrator, personal secretary, and the city recorder.

The Assyrian spokesman had obviously been chosen for his loud clear voice, for he delivered the message to the three-man delegation in a voice loud enough that the throng on the city walls could clearly hear what he said, "Citizens of Jerusalem, why are you so foolish as to trust the feeble protection of the walls of your city? 'The Lord will protect us!' Is that what Hezekiah is telling you? Hunger, thirst, and a slow lingering death are all you have to look forward to. Haven't you heard what we Assyrians have been doing all over the world? Has any other nation been able to withstand us? Were any of their gods strong enough to protect them? So what chance that your god can do any better? Don't believe a word Hezekiah tells you.

"And you can tell Hezekiah that this is what the Great King of Assyria has to say: 'Don't imagine that anyone is coming to your rescue. You are all alone. And do you suppose that you are the only one who has a direct line to heaven? It was the Lord himself who told me to march against this land and destroy it!'"

Not wanting the crowd on the city wall to understand what was being said, Hezekiah's administrator called back in Aramaic, the lingua franca by which many people communicated in those days. "Please don't speak to us in Hebrew. We understand Aramaic and would rather this conversation were kept confidential."

"Not at all," shouted back the Assyrian in Hebrew. "This is no private message for the king's ears alone, but for all the people of this city who will soon be reduced to eating their own excrement and drinking their own urine. Now listen up, all you people! Surrender, and I can promise that you will all live out your days in peace. I will take you to a better land and settle you in your own farms and homesteads on good productive land. Haven't you heard what happened up the road in Samaria? They are all now happily settled in a new and better place. So choose to live, not to die!" The crowd remained silent and said not a word in response.

When he had finished his speech, the Assyrian handed the administrator a letter, expressing much of what he had just been saying, but in writing. Hezekiah was distressed when he read the letter. He told the three-man delegation to go and tell Isaiah the prophet what had happened. "Tell him to pray!"

Meanwhile, Hezekiah went into the temple. He spread out the letter before the Lord and read it to him. "The worst of it is," he concluded, "that much of what this letter claims is true. These fellows have conquered many cities and have burned their so-called gods. But should they be permitted to insult you, the living God, and get away with it? Deliver us, oh Lord, so that it will be known all over the world that you alone are God."

Isaiah sent an encouraging message to Hezekiah: "This is what the Lord has to say to you: 'I have heard your prayer. There is no need to be afraid of Sennacherib's blasphemous words. He won't be able to enter this city, or even so much as to shoot an arrow over the walls. I myself will defend you, and Sennacherib is soon going to limp back to his own land, where he will be cut down.'"

Next day, Sennacherib sounded reveille to rouse his troops, but not a man stirred. When he checked their tents, they were all dead men, officers and soldiers alike – 185,000 corpses. There was nothing for it but to take the long road back home to his native Nineveh, every step mired in disgrace. First thing he did when he got home was to go and have a talk with his god in his temple. But while he was praying, his sons snuck up behind him and killed him.

Some time later, Hezekiah fell sick. The prophet Isaiah paid him a visit, but his bedside manner left a little to be desired. "The Lord says that you should put your house in order, because you are going to die."

As soon as the prophet left the room, Hezekiah burst into tears. Choking through his grief he prayed. "Lord, I have sought to serve you faithfully. Please don't forget me."

Isaiah had not even left the building before the Lord turned him around and sent him back. "The Lord has heard your prayer and seen your tears. He now promises to heal you. He will give you fifteen more years."

One might have imagined that Hezekiah would accept this reversal with unquestioning gratitude, but not so. "What sign will you give to assure me that what you promise is true?" he asked suspiciously.

Far from taking offense, Isaiah enquired, "Well, would you like the shadow of the sun to jump forward ten treads on that stair way over there, or to go back ten?"

"Well, ten treads back would be more convincing." And so it happened.

Isaiah prescribed a poultice of figs to be applied to Hezekiah's pernicious boil. That seemed to do the trick, and three days later, Hezekiah was once again up an about.

But something about having cheated death made Hezekiah arrogant. His royal success was outstanding, for by now he was a very rich man and had built huge storehouses to keep his resources and barns for his animals. So when ambassadors came to town representing the king of far-off Babylon, enquiring after his health, Hezekiah was flattered. He showed them everything he had: his palace, storehouses, treasures. They saw it all.

When they had gone, Isaiah called in on the king: "Where did those ambassadors come from?"

"Oh, they came from a very distant country. From Babylon, actually."

"And what did you show them in your palace?"

"Everything. I have no secrets."

"Well, this is what the Lord has to say: 'The day will come when all you have shown off will be carried away to Babylon, along with some of your own descendants.'"

"That's fine," conceded Hezekiah, but secretly he thought, *Not in my lifetime, at least,* smug in the assurance that he had another fifteen years to look forward to.

But alas, it was during those fifteen years that a terrible legacy was hatched, to be foisted on the next generation: a son named Manasseh. The promised fifteen years dwindled and eventually ran out. Hezekiah was given a royal send-off by the grateful citizens of Jerusalem. But their gratitude quickly wore thin when the young Manasseh took over the reins of power.

Manasseh was but a child of twelve years when he was made king, and such power inherited by one so young must have turned his head, for he set to work with a will to undo all the good accomplished by his late father. He rebuilt the pagan shrines on the very foundations of those so recently destroyed. He copied the evil deeds of King Ahab of Israel by building altars to Baal and chiselling Asherah poles. He worshipped the stars and practiced sorcery. He sought his wisdom from psychics and mediums. He even went so far as to burn his own son as a sacrifice. Violence was the norm, and the streets ran red with the blood of the innocents. Perhaps the greatest insult that he paid to the Lord was by carrying on these evil practices in the Lord's own temple. It was precisely because the previous inhabitants of the land had so flouted the laws of the Lord that they had been dispossessed. Now here was Judah doing exactly the same things, only worse. The Lord therefore sent his prophet to warn Manasseh of the jeopardy in which he was placing his people: "I am going to bring such disaster on Jerusalem that the ears of all who hear of it will tingle. I will wipe Jerusalem clean like a dishrag to a dirty plate."

The dishrag turned out to be the army of the Assyrians, back for a second attempt. They besieged Jerusalem, taking prisoners, including King Manasseh. Bronze shackles were clamped to his wrists and ankles, and a cruel ring was punched into his nose. He was ignominiously dragged hundreds of miles to Babylon. Gone now were his lofty and rebellious notions of paganism. In his misery, he cried out to the God he had insulted, begging him for mercy.

And mercy is what he got, for not long after, he was released and found himself back in Jerusalem, sitting on his old throne. But now things were different, very different. Now he knew who God was and went about undoing all the mess he had made in his arrogant youth. He threw out all his pagan altars and restored the true altar of the Lord, offering sacrifices of gratitude to the one who had shown himself faithful and merciful. But the same could not be said for his subjects, who, having started down the road to perdition, were not easily turned.

After fifty-five turbulent years, Manasseh died and was buried, not in the kings' cemetery but rather in his own palace garden.

Amon, his son, was a chip off the old block, except that he never mended his ways or humbled himself before the Lord. The only good thing that could be said of his period in office was that it didn't last long. After just two years, his officials ran out of patience and assassinated him.

Josiah was next in line, and he was just eight years old when they crowned him. Right from his earliest days, Josiah had a yearning to know the true God and began to actively seek him. Instinctively, he started in his teens to demolish some of the pagan shrines around Jerusalem and to hack down the Asherah poles that littered the landscape.

When he was twenty-five, he gave orders for a major restoration of the temple. While this was being undertaken, they came across an old scroll that looked as if it might be important. So they took it to the king.

"Well, read it to me, would you," he ordered.

They did.

"So no wonder the Lord has been angry with us," the king said, tearing his robe in horror. "We have been flagrantly disobeying the words written in this book."

With urgency, Josiah called a general assembly in the temple of all the people of the land: priests, prophets, and laymen. There he stood on his royal platform, and in a clear voice that all could hear, he read the words of the scroll. When he had finished, he led the people in a prayer of repentance, and they all swore an agreement to keep God's commands in future.

Then began a national purge, the like of which had not been seen for generations. All the pagan junk was dumped in the Kidron Valley and burned. The pagan priests all over the land were done away with, together with the shrine prostitutes, the mediums, and the spiritualists.

Many of the remnants of Israel simply wandered back to find shelter under the wing of Judah and were present at the renewal of the covenant in the temple, even donating toward the restoration project. With no Israeli king to oppose him, Josiah was now able to clean house far and wide, including the former Israeli territory. Somewhere near Bethel, he came upon an ancient altar that, despite being split, had survived for three centuries. Records showed it to be the same altar where Jeroboam had "caused Israel to sin," where he had cast his gold cows and pronounced them to be gods. That single act of defiance had set a precedent of idolatry that had led Israelis to anger the Lord for centuries. It had been to that altar that a prophet from Judah had prophesied: "This is God's word to this altar. The day will come when a descendant of David named Josiah will burn the bones of your self-appointed priests on this altar. And today this altar shall split asunder."

Josiah finished off the good work that the original split had started. He ground the altar to dust. Here he was, King Josiah turning prophesy into history. He slaughtered the pagan priests and burned their bodies where the altar had stood.

When the purge was completed to Josiah's satisfaction, the priests organised a celebration of the Passover on a grand scale. There was music and dancing and feasting, but care was taken to do everything according to the book.

Sadly, Josiah was still a relatively young man in his late thirties when he died in Megiddo, fighting a pointless battle against Pharaoh, king of Egypt, in a vain attempt to assert his sovereignty. His body was carried back to be buried with full honours in the royal tomb in Jerusalem.

So that left the Egyptians as controllers of Judah. Pharaoh took a dim view of Judah's choice of Jehoahaz, Josiah's son, as a successor to his father's throne. Pharaoh had him arrested and taken off to Egypt, where he finished his life in chains. Pharaoh replaced him with his brother Jehoiakim, a puppet king, willing to comply with the demands of Judah's new masters.

Judah was in limbo, threatened by the Assyrians, who had already taken her sister Israel into exile, and now defeated by the Egyptians: virtual slaves in their own land, groaning under the burden of punitive taxation.

25

The Prognosis

As a mackerel sky is often the harbinger of a change in the weather, so a pattern of outspoken prophets spoke of changes just over the political horizon.

Habakkuk was grieved over the injustices inflicted on both Israel and Judah by the Assyrians and now by Egypt, so he begged the Lord to intervene. "How long, oh Lord, must I call for help, but you don't seem to listen? Why do you tolerate wrong? Why do you remain silent while the wicked take advantage of those more righteous than themselves? Lord, I have heard about your fame, and I stand in awe of your deeds in years gone by. Oh Lord, renew them in our day."

And God gave him a reply: "I am going to do something in the near future that you will find hard to believe. I am going to raise up the Babylonians, a ruthless and impetuous people, who will sweep across the earth."

The threat of storm clouds on the horizon did little to ruffle Habakkuk's own composure, for he had complete confidence in the kindness of God. "Even though the fig tree should fail to bud and no grapes grow on the vines, though the olive crop fails and the fields produce no harvest, though no sheep be found in the pens or cattle in the stalls, yet I will rejoice in the Lord and will be filled with joy because of God my Saviour. For the Lord is my strength, and one day the earth will be filled with the knowledge of the glory of the Lord as water fills the ocean."

Zephaniah, a blue-blooded prophet of royal descent, also saw the coming demise of the Assyrians, as did Nahum, a poet who vividly painted a picture of the downfall of Assyria in verse:

"The crack of the whips,
and the clatter of wheels.
The galloping horses
and jolting of chariots!
The flashing of swords
and the glittering spears!
The piles of dead,
and streets clogged with corpses."

Jeremiah never wanted to be a prophet. When first called to this ministry, he insisted that he was far too young. "Don't say that," the Lord told him. "I have touched your mouth with the words that I will give you. No fear!" That had been back in the days of King Josiah, when Jeremiah had still held out hopes that Josiah's reforms might prove to be the salvation of the nation. He had even seen visions of spring blossoms and baskets of fruit that he used as illustrations to his optimism for the future. But then Josiah had been killed, and Jeremiah became deeply disappointed.

In his chagrin, he wrote a message to Pharaoh Neco, king of Egypt: "Prepare for battle. Polish your spears. Put on your armour. Yes! But what do I see? Terror and defeat! Men fleeing without a backward glance. There in the north by the Euphrates River, you will fall."

And there he did fall at the hand of King Nebuchadnezzar of Babylon. There on the banks of the Euphrates River, near the city of Carchemish, a battle of the titans was joined. Superpowers were toppled and others arose. Assyria was all but obliterated from the political landscape, and Egypt limped home in ignominy. Babylon was now supreme and assumed dominion of all vassals previously controlled by Egypt and Assyria.

On his way home from the battle, Nebuchadnezzar paid King Jehoiakim a visit in Jerusalem, to make it clear to what address taxes were to be sent in future. Jehoiakim wanted to keep his job, so he swore to be Nebuchadnezzar's faithful vassal. The agreement was made, but Nebuchadnezzar took hostages – members of the royal family and a few bright young men of the nobility – just to keep Jehoiakim honest. Amongst the hostages was a young man named Daniel, with his three buddies Shadrach, Meshach and Abednego.

The following years were tough for those who remained in Jerusalem. Heavy taxes and the endless incursions of the Arameans, Moabites and Amorites who set out to profit by the political confusion.

Jeremiah's message of "I told you so!" did little to improve the mood in Jerusalem. So volatile were his words that his movements were restricted. Access to the temple was denied him, so delivering the messages God gave became increasingly difficult. But sometimes necessity proves to be the mother of invention, and Jeremiah, with the help of his secretary Baruch, set about committing to paper the message that had been burning in his heart for the past twenty odd years. It took months to accomplish, but when it was all finished, Jeremiah commissioned Baruch to take his precious scroll to the temple so he could read it out loud on a feast day when people from all over the nation would be in town. In a clear voice and from an elevated vantage point, the words of God through Jeremiah were proclaimed for all to hear.

When he was done, Baruch was alarmed to find himself summoned to the palace to meet with some of the chief men of the land. But when he was shown into the room where they were meeting they quickly put him at ease. "Sit down, please. We want to hear what you have been reading to the people." So Baruch went through it all once again.

When he had finished: "How did you come to write all this? Was it Jeremiah who dictated it to you?" Clearly they were seriously challenged by what they had heard.

"I think the king should hear this," they all agreed. "But you and Jeremiah might be smart to make your selves scarce. Who knows how the king will react."

King Jehoiakim was trying to keep himself warm from the December cold with the aid of a brazier when the scroll was brought in. The reading commenced, but when a few paragraphs had been read, the king called a halt. He produced his pocketknife and cut off the section from the scroll he had just heard, contemptuously tossing it into the fire. "Carry on!" he ordered.

And so it continued with the king systematically incinerating it, section by section. Not a flicker of remorse, not a whiff of repentance.

But God's word cannot be dismissed that easily. So Jeremiah and Baruch went back to work and rewrote the whole scroll, with a few pithy additions.

Jehoiakim's life didn't last much longer than it took to complete the scroll, and he was succeeded by his eighteen-year-old son, Jehoiachin. During his brief reign, he did nothing to break the pattern of evil established by his father and uncle before him. He must have had a shrewd idea of what was coming his way, for when Nebuchadnezzar marched up to the walls of Jerusalem, Jehoiachin surrendered without a shot being fired. The Babylonians stripped the temple and the royal palace of anything of value. They rounded up the best educated people – the nobles, craftsmen, fighting men, and even a priest named Ezekiel – and marched them all off to Babylon, leaving Jerusalem populated only with second class citizens. Someone had to be left in charge, so Nebuchadnezzar appointed Jehoiachin's uncle Zedekiah as king.

Jehoiachin was taken to Babylon where he would spend the next thirty-seven miserable years in prison.

The priest Ezekiel, however, enjoyed a measure of freedom in his new home among his fellow exiles in Babylon. To all of their relief, they found themselves to be treated more as colonists than slaves, and were settled just outside the city of Babylon in a community situated by the Kebar River. It took Ezekiel a while to adjust to his surroundings, but five years after arriving a dramatic event changed everything.

At first he thought it was the approach of a tornado, but as it grew closer he saw that at its centre was brilliant light. In it he made out the forms of four creatures with four faces like those of lion, cow, eagle and man, riding on what appeared to be a chariot with four wheels each with a wheel intersecting itself. Above it hovered a sapphire throne, but it was the one who sat upon the throne that held Ezekiel's attention. After the vision was over he would be at a loss for words to describe him. It was as though human language was inadequate to express the wonder. He had the likeness of a man, but infinitely more wonderful. His body had a radiance like that of fire but much brighter. He was surrounded with dazzling light with all the colours of the rainbow. Next thing he knew he was face down in awe.

Then a voice spoke to him and a hand raised him to his feet. "Son of man, I am sending you to the Israelites, to an obstinate and rebellious people. But you must not fear them."

He held out to Ezekiel a scroll. "Take this and eat it. Now you can speak my words to the people. You are as a watchman to Israel, warning them of coming danger."

Ezekiel was indeed to be a watchman, sending devastating messages to those who remained in Jerusalem, and the surrounding nations. Though absent from the scene, he saw clearly what those with physical eyes perhaps failed to see. He saw the secret idolatry in the temple, hidden away in the hearts of the worshippers. He berated the prophets for their false words, promising peace when there was no peace and declaring: "Thus saith the Lord!" when the Lord had said no such thing.

He described Israel as a young woman on whom the Lord had at first lavished his loving attention, but who later had turned her back and behaved as a degraded prostitute.

His most vivid communication was an acted parable depicting the coming siege of Jerusalem. He created a scale model of the city, then mounted siege works around it. For over a year he lay silently beside his model, nearly starving himself to death as he demonstrated the horrors to come for those who would remain in the city.

Perhaps the most costly message he sent involved the death of his own dear wife whose passing he was not permitted to mourn. If God would permit the death of Ezekiel's wife with no tears, then who would weep for Jerusalem?

Meanwhile, back in Jerusalem things were not good. At his coronation Zedekiah had sworn to obey the Lord, but once Nebuchadnezzar was safely over the horizon, Zedekiah reverted to type. Evil was the fashion and evil was what Zedekiah was good at and evil was what he did.

During those years Jeremiah maintained a powerful presence in Jerusalem. He was an eloquent communicator who employed visual aids to speak into the times. He used a clay pot that was spoiled in the hands of the potter as a picture of the nation spoiled under the hands of the Creator. Then he shattered a completed pot to illustrate the violent end towards which Judah was headed. He carried on his shoulders an animal yoke to symbolise the slavery that awaited the unrepentant citizens.

"Listen up, people! This is what God says to you. 'I am going to bring on this city every disaster of which I warned them, because they are stubborn and will not listen to my words.'"

Pashhur, chief of police, interpreted Jeremiah's words as bad for morale at best, treason at worst. He had Jeremiah arrested, flogged and put in the stocks over night. But in the morning Jeremiah was unrepentant and had changed his message not a whit. In fact he made his message personal. "Yes, the Lord will surely hand over all who live in this city to the king of Babylon, and you, Pashhur, and all who live in your house, will be among the first to go."

Jeremiah did not enjoy his job. Clearly it was not designed to win him popularity. He suffered from periodic bouts of deep depression. "Lord you have deceived me and I was deceived!" he moaned. "Delivering your words brings me nothing but insults and reproach. Yet what can I do? I am incapable of holding back the things you give me to say. Your words are like a fire shut up in my bones that must out."

Was he suicidal? He certainly cursed the day of his birth. He would later write a whole book that because of its mournful content would be known as 'Lamentations'. Yes, being a prophet was no laughing matter.

King Zedekiah maintained a love hate relationship with Jeremiah. He paid scant attention to his prophecies, yet when in trouble he would contact the man of God: "Please pray for us."

Many were suspicious of Jeremiah's motives. "Whoever stays in the city will die, but whoever surrenders to the Babylonians will live," he would say.

"Just whose side are you on?" people would ask.

One day while heading out of town, Jeremiah was accosted by a captain of the guard. "Where do you think you are going?"

"I am off to inspect a parcel of land I have recently purchased."

"Is this some kind of a joke? No one is buying property these days. Haven't you heard? Babylon is about to invade!"

"But God told me to buy it, and the day will surely come when the property market will once again rebound."

"Well I don't believe a word of it. You are deserting and leaving the city to join the enemy."

"No, I am not deserting."

But no one believed him. He was arrested, beaten and thrown in jail. And there he stayed for a long time.

Eventually it was King Zedekiah who had him released. "Have you heard anything from the Lord?" Zedekiah asked anxiously.

"As a matter of fact, yes I have. You are going to be handed over to the king of Babylon." He could hardly expect a favour after delivering such a message, but Jeremiah was desperate. "But please don't send me back to jail. I will die there."

Zedekiah was merciful and instead of jail, Jeremiah was confined to barracks.

But Jeremiah's opponents judged such treatment to be much too lenient. "This man should be executed," they insisted. "His negative prophecies are discouraging the soldiers and all the people."

"Have your own way," relented the king. So they took Jeremiah and threw him into a filthy cistern right there in the parade ground of the barracks. The water was all gone. Putrefying mud was all that remained and Jeremiah sank up to his waist, choking in the stench. And there he might well have died had it not been for the intervention of Ebed-melech, an African who served in the royal court. He begged the mercy of the king, then pulled Jeremiah up with ropes, thoughtfully providing rags to protect his arms from rope burn. Confinement to barracks felt like freedom after that.

Once again the king summoned him. "I want you to give me a straight answer."

"But won't you kill me if I do? And if I give you good advice, you won't act on it, will you?"

"I swear as the Lord lives that I will neither harm you, nor hand you over to those who would."

"Very well. Here is what the Lord says. If you surrender to the king of

Babylon, you and your family will live, and the city will not be destroyed. But if you refuse, the city will burn and you will not escape."

"It's not as easy as that. I fear what my fellow Jews may do to me if I surrender."

"Obey the Lord and they won't touch you."

But Zedekiah had long refused to obey the Lord's commands, so neither could he now find rest in the Lord's promises.

The warnings of Jeremiah were reinforced by a message that reached Jerusalem from Babylon. Apparently Ezekiel had seen a vision and acted out the revelation to his mystified fellow exiles. They watched as he packed a few belongings in his backpack, as though preparing once again for exile. Then at dusk he had broken a hole in the village wall and headed out into the night, blindfolding himself as he stumbled into the darkness.

"What in the world are you doing?" they called after him.

"This is an oracle for the king in Jerusalem. I am an omen to him. As I have done, so will he do. The king will shoulder a few possessions and escape through a hole in the wall at dusk. But he will not get away. He will be brought here to Babylon, yet he will never see it and all he loves will be scattered to the four winds."

When Nebuchadnezzar eventually marched his army right up to the walls of Jerusalem he found the natural defences of the city to be impregnable. For two long years the Babylonians were content to bide their time, simply choking off the food supply. Starvation was staring the citizens in the face, so one evening at dusk, King Zedekiah, his family and his bodyguards made a break for it through a hole in the wall. They fled east in an attempt to get lost in the badlands beyond the Jordan. For a time it looked as though they had got clean away, but the Babylonians tracked them and caught up with them in the plain near Jericho. The soldiers scattered, and the king and his family were captured. It was significant that it should end in that particular location, for that was where Israel had first set foot in the promised land under the leadership of Joshua, nearly nine hundred years previously. Now this is where it would all end.

Zedekiah was dragged before Nebuchadnezzar. Before his eyes were gouged out, they treated him to one last horrifying view of his family being hacked to death. Zedekiah was taken to Babylon in chains, but as Ezekiel had foretold, he had no eyes to see it. If only he had heeded the warnings of Jeremiah.

So Jerusalem was defeated and the Babylonians set about the business of reducing that magnificent city to rubble. The wall was broken down and the whole city was ransacked. All those fine buildings that had survived since the heady days of David and the great builder Solomon were torched and razed to the ground. The valuable relics that Solomon had designed and had cast from bronze and clad with gold were all broken up and taken away as scrap. No one ever knew what happened to the ark, but what use had Israel for the ten commands since they had systematically broken every one of them.

The words of Jeremiah echoed after the retreating footsteps of the exiles as they dragged their chains towards Babylon. "This is what the Lord, the God of Israel, says: 'The days are coming when I will bring you back from captivity and restore you. I have loved you with an everlasting love; and I will draw you back with loving-kindness. I will rebuild you again and there will be dancing in the streets. I will gather you from the ends of the earth and you will come home with weeping, praying as you come. Rachael, weep for your children no more! There is hope.

"'The time is coming when I will make a new covenant with all Israel. This will not be a covenant written on stone tablets, but I will write it on your hearts. No longer will it be necessary for a man to teach his neighbour about God, because everyone will know me.'"

By the time the exiles reached Babylon, Jehoiachin had already been in a Babylonian jail for eleven weary years. But a further twenty-six years would pass before he once again saw the light of day. He had been eighteen when he was imprisoned, but was in his midfifties when Evil-Merodach, new king of Babylon, brought him out. He spoke kindly to him and gave him robes to replace his prison rags. He even gave him a seat of honour at his table where he enjoyed a regular allowance for the rest of his days. So the last king in the royal line of David died in far-off Babylon.

But the ember of hope never died in the hearts of the exiles. Yes, they remembered the words Jeremiah had spoken back in Jerusalem, but the sparks of hope were fanned daily by the eloquent words of Ezekiel who was one of them, a fellow exile in a foreign land.

Ezekiel told them he had seen a vision of a whole valley full of dry bones scattered on the ground. "Do you believe these bones can live again?" God had asked him.

"You alone know the answer to that one," Ezekiel had replied.

"So speak it, Ezekiel. Prophesy!"

"Very well. Dry bones, hear the word of the Lord ..."

As he had begun to speak, a rattling noise had filled the valley and the bones began to organise themselves into definable skeletons. Then flesh and skin had clothed them and soon the valley was full of fresh corpses.

"Now prophesy to the four winds. 'Breath on these slain that they may live again!'" And as Ezekiel had obeyed, a breath of wind filled the valley with life, and the corpses had stirred, sat up, then risen to their feet to stand at attention.

"Now tell your people, 'I am going to open your graves and give you life. I will gather you from all the countries where you have been scattered and will bring you back to your own land. I will wash you with clean water, and make you clean; I will cleanse you from all your impurities and your idolatry. I will give you a new heart and put a new spirit in you; I will remove your hard heart of stone and give you a heart of flesh. I will put my Spirit in you who will move you to obey my laws. You will be my people, and I will be your God."

26

The Exile

Things in Babylon were not so bad as might have been imagined. Nebuchadnezzar viewed his new immigrants as valuable assets, and took care to maximise their potential. He identified the brightest of the group and determined to teach them local culture. Among those who were admitted to the university of Babylon were four friends, Daniel, Shadrach, Meshach and Abednego. Unlike most of their contemporaries, they feared God, and now that they found themselves as exiles in a foreign land, were more than ever determined to obey him in all things.

As is often the case, it is in the small things that compromise has the potential to take root, and such might well have been the case for these four young students had it not been for their resolve to abide by God's commands. It started in the school cafeteria, where to their amazement, they were presented with a veritable smorgasbord of fine food and drink.

"Where did all this come from?" inquired Daniel.

"This? Oh this is only leftovers," replied the steward in charge of their welfare. Seemed it had first been offered to the gods and since they didn't eat much, it had been sent on to the king, whose appetite being also limited, sent it to the school kitchens.

Daniel was uncomfortable and shared his misgivings with his buddies.

"If we eat this meat and drink this wine that are purported to be the gifts of the local gods, who knows what concessions we will be making next."

They all agreed, and restricted themselves to drinking only water and eating only vegetables. The steward was concerned that his job might be in jeopardy if their health were to suffer. "So you be the judge," they conceded. "If after ten days we are looking off-colour, then okay." At the end of the test period it was apparent that this vegetarian regime suited them, and they were permitted to continue. Round one!

Next test was their final examination at the end of the course. The examiner turned out to be King Nebuchadnezzar himself. To their great joy, the four friends came out top of the class, and in consequence were offered positions in public office. Round two!

The third test was more challenging. King Nebuchadnezzar had a disturbing dream, but as often happens, he had trouble recalling the details next morning. Yet the nagging sense that it was an important revelation would not leave him. So he summoned his advisors. "I want to know the meaning of my dream," he demanded.

"So tell us the dream."

"Anyone can make up a convincing interpretation for a dream! I want to know that your version is genuine. So first tell me what I dreamt, then tell me what it means." They were dumbfounded.

"No king has ever asked such a thing of his advisors," they whined.

"Well, I'm asking you now!" he roared. When they failed to come up with anything coherent, the king ordered their execution. A warrant was also issued for the arrest of every member of the advisory council, a list that included Daniel and his friends. They spent the evening praying, and that night, Daniel himself had a vivid dream.

First thing next morning he got a message through to the king who summoned Daniel to his presence. "Are you able to tell me my dream?" the king demanded sceptically.

"No man could do that! ..." Nebuchadnezzar was about to explode when Daniel continued ... "but God can."

Daniel related his dream to the king and it was clear from the expression on the royal face that Daniel was hitting the mark.

"So what does it all mean?" stammered Nebuchadnezzar.

Daniel explained that the king had dreamed about a huge statue, symbolic of successive kingdoms to come, but that would eventually be toppled by a rock of divine origin. "That rock represents a kingdom that will never be destroyed, established by God himself. But, for the time being, you, oh King, are the head of gold."

That part of the interpretation proved to be to the king's liking, so he promoted Daniel to the position of chief advisor, with Shadrach, Meshach and Abednego as his associates. "There is no doubt that your God is God of gods and Lord of kings," Nebuchadnezzar concluded.

Round three.

But his apparent conversion was only skin deep, for shortly after, Nebuchadnezzar built his own god, a huge statue one hundred feet tall, much like the one in his dream. Mindful that he was the head of gold, he had the whole image covered in gold leaf, head to toe. And there it stood, dominating a great square. Dignitaries gathered from all over the world to attend the dedication. When the hour struck on the appointed day an expectant hush fell over the assembled throng.

"Listen up, you peoples from all over the world," announced a herald with a speaking trumpet. "You are hereby ordered to worship this great god. As soon as the band starts to play you are to prostrate yourselves before it. Be it clearly understood that anyone failing to fall face down will be burned to death." The nearby roar of a great furnace lent menace to his words. But for most of the crowd the threats were unnecessary, for who amongst them had ever seen so impressive a god?

For some reason, Daniel was out of town that day, but standing in the crowd were his three buddies, Shadrach, Meshach, and Abednego. It was no mere compromise that they were facing now, but a direct challenge to the second of the great commands: *"You shall not bow down to or worship a man-made idol; for I, the Lord your God, am a jealous God."*

So long as they remained just three members of the crowd, they went unnoticed. But the moment the band began to play, they stuck out like sore thumbs from the otherwise horizontal sea of humanity.

"Arrest those men!" someone shouted, and they found themselves dragged before the king.

Nebuchadnezzar was incredulous. How could anyone be so foolish as to defy his order and decline to worship so magnificent an image? "Is it really true that you refuse to worship my god?" Then because he frankly believed that it must all have been a misunderstanding, he went on, "Look, next time the band plays, all you have to do is bow down like everybody else." Then, conscious of his audience of dignitaries from all over his realm, he hardened his tone: "But be sure of this, if you do not bow down you will immediately be burned alive. And then what kind of god do you have that could rescue you?" Nebuchadnezzar had been to Jerusalem and seen the temple of their god, but though he had searched, he found no trace of him. Just an empty box. So he had burned the temple to the ground.

With no hesitation, one of the three spoke up: "We have no defence of our own to offer, but we are confident that the God we serve is more than able to save us from you and your furnace. But even if he should choose not to save us, there is no way we will ever bow down to your image."

The most powerful king on earth, challenged by three insignificant nobodies, was enraged beyond measure. "Bind them and burn them!" he roared. Big, burly soldiers stepped forward, trussed the three men with ropes, and then dragged them towards the inferno. They hesitated as they approached the threshold, since the heat was so intense. "Throw them in!" screamed the king, and because they feared his displeasure more than the flames, those soldiers staggered forward to obey; they shrivelled and died as they did so.

Nebuchadnezzar and his guests, who were watching the spectacle from a safe distance, were amazed to notice that the three bundles of rags that they took to be the offenders were still moving. Yes, they were burning nicely, but soon it became apparent that the only thing actually alight was the rope that bound them. And now they were getting to their feet and walking around in the middle of the flames, cool as you like.

"Am I not right in saying that we threw but three men into the furnace?" When that was confirmed, he continued, "But I see four men, walking free. And that fourth man has the appearance of a son of the gods."

When the flames had died down somewhat, Nebuchadnezzar shouted into the smoke: "Shadrach, Meshach, and Abednego, servants of the most high God, come out here!" And out they walked, unsinged. "May your God be praised!" he said. "You trusted him to save you, and he did. You were willing to defy my orders and to sacrifice your very lives rather than to serve any god other than your God."

He then turned to the assembled throng: "I hereby decree that anyone anywhere who says a word against the God of Shadrach, Meshach, and Abednego shall be cut to pieces and their houses reduced to heaps of rubble." Nebuchadnezzar liked powerful incentives! Be sure that those delegates returned to the four corners of the realm, saying little about the spectacle of a one-hundred-foot image of gold and much about the invisible God of the Hebrews.

One might imagine that after two such brushes with God, Nebuchadnezzar might be set to be a believer for life. But such was not the case. He was self-obsessed and boasted in his arrogance that he could accomplish anything he gave his mind to. Once again, it was a dream that forewarned him of what was to come, and it was Daniel who gave him the interpretation. This dream was of a great tree, cut down in its prime, its stump clamped with an iron ring. The fulfilment of the dream was seven years of insanity, during which time Nebuchadnezzar lived in the wilderness like a wild animal. Eventually, as predicted, he humbled himself and acknowledged the King of heaven. "Everything he does is right, and all his ways are just. And those who walk in pride he is able to humble," he concluded.

Daniel was a survivor. In fact, he survived several Babylonian monarchs who succeeded one another either because of natural cause or assassination. So Daniel was an old man when Belshazzar became king.

During the early years of Belshazzar's reign, Daniel passed much of his time in prayer and meditation. Rather than playing the role of interpreter of dreams, he himself became the dreamer. He foresaw events to come in the most vivid and alarming allegories. He even caught a glimpse of one he called "the Ancient of Days." He described him as shining white, sitting on a great fiery throne, attended by a billion people. Then he saw one like a son of man, riding on the clouds of heaven, who approached the Ancient of Days and was given authority, glory, and sovereign power. People from all over the world worshiped him. His dominion was to be an everlasting dominion that would never pass away or be destroyed.

For the ten years of Belshazzar's reign, Daniel continued his public office in a very private way, never so much as catching the eye of the king. Belshazzar rested easy on his throne. Babylon was an impregnable fortress. No enemy had succeeded in taking it in a thousand years. So when Cyrus, king of Persia, laid siege to the city, Belshazzar treated the threat with the contempt it deserved. He threw a banquet for a thousand of his lords. In an attempt to impress the company, he served the drinks in the antique gold and silver chalices that had been made by the great King Solomon over four hundred years earlier. They had been brought from Jerusalem almost half a century previously by his grandfather-in-law, King Nebuchadnezzar. With these goblets, the drunken toasts were raised in honour of the man-made gods of silver and gold, bronze, iron, wood, and stone.

Doubtless Belshazzar had heard the stories of how the God of the Hebrews had humbled Nebuchadnezzar. But he was now long dead, and what did he, Belshazzar, care for such superstitions anyway? So the wine flowed free. The music played. The people danced, and the sentries on the walls kept watch.

Suddenly, the hubbub died away. The music ceased, and the dancers stood still. Silhouetted against the wall were the fingers of a hand, writing, writing. Then the hand faded, but what was written remained.

No one could make head nor tail of what the writing meant. Experts were called. Baffled. It was the queen who reminded her husband of Daniel: "He was able to interpret the meaning of riddles and dreams in the days of your grandfather Nebuchadnezzar. I believe he is still alive. Why not call him?"

Daniel was wheeled in and promised the earth if he would but explain the meaning of the inscription.

The old sage reminded the king of how his grandfather Nebuchadnezzar had been humbled. "Yet, despite the fact that you well know this, you have not humbled yourself, but rather have vaunted yourself against the Lord of heaven. You insulted him by drinking from his holy goblets to honour gods that are not gods at all – dumb idols. You have dishonoured the God who holds in his hand your very life."

The atmosphere was tense. Would the king strike down the old fool?

"So this is what the inscription means," continued Daniel. "'*Mene, Mene, Tekel, Parsin.*' Your days are numbered, and your number is up. You have been weighed in the balance and found lacking. Your kingdom is now divided and given to the Medes and Persians."

Unknown to the revellers, the Persian troops had been working hard to reroute the Euphrates river that flowed through the city too deep and swift to be crossed. And that was the very night the waters were diverted and the level in the usual channel dropped sufficiently to enable the Persians to wade down the riverbed, under the walls, and up into the city before the defenders knew what was happening. Belshazzar was killed, and Cyrus took over Babylon. He left his trusted surrogate, Darius the Mede, to reign in his place till he could return from conquering the rest of the world.

Darius was an old man of sixty-two, but wise. He liked Daniel, whom Belshazzar had promoted as his last royal act before being killed. Darius made him one of three administrators over Babylon and had plans to promote him to overall authority.

As an octogenarian, Daniel couldn't do much, so he prayed more. He had read the prophecies of Jeremiah and, having carefully analysed what he had written, discerned that the exile would come to an end after seventy years. There was, therefore, but another twenty years to run. So Daniel fasted and prayed, with increasing expectation that God would soon have mercy upon his wayward people.

But prayer is a dangerous habit, so the enemy did his best to gag Daniel.

A delegation of leading men who were jealous of Daniel's position came to King Darius: "Oh King, live forever." Not that they expected he would, but the sentiment was nice. "We have all agreed that as a measure to unite your kingdom, it would be good to set a token precedent that for one month, prayers should be offered to no one other than to your good self. We feel that this decree should be irrevocable. We are also agreed that it should have teeth, enforceable on pain of death – by lions."

Why the king neglected to bounce the proposal off Daniel, his administrator-in-chief, before making it law is uncertain. But the deed was signed, sealed, and proclaimed before Daniel even knew about it.

A sensible precaution might well have been for Daniel to restrict his praying to a private conversation between himself and his God, but he would brook no such compromise. Daniel had read the words of the prayer that Solomon had offered on the day he had dedicated his temple to God as a house of prayer: *"If ever your people should so sin against you that you permit them to be taken into exile in a foreign land, then if they pray toward this temple, hear from heaven and forgive."*

So Daniel continued his practice of praying three times daily at his open window, which faced towards the ruins of the temple in Jerusalem. He was not going to let a small thing like a royal decree get in the way of so important a responsibility.

Of course, the violation was reported, and Daniel was arrested. King Darius was not at all pleased. He had high regard for Daniel, and the thought of throwing him to the lions did not sit well with him. He tried all day to find a legal loophole whereby the irrevocable might be revoked, but to no avail. At sun down, Daniel was taken to the pit, where the lions snarled and paced in anticipation of fresh meat.

"May your God rescue you!" were the parting words of the king. Then the old man was dropped into the dark hole, and the pit was sealed shut.

King Darius passed a sleepless night. Nothing could take his mind from the thought of Daniel's bones being chewed by lions at the bottom of a deep, dark hole. So at first light, there was the king, visiting the lion pit. He ordered the hole to be opened and called down into the darkness, "Daniel, are you there? Did your God rescue you?"

"Oh King, live forever!" came the reply from the darkness. Daniel knew something about living beyond normal expectations, so his words were more than mere sentiment. "Yes, God sent his angel to protect me, since I was innocent before him, as indeed I am before you."

Daniel was hoisted up, and to everyone's amazement, he had not a scratch on him, not a claw nor a tooth mark to hint at his ordeal.

The joy of the celebration was perhaps a little tainted by the king's order that those who had inveigled him into passing that foolish law be thrown to the lions, together with their wives and children. On that occasion, nature took its course.

So Daniel lived to continue his ministry of vigilant prayer.

Sometimes, he would set aside weeks on end to go without food so as to concentrate his whole being on his earnest request: "Oh God, hear the prayers and petitions of your servant. For your name's sake, remember your desolate sanctuary. Open your eyes to the rubble of the city that bears your name. It is not because we are righteous that we expect an answer, but because you are merciful. Oh Lord, hear us! Oh Lord, forgive! Oh Lord, act!"

At the end of one such three-week fast, Daniel and his entourage were up north on the king's business. They were travelling along the Tigris River when an unaccountable terror suddenly gripped his companions and they fled, leaving Daniel standing on his own on the riverbank. There before him stood a man, if indeed it were right to describe him as such, for his face was dazzling like lightning and his eyes burned with the intensity of fire. His arms and legs were like polished bronze, and when he spoke, it sounded like a multitude of voices speaking as one. So terrified was Daniel that he collapsed in a dead faint.

Then a hand was laid gently on his back and helped him to his feet. "Daniel, you are greatly loved. Your prayer has been heard since the first day you started. In fact, that is why I have come to you." Daniel was quite unable to reply, still breathless with fear. But the one in whose presence he trembled gave him strength to listen to the amazing message he had to deliver.

The message was made up of mysterious pictures of things to come: of the rise and fall of the mighty, of an eternal kingdom, of the end of days when the books would be opened and the hearts of men would be laid bare.

What a way to conclude a long life. What a way to pass seventy years of exile!

-- 27 --

The Queen

Generation succeeded generation, and the exiles were scattered far and wide. Some found themselves in the fortress city of Susa, three hundred miles further east, beyond Babylon. They had never known their native land, and the stories of Jerusalem were but memories passed down, father to son. In Susa, there was a large Jewish community who maintained their identity and traditions. Amongst them was a eunuch named Mordecai. Families looked after their own in those days, and Mordecai had an orphaned niece, a cute little girl named Esther, who he had taken in and raised as his own daughter. She grew up to be a real head-turner, with a nature to match. All agreed that she was a stunningly beautiful young lady.

King Xerxes, king of all Persia, whose kingdom extended from North Africa in the west to India in the east, ruled his vast empire from Susa. An invitation was extended to his nobles and officials all over the world to attend a celebration of his greatness. Camel trains of mighty men streamed into town for the event. For some, the journey had taken weeks, so it was no one-day event. In fact, it lasted for six months, culminating in a seven-day banquet. Wine knew no limit, and the waiters were instructed to serve every man just as much as he wanted.

While all this was going on, the queen threw a banquet of her own for the women folk, a much more sedate affair. Queen Vashti was a beautiful woman, and the king, who was justly proud of her, wanted to show her off to his guests. But when he summoned her, Vashti was unwilling to leave the civilised company of her ladies for the bawdy, drunken binge going on next door. The king took her refusal to attend as a personal affront and foresaw that this could well be interpreted as a slight on male dominance in general. Having taken advice, he had Vashti banished from his presence forever and sent a message to every corner of his realm, affirming every man's right to be head of his own household. Women! Who needed them?

But King Xerxes did. There was only one thing worse than having a rebellious wife, and that was having no wife at all.

"So hold a beauty pageant, and let the winner become the new queen," someone suggested. The king thought that a capital plan, and the contest was announced. Beautiful women were sought far and wide and brought to the royal spa to undergo a whole year of intensive treatment. Among those who entered the program was Esther, adopted daughter of Mordecai. She kept quiet about her Jewish origins, since the fact that she was an exile might not have worked in her favour. The executive producer of the pageant was a man named Hegai, who took an instant shine to Esther and gave her preferential treatment.

Unlike some pageants, where there was a panel of judges, there was but one judge, and he did his judging in private, in his bedroom. The girls would be brought to the king for a one-night stand, and if they didn't shine, they were never heard of again. Esther, however, was an instant success and was pronounced the winner of the contest before breakfast was served next morning. Banquets were held and celebrations broke out all over the kingdom. Long live the queen!

Mordecai kept as close as possible to Esther but was not permitted to enter the palace. So every day, he would come and stand at the palace gate, in the hope of catching a glimpse of her. He would send messages to Esther, giving advice and offering her wisdom on how best to act in many situations, guidance that she gladly accepted.

Mordecai heard all kinds of gossip as he stood incognito at the palace gate. No one knew he was the father of the queen. So one day, some important information came to his ears. A couple of disgruntled officers of the guard were planning to take out the king. Mordecai got word urgently to Esther, who passed the intelligence on to the king. The offenders were arrested and hanged, but a reward for Mordecai was somehow overlooked.

Five years passed, and then something happened that might have gone unnoticed had it not been for Mordecai's reaction. An official by the name of Haman won the king's favour and was promoted to be prime minister. Along with this exalted position came the honour of being bowed to by all and sundry wherever he went, a ritual to which everyone submitted; everyone except Mordecai, that is. "Jews don't bow to anyone," he growled.

The noncompliance was reported to Haman, who from then on could not enter or leave the palace without noticing the one stubborn member of the crowd standing upright. "I'll have his head for this" – but then, on reflection – "No. That would be too easy. I'll kill anyone who shares his miserable race. I'll kill every Jew in the kingdom." And the first holocaust was planned.

With the king's assent, an edict was relayed to every province of the kingdom, requiring officials to exterminate all Jews on a given date. That date had been determined by the casting of the Pur, or lot. Because the kingdom was so large, and communications were so convoluted, the best part of a year's notice was given before the terrible day would take its toll.

But it didn't take long for the edict to be proclaimed in Susa. Understandably, the Jewish community was in turmoil. What was to be done?

In the royal palace, Esther was sheltered from the realities of life at street level. The first she heard of what was going down was a report that Mordecai appeared to be in mourning at the palace gate. So she sent a message asking what was the matter. By way of explanation, Mordecai sent her a copy of the edict. "Go to the king and beg for mercy for your people," he had scribbled on the reverse side.

"You tell Mordecai that I can't possibly do that," Esther replied, via the messenger. "No one can just barge into the king's presence without being summoned, on pain of death. If he happens to see me, and is not busy at the time, he may hold out his sceptre. Only then would I be spared."

Mordecai's reply was harsh, but the circumstances demanded it: "Don't imagine for one moment that just because you live in the palace that you alone of all the Jews will be spared. You will perish along with the rest of us. Yes, a rescue for the Jews will certainly come from somewhere, if not from you. But if you remain silent at so crucial a time as this, then you can be sure that you and your family will all perish. And one more thought. Perhaps the whole reason that you have been promoted to royal position is for this exact purpose. Don't miss it!"

"Very well," Esther replied. "Get all the Jews in Susa together, and spend three days praying and fasting. My maids and I will do the same. Then I will go to the king. And if I perish, I perish."

Three days later, dressed in her royal finery, and with her knees knocking together, Esther went and stood in the entrance to the court. There was a sharp intake of breath by those who witnessed her arrival, and they waited with bated breath to see what would transpire. The king saw her standing there and loved her. He held out his sceptre. She approached and touched it as she bowed.

"What it is you want, my queen?" he enquired kindly. "I will give you anything in my power to give, up to half my kingdom."

She could have blurted the whole problem there and then in the presence of the whole court, but she was too smart for that: "I have come to invite you to lunch, you and Prime Minister Haman."

The king was mystified. He didn't receive too many invitations to dine out, so he readily accepted. He and Haman arrived at the appointed hour and enjoyed a delightful meal in her radiant presence. Over dessert: "So tell me, my dear, what is all this about? What can I do for you?"

Still hesitant to spill what was on her mind, she invited them both to return for a second lunch party: "Come tomorrow, and I will tell you all." The mystery of the second invitation made the tension all the sweeter.

Haman went home ecstatic. He told his wife and all his friends where he had had lunch and that he had a second lunch date for the morrow. "But all that gives me no pleasure because of that cursed Mordecai fellow, who day after day still refuses to bow to me."

"So why wait for the big day?" his wife asked. "Build a gallows here in our back yard and hang the so-and-so tomorrow." That put a smile on his face, and he gave orders for the carpenters to get busy.

Next day, Haman headed to work early and with a light heart. There was the gallows all ready, with the noose swinging in the breeze. Today he was to take lunch with the king and queen. How special was that? But first he must get royal assent to hang Mordecai. He headed to the palace.

"Good morning, Haman," wished the king as he entered. "I was wondering if I might ask your advice on a matter that is troubling me. What should be done for a man the king wants to honour in a special way?"

Who could he have in mind, but me? Haman thought to himself. "Well …," he said, smirking, "if you really want such a man to feel special, have him dressed in royal robes and then seat him on the king's charger and parade him through the streets, led by a high official, proclaiming, 'This is how the king honours he in whom he is well pleased.'"

"Excellent plan!" declared the king. "I was rereading the palace records last evening and came to the part that referred to that plot by two of my bodyguards to assassinate me. I find that nothing was ever done to reward the man responsible for uncovering that attempt on my life. So I would like you to seek him out and give him the royal treatment that you suggest. I think you will find him at the palace gate. His name is Mordecai."

Haman was mortified but carried out the king's instructions to the letter. When it was done, he returned home to quickly change for the queen's luncheon and to tell his wife his troubles.

It was with a terrible sense of foreboding that Haman now went to the palace. The food was all done, and over drinks, the king once again asked Esther the nature of her petition, promising her up to half his kingdom. "Now what is your request?"

"I simply ask that you would spare my life and that of my family and my people. If it were simply a matter of sparing us all from slavery, I would not have troubled the king with so trifling a matter. But it is our lives that are in jeopardy."

"Who is it that dares to threaten you?" the king demanded, furious.

"It is this vile man, Haman," Esther said, turning towards the prime minister. "I am a Jewess, and at this man's instigation, a date has been set for my extermination and that of my people."

King Xerxes was so enraged that he might well have murdered Haman there and then with his bare hands, so he walked out into the garden to cool off. As soon as he was gone, Haman went over to Esther, who was reclining on a couch. So passionate was he as he begged for his life to be spared that in his inebriated state, he toppled over and sprawled on the couch on top of Esther. Which was unfortunate, for that was the very moment the king chose to come back into the room. If he had been successful in cooling off in the garden, the good was instantly undone at the sight of Haman apparently in the very act of molesting his queen.

"Hang this man!" roared the king. Someone told the king about the newly constructed gallows at Haman's house, intended for Mordecai. "Hang him on his own gallows."

That day was a day of great reversal. Haman was hoist on his own petard, and Mordecai was promoted to the position newly vacated by the late Haman: prime minister.

But their troubles were not over, for the terrible day of the planned genocide was looming. Esther once again risked her life by entering the king's presence, and a second time he extended to her his royal sceptre. "What now can be done for you?" asked the king.

"If it please the king, and if I have found favour in your eyes, please let the edict to destroy the Jews all over your great kingdom be reversed, and spare our lives."

"I regret that the laws of the Medes and Persians can never be revoked, so that is not mine to give. However, I could issue a second edict ordering the Jews everywhere to unite in their own defence, and with my express permission."

The edict was signed, sealed, and communicated, so that when the day came, the Jews were ready, and no one dared lift a finger against them for fear of incurring the wrath of King Xerxes.

So that day was written into the Jewish calendar in perpetuity to be a day of celebration. It was known as Purim, the day of the lot. With God, there is no such thing as chance or luck, good or bad.

28

The Return

Jerusalem was a ruin. Heaps of rubble overgrown with thorns and brambles topped the once proud mountain. In the absence of human inhabitants, the wild life had multiplied, and all manner of creatures picked a meagre living from amongst the fallen stones and charred timbers. The people who once had lived there may have been homesick, but for what? For a memory of what used to be? But who would want to live there now?

Yet the words of the prophets never failed to stir sparks of hope in the ashes of despair that choked the ambitions of the exiles. But all the while, the sand was running, running, running, and seventy winters had been succeeded by summers when King Cyrus turned prophesy into a proclamation: "Let the foundations of the temple in Jerusalem be re-established!" He committed it to paper and distributed copies all over his realm, for all the world to read. Cyrus may have never heard of Jeremiah, yet it was his words spoken years earlier that moved his heart to act that day.

The proclamation ran: "This is what Cyrus king of Persia says: 'The God of heaven has appointed me to build a temple for him in Jerusalem. Any of his people who are willing may now return to Jerusalem to rebuild the temple of the Lord, the God of Israel. I command their neighbours to provision them with gold and silver, food and livestock for their mission.'"

Exiled Jews, as they were now called, started to arrive outside the gates of Babylon, and before long a huge throng of forty-two thousand excited people was milling about, eager to be on their way. They were indeed laden with provisions and encumbered with livestock. To crown it all, Cyrus entrusted to their safe keeping over five thousand priceless treasures: the gold and silver cups, chalices and bowls that King Solomon had made but had been carried into exile by Nebuchadnezzar on that terrible day, decades earlier. A huge caravan set off, thousands of camels, horses, mules, and donkeys all laden with provisions and precious cargos.

In overall command was the nearest thing the Jews had to royalty, a true descendant of King David: Zerubbabel, son of King Jehoiachin, who had died in captivity in Babylon. The journey was long and slow, over six hundred miles, but every step got them closer to the city of their dreams. Their arrival must therefore have been an anticlimax. Desolation!

The first priority was to find a roof to sleep under. Some of the seniors, who had been children when they left, remembered exactly where their family homes had been and gladly returned to the ruins of what had once been their ancestral heritage. But the younger ones had to find their way from directions passed on to them by their parents and grandparents.

On an agreed day some three months after their arrival, they all assembled in the ruins of Jerusalem. There was their leader, Zerubbabel. No one liked to call him "king," for fear of upsetting King Cyrus. Together with Jeshua, the high priest, Zerubbabel led them in making a start to clear the rubble and rebuild the altar of the Lord. The completion of the project coincided with the right dates for the Festival of Tabernacles, a holiday that lasted a whole week with campouts, campfires, and singing. The sacrifices on the new altar were the focus, and the joy of the returned exiles knew no limit.

The words of the prophets were a constant source of encouragement. "My temple will be rebuilt," the Lord promised through the mouth of Zechariah. "Plans will be drawn up for the reconstruction of this city."

Zechariah told the people that he had seen a clear vision of a mighty angel with measuring line in hand, drafting the dimensions of the city.

"What will it be like?" the people enquired.

"Jerusalem will one day be so full of people that there will not be room enough to house them all, and they will have to expand into the suburbs.

Old men and women will walk the streets in safety and will sit around in the city squares. Children will play in the parks. And the Lord himself will be a fiery wall of protection around them all."

"But how will this be?" the people wondered.

"'This may all seem impossible to you now, but it's not impossible to me,'" Zechariah quoted the Lord Almighty. "'I will rescue my people from east and west and bring them home to live safely in Jerusalem. You may depend upon it.'"

Then Zechariah turned to Zerubbabel: "And this is what the Lord has to say to you, Zerubbabel: 'It is not through human strength or effort that you will succeed, but by my Spirit. Nothing will stand in your way, even though it seems as immovable as a mighty mountain. You will one day set the final stone in place on the temple. So do not despise this small beginning.'"

Spurred on by these encouraging words, the people set to work with a will. The next project was the temple itself. With King Cyrus' permission, they imported logs from Lebanon and floated them in rafts down the coast as far as Joppa, just at Solomon had done. Supervising the work were some of the older priests, with the younger fellows doing the grunt work. When the foundations were in place and the footprint of the great building was clearly distinguishable from the confusion, they stopped to give thanks to the Lord. They sang a joyful refrain of "*The Lord is good, and his love endures forever.*" Those who had never seen the former temple shouted for joy in anticipation of what lay ahead, but the old people, who remembered the glory of Solomon's temple, wept for the good old days. The noise of the combined cacophony was deafening and could be heard for miles around.

Then rising above the hubbub came the clear sound of a confident voice, demanding, "Who here saw this house in its former glory?" Everyone turned to look. It was Haggai, the prophet. Some of the seniors raised their hands. "So what do you think of it now? Seems like nothing, eh?" There were mumbles of assent. "But now here is a word from the Lord for you, Zerubbabel and Jeshua, and all you people today: 'Be strong, for I am with you. I have all the silver and gold you need. The glory of this house you are building will be greater than the glory of the house that formerly stood on this ground. Soon I am going to shake the heavens and the earth and all nations with them. Then the desired of all nations will come, and I will fill this house with glory,' says the Lord Almighty."

The local inhabitants who lived around Jerusalem were a little alarmed by this sudden influx of thousands of strangers from Babylon. These newcomers laid claim to the territory as though they owned the place. But it had been the king of Assyria himself who had given this land to them, nearly a century ago. Not only had he given the land to them, but he had also taught them to worship the God of the land by providing one of his priests to be their mentor. So yes, they had learned to worship the God of their new land, but they also maintained the traditions of the gods from the lands from which they had been relocated. So it was somewhat threatening to find these Jews not only commandeering their land, but also taking charge of their religion.

Conforming to the old maxim that if you can't beat them, you should join them, they came and offered their help in the reconstruction of the temple. "We also are worshippers of your god and have been sacrificing to him ever since the king of Assyria settled us here."

But, recognising the potential for compromise, Zerubbabel refused their kind offer. This rebuttal was not well received by their neighbours, who from then on made it their business to impede progress with threats and frustrations of every kind.

Eventually, they wrote an official complaint to the new king of Persia. The letter was addressed to King Artaxerxes. The gist of the letter was that troublemakers were attempting to rebuild Jerusalem, and that if this outrage were permitted to continue, it would spell serious trouble. Taxes due to the royal treasury would undoubtedly be curtailed, and dishonour would be brought to the king's good name. "A cursory check of the records would quickly reveal the sad fact that Jerusalem has long been a rebellious and troublesome province, right from ancient times," and so on. Signed: "Your loyal servants, the men of Trans-euphrates" – that being the nomenclature by which the region was now tagged by their lords and masters.

Some months later, and with smug expressions on their faces, the leaders of Trans-euphrates arrived in Jerusalem, waving a reply from the king. "You are to cease and desist forthwith," they announced. The work ground to a sorry standstill and stayed that way for fifteen years.

The people used the delay to work on their own homes, which were in urgent need of repair, having been left uninhabited for decades. And things might well have stayed that way, were it not for the insistent words of the prophet, Haggai. Standing on the abandoned foundations of the temple, he raised his voice: "Give a thought to how things stand. You plant much, but harvest little. You eat but are never full, drink but are always thirsty. You put clothes on your backs but still shiver with cold. You earn wages, but there are holes in your pockets. Your expectations prove disappointments. And why this famine, you ask? It is because my house remains a ruin while you live in your fancy houses. Go get lumber and build this house so that I may take pleasure in it, says the Lord."

Shamed by his words, Zerubbabel and Jeshua swung into action, and work on the reconstruction of the temple once again got moving. Even Haggai rolled up his sleeves to lend a hand. But it wasn't long before some civil servants from the regional district of Trans-euphrates arrived, long faced: "Who authorised you to rebuild this temple? We want a list of the names of all the men working on this construction site."

Another official letter was sent to the king, now King Darius. But since the mail was slow in those days, the Jews continued with the work till a reply could reasonably be expected.

Apparently, the letter had included the list of offending names, underscoring the ringleaders: "They claim to be servants of the God of heaven and earth and say something about their forefathers having offended him in some way, which explained why the Babylonians had destroyed the city in the first place. However, they do claim that this rebuilding project was authorised by King Cyrus. So if it please the king, it might be judicious if the royal archives were to be searched for any record of such a permit being issued."

Well, surprise, surprise! A letter came back to the Trans-euphrates municipal hall, bearing the royal crest. It was brief and to the point: "Stay out of the way! Do not interfere with the work of rebuilding this temple of God. Furthermore, I hereby decree that the expenses for this work are to be met from the revenues of Trans-euphrates." If that was not enough, the king added one last stinging paragraph: "If anyone changes this edict in any way, a beam is to be extracted from his house and he is to be impaled thereon, and his house left a heap of rubble." Nobody argued with that, and work on the reconstruction of the temple continued till completion.

The dedication of the temple was cause for great celebration. Soon the priests and Levites were organised to undertake their duties according to the traditions handed down to them since the days of Moses. Passover was celebrated for the first time since the exile, and some sense of normalcy was re-established.

A significant new addition to the team of returned exiles was a priest named Ezra, with a pedigree as long as your arm that recorded his ancestry right back to Aaron, Moses' brother. Ezra was a teacher and a historian who had taken care to fill in many of the gaps in the history of the kings of Judah and Israel that other writers had omitted. He arrived much relieved after his long and dangerous journey from Babylon, in company with a fine group of reinforcements, which included some carefully selected Levites and temple servants. He carried with him a bag of cash for the building fund and, perhaps most valuable of all, a letter from the king exempting from taxes all priests, Levites, and others involved in the work of the temple. As a teacher, Ezra was particularly thrilled to have in his possession a comprehensive mandate to teach the law of God, the observance of which could be enforced by imprisonment or, in extreme cases of disobedience, by death. There were joyful reunions between the newcomers and those who had arrived back in Jerusalem earlier.

In the absence of a clear leader since the death of Zerubbabel, the people were glad to have among them a new boss with a clear sense of purpose. But their joy was short lived. It quickly became apparent to Ezra that things were not as they should have been. The early returned exiles had taken local girls for wives, and the purity of the holy race was being polluted. While they had been in far-off Babylon, they had managed to keep themselves to themselves, but back in their own land, the lines of distinction had become blurred. It wouldn't be long before these women introduced into the family circle the worship of their pagan gods, and the whole messy cycle would begin all over again.

Ezra tore his clothes in dismay, particularly when he realised that it was not just among the rank and file that this was prevalent, but it was the leaders who were setting the example. He sat down on the ground in the temple and, pulling the hair from his head and beard, wept aloud.

It didn't take long for a crowd to gather. "Whatever is the matter?" they asked. When he explained, they sat down and joined him in an ever-widening circle.

All day they sat there, and then when evening came, Ezra started to pray: "I am too ashamed to lift my face to you, oh God. We have just returned from the exile that our sins so richly deserved, and now look at us! You clearly warned us not to make any kind of treaty with the idolatrous people who live here, and now here we are, married to them. Oh God, you must be angry enough to destroy us completely. So we stand before you today, guilty."

Soon the crowd grew, and the sound of weeping filtered throughout the sorry throng: "Yes, we have been unfaithful to God by marrying foreign women, but surely there is still hope for us. Why don't we make a covenant together to divorce our foreign wives and to agree that in future, we will obey all God's commands? Ezra, you lead the way, and we will gladly follow."

There and then, those present took a solemn oath to take appropriate action. Messages were sent to all the exiles to assemble in Jerusalem three days hence. It was a bedraggled assembly that came and stood before Ezra in the temple square that cold and rainy winter's day. So Ezra's message was brief and to the point:

"You have sinned by marrying foreign women. Therefore, confess your sin and agree to do his will in this matter. Distance yourselves from your foreign wives and the people around us."

Wisdom prevailed when someone pointed out that this matter could not be settled in a day, and besides, the people were too cold and wet to think clearly. So they all went home, and the matter was delegated to the judgment of family heads in each community. Within three months, the matter was resolved. A legal divorce and the sacrifice of a ram ended each offending marriage. It turned out that of the 111 mixed marriages, most had been among the laity, with but 23 priests and Levites involved.

Meanwhile, nearly a thousand miles east, in the citadel at Susa where Esther had been crowned queen a half century earlier, news reached the remaining Jews that while the temple had been rebuilt, the majority of the city of Jerusalem was still in ruins: "It's a disgrace. The wall is broken down, and the gates are broken and burned."

In the royal palace of King Artaxerxes, the butler was a Jew named Nehemiah. He was devastated at the news and spent all his off-duty time praying and fasting for something to be done. As one of a very select group who had access to the king on a regular basis, Nehemiah had to guard his appearance in the royal presence. But his fasting and heartache did not long escape the king's notice.

"Why do you look so sad these days?" demanded the king.

Nehemiah's heart skipped a few beats: "I grieve for the city of my ancestors that lies in ruins, oh King." Was he about to be fired, or was this a once-in-a-lifetime opportunity?

"So what do you want to do about it?" replied the king.

In the time it took him to draw breath, he offered a swift and silent prayer. Then: "If it should please the king, send me on a mission to rebuild that city." Might as well put your mouth where your heart is.

"When would you be back?" asked the king. Hard to say exactly how long it would take to rebuild a city he had never seen, but Nehemiah set an arbitrary date. Recognizing that he might never get another opportunity to petition the king, he quickly added a request for a letter of authorisation to the governor of Trans-euphrates and another to the keeper of the king's forest to provide lumber.

Nehemiah was walking on air after the king's secretary delivered the letters to him. But when he came to set out on his journey, Nehemiah was overcome with gratitude to find a detachment of the king's cavalry riding along with him, with orders to accompany him safely to his destination. The governor of Trans-euphrates was not at all pleased to receive the royal missive, but what could he say with a company Persian soldiers at his gate?

Nehemiah said not a word to anyone about the purpose of his mission when he arrived in Jerusalem. He took a midnight reconnoitre so he could see for himself just how bad the situation was. So when he finally met with the leaders of the Jewish community, he knew whereof he spoke. "Look," he said. "I have come with the permission of King Artaxerxes to rebuild Jerusalem. I propose that we start with the walls, so that we will no longer appear a disgrace to all who see the city from the outside." It is difficult to tell if Ezra was present on that occasion, but if he was, he raised no objection to a newcomer taking the lead. "Let's get cracking!" they all agreed. And so they did.

The project was divided into segments, with different families or interest groups each taking responsibility for a section of the wall. Those who lived near the wall naturally were allocated to the sections that were closest to home. People from out of town worked together with others from their own village: nobles and peasants working shoulder to shoulder. A guild of goldsmiths combined their efforts to work with a very different mineral from their usual, and next to them laboured a group of workers from the perfumery. No less a person than the mayor of the city knuckled down to the task, aided by his daughters. Even the priests and Levites did their part. Credit was given to each individual who took responsibility as assigned, men like Hashabiah, ruler of half the district of Keilah, and his counterpart Binnui, ruler of the other half. And there were a host of ordinary folks who worked their fingers to the bone, men like Baruch, Meremoth, Benjamin, and Hasshub. The list went on and on, but each was immortalised by being written into the story of the great restoration.

The governor of Trans-euphrates, an unpleasant piece of work by the name of Sanballat, was greatly upset when he heard that the wall was now shoulder high all the way round. He was based in Samaria, the former capital of the northern kingdom of Israel. Sanballat and his colleagues jeered at the efforts of the builders: "If even a fox were to walk along that wall, it would collapse!" Rumours were circulated that the fighting men of Samaria might launch a surprise attack at any moment, but Nehemiah prayed and posted a guard. Nothing happened.

After several weeks, the people became weary. There was just so much rubble to move, and as the wall grew higher, it became increasingly difficult to hoist up the heavy blocks of stone. Nehemiah was a master of encouragement and reassured the fearful by posting guards all round the perimeter. As the rumours of imminent attack intensified, he went so far as to divide the people into two groups: half the people to stand guard while the others worked on the wall. And no matter what they were about, each man carried a sword in his belt. A system of signals was agreed so that if an attack should be launched in any quarter, everyone was to rally to the sound of the trumpet. "And never forget," Nehemiah reminded them, "God is for us and will fight on our side."

It was slim pickings for some of the poorer people during those days. They could not pursue their own businesses while working on the walls. So some of them were forced to borrow from their neighbours who had reserves. It was the property taxes that crippled them, and as a result many homes were mortgaged to the hilt. Some were so desperate that they were forced to sell their own children as slaves just to have enough money to eat.

Conversely, others who were better off were turning a nice profit from the misfortunes of their fellows. When Nehemiah realised what was happening, he was furious and demanded that all charging of interest on loans should not only cease immediately, but the 1 percent interest that had already been exacted should be returned. As for the mortgaged property that had been confiscated by the lenders, it should all be returned to the original owners. "And whatever do you think you are doing, taking each other into slavery? Have we not all recently returned from exile as slaves in a foreign land?"

The old prophet Zechariah added his two bits: "The Lord Almighty says, 'Be fair and honest, and show kindness and mercy to each other. Never oppress the widows, orphans, foreigners or the poor people among you. See, I am planting seeds of prosperity among you. Your vines will become heavy with fruit and your harvests will be plentiful.'"

Amazingly, they all agreed to return every penny and promised never to take advantage of their brothers again. Nehemiah himself set a fine example for the others. He was now officially recognised as governor of Judah and, as such, was entitled to a generous income. Yet he never accepted a penny, insisting that since everyone else was working in a voluntary capacity, so would he.

There were many distractions directed at Nehemiah personally. Sanballat attempted to lure him out of the city, with the intention of doing him mischief. And when that didn't work, he threatened to circulate a story that Nehemiah was planning to make himself king and to lead a revolt against Persia. Nehemiah told Sanballat not to be so silly and got on with the job.

Next, Sanballat hired a priest to lock himself into the temple and then lure Nehemiah to join him, for fear of an imminent assassination attempt. Nehemiah pooh-poohed that suggestion also. Nothing was going to distract him from his God-given mission to get those walls finished. And finished they were, in the remarkable time of fifty-two days.

A great celebration was planned for the dedication of the new wall. Two distinct choirs of Levites were formed, each with its own orchestra to accompany it. Nehemiah divided the people in half, and with the choirs leading the way, the two processions set off to walk right round the wall, one going right, the other left. Ezra led one group and Nehemiah the other. As they walked, they sang and the orchestras played. The music echoed antiphonally across the city. When the circuit was done, they all met up in the temple as one mass choir, and the sound of their rejoicing could be heard for miles.

Nehemiah, just as he had promised, made the long journey back to Babylon to report to King Artaxerxes. As soon as his back was turned, however, things began to go pear-shaped. The contributions were not being brought to the temple as promised, and many of the Levites were forced to return to their own farms to grow food. Even some of the rooms in the temple were rented out to Tobiah, of all people, the dreaded Sanballat's sidekick. Worse, trading on the Sabbath was being carried on, and some were back to intermarrying with local girls.

Malachi, a prophet with an in-your-face style that rivalled that of Ezra (so much so that some even mistook him for Ezra), jumped into the breach.

First, he took on the Levites for dereliction of duty: "'If only someone would simply lock the doors of the temple to prevent hypocritical fires being kindled on my altar,' says the Lord. 'I am not at all pleased with you. You profane my name by suggesting that my service is disreputable.

"'What a chore!' you sniff disdainfully as you bring diseased animals to offer as sacrifices on my altar. I am a great king and you fail to honour me! Your forefather Levi was not like that. He reverenced me and stood in awe of my name. True instruction came from his mouth, and he spoke no falsehood. He walked with me in peace and righteousness, and brought many to repentance. But you have violated the covenant of Levi and caused many to stumble.'"

Then he turned on those who had failed to financially support the priests and Levites, accusing them of being responsible for the failure of the very people they were supposed to be upholding. "Will you rob God?" he blazed. "Yet you are doing exactly that.

"'How?' you ask.

"'By failing to bring your tithes and offerings to my house,' says the Lord. 'So bring the full amount into my house so there will be food on my table. Then watch what will happen as I open the flood gates of heaven to pour down on you such an overflowing blessing that you will not know what to do with it all.'"

Finally, it was on those who had married foreign women that he directed his ire: "You have done a detestable thing. You have desecrated the Lord's temple.

"'How so?' you ask.

"By marrying the daughters of a foreign god. And now you weep and wail at the Lord's altar. Do we not all share one Father? And was it not one God who created us all? Yet you have compromised the very unity of who God is. Yes, you hate the idea of divorcing your foreign wives. Well, know this. The Lord hates divorce too. He was witness to your marriage vows when you swore fidelity to each other. And it was the one Lord who made you one, body and spirit. Why did he make you one? Because he wanted your children to be one, just as he is one. But you have brought violence upon yourselves, tearing your union apart, as a cloak is torn to shreds."

Then Malachi addressed the whole assembly: "You have wearied the Lord by saying that those who do evil are okay in the eyes of the Lord and suggesting that he is somehow pleased with them. Whatever happened to the God of justice?"

But despite all his strong words, the situation that faced Nehemiah on his return was not greatly changed. In a fury, he threw all Tobiah's belongings out into the street, insisting that the storerooms in the temple be sanctified once again for their holy purpose. Then he threatened violence to the foreign merchants should they ever set foot in the city again on a Sabbath. He physically attacked those who had intermarried, beating them and tearing out their hair. Nehemiah was a force to be reckoned with.

Since his arrival from Babylon, Ezra had been patiently waiting for the right moment to present itself for him to fulfil his mandate from King

Artaxerxes to teach the law. What with the building of the temple and then the wall, the people had been too preoccupied with physical work to set aside the time to listen to an old man. But now with the wall finished, everyone was in a good space to listen.

A general assembly was called, and the people massed in the great square by the temple. A high wooden platform was erected in front of the Water Gate, and at the agreed hour, Ezra mounted the steps, flanked by a dozen priests. As the book of the law was opened, the people rose to their feet, and an expectant hush fell on the throng.

Ezra cleared his throat. "Praise the Lord!" he cried in a clear voice that could be heard even at the far side of the square.

The people raised their hands high and responded, "Amen!" Then they all bowed, faces to the ground.

When they had resumed their places, the reading of the law began and continued all day. Whenever he came to a section that he considered difficult to understand, Ezra would take time to explain the meaning. From time to time, and to give Ezra a break, some of the Levites would take over the reading so there would be no interruptions in the flow.

The effect on the crowd was amazing. First, there were tears and then open weeping as the people were pricked to the heart by the gravity of what they were hearing.

Nehemiah addressed the grief-stricken crowd: "Don't be sad, people. This is a sacred day, a day when we should be rejoicing. Go have your supper and celebrate. Remember that it is the joy of the Lord that makes you strong."

So the crowd dispersed for an overnight break and shared what they had with each other so that nobody would go hungry. Everyone was thrilled to have heard and understood the things that had been written so long ago by the likes of Moses and King David.

Next day, they were all back, eager to hear more. As it turned out, they spent a whole week enjoying the open-air life, inspired by the Festival of Tabernacles, and listening to the careful reading and explanation of the Scriptures.

When the whole book had been read cover to cover, it was obvious to everyone that they and their forefathers had been negligent of the requirements of the law that were set out so clearly in what they had been reading together. A corporate act of confession and repentance seemed the appropriate response.

It was a team of Levites who led the people in prayer. They stood on the steps and prayed aloud, taking turns to voice the passion of all their hearts: "Blessed be your glorious name, oh Lord. May it be exalted high above all blessing and praise. You alone are God. It was you who created all things, and you are he who alone gives life."

Starting from the account of creation, they used the story from the Scriptures to inspire a prayerful response. They recalled Abram's migration from Ur of the Chaldeans to Canaan. They followed their history through the days of slavery in Egypt and their miraculous delivery from Pharaoh's clutches. They traced their path through the sea dry-shod, and the subsequent provision of food and water during those long years in the wilderness. The giving of the law at Mount Sinai inspired them to recall the unchangeable commands that God had given. But they did not gloss over the shame that they had all but turned back to Egypt through fear and unbelief, and didn't ignore their constant grumbling. They reminded each other in the Lord's presence of their rebellion on the occasion when before the ink was even dry on the commands, they had made an idol shaped like a calf. Yet God had remained faithful to them through it all and never once had withdrawn his generous provision for all their needs till they arrived in the promised land, where God had helped them subdue the inhabitants.

Yet even after he had brought them that far, they had still turned their backs on the Lord and time and again had suffered the miserable consequences of their sin, only to cry out to the Lord for help that he never failed to give.

Then their praying turned to more recent history. They recalled how they had been taken into exile by the kings of Assyria and Babylon, yet even there in far-off exile, the Lord had heard their cry.

"So now today, here we are back in the land you gave to our forefathers. We wish to make with you a binding agreement in writing that from now on, we will wholeheartedly obey you."

When the deed was signed and sealed, the prophet Malachi spoke: "You have this day signed this scroll of remembrance that was written in his presence. This is what the Lord says to you who fear the Lord and honour his name. 'You are my treasured possession,' says the Lord. 'The sun of righteousness will shine on you with healing rays. Go forth in freedom and dance like calves released from their stalls.'

"The day is coming when the Lord will suddenly appear in this temple. But before he arrives he will send his messenger to prepare the way for his coming. He is going to send you the prophet Elijah, who will restore parents and children to each other to make families ready for the Lord.'"

The story continues...

TO MAKE A LONG STORY SHORT
A compelling retelling that makes the Bible's New Testament dance with life

A baby is born to an unwed mother in a barn. The child grows up in an obscure mountain village until he emerges—a man with a revolutionary message. His out-of-the-box thinking and non-conformist charisma infuriate the guardians of the status quo who determine to destroy him, along with his dangerous ideas. Love and hate; life and death stand their ground in the ultimate face-off. But who will have the last word? Fascinating characters and fast-moving action, laced with humour, trace the thread of the original Bible story, allowing the narrative to live afresh today.

CONTACT JUSTYN REES:
www.justynrees.com
jrees@upstream.ca

About the Author

 Justyn Rees is a lifelong student of the Bible. His deep understanding of the book enables him to make its profound truths accessible to ordinary people. He is a storyteller whose ability to keep audiences of all ages on the edge of their seats has taken him to several continents as he tells the greatest story ever.

Born in the United Kingdom, Justyn uses his many British dialects to lend colour to the characters he portrays, while his sense of humour brings the truth he relates to street level.

Justyn's career has included directing a conference center near London, England; serving as pastor for one of Canada's largest churches; leading a team of musicians and actors across Canada on a five-year mission of reconciliation; and facilitating a delegation of church leaders from a dozen denominations to Rwanda. He has authored several books and is in demand as a speaker at conventions and conferences on both sides of the Atlantic. Justyn now lives in the province of British Columbia in Western Canada with his wife Joy.

CPSIA information can be obtained
at www.ICGtesting.com
Printed in the USA
LVOW12s0743171117

556676LV00001B/83/P